History

for the IB Diploma

Nationalist and Independence Movements

Stephen Nutt and Jean Bottaro

Series editor: Allan Todd

Cambridge University Press's mission is to advance learning, knowledge and research worldwide.

Our IB Diploma resources aim to:

- encourage learners to explore concepts, ideas and topics that have local and global significance
- help students develop a positive attitude to learning in preparation for higher education

CAMBRIDGE UNIVERSITY PRESS
www.cambridge.org

CAMBRIDGE UNIVERSITY PRESS
Cambridge, New York, Melbourne, Madrid, Cape Town,
Singapore, São Paulo, Delhi, Tokyo, Mexico City

Cambridge University Press
The Edinburgh Building, Cambridge CB2 8RU, UK

www.cambridge.org
Information on this title: www.cambridge.org/9780521189385

First published 2011

Printed in the United Kingdom at the University Press, Cambridge

A catalogue record for this publication is available from the British Library

ISBN 978-0-521-18938-5 Paperback

Contents

1 Introduction

Overview

This book will examine themes relating to nationalist and independence movements in Africa, Asia and post-1945 Central and Eastern European states. The themes are organised within chapters focusing on case studies across these regions. Chapters 2–4 deal with African and Asian states that moved from colonial rule to independence in the period after the Second World War. Chapters 5 and 6 cover the challenges to and the collapse of Soviet or centralised control in Central and Eastern European states, as well as the post-communist regimes in these countries.

The African and Asian examples – Zimbabwe, India and Pakistan, and Vietnam – have much in common with each other. Each was a colonial possession under the control of a European power. They all gained independence from colonial rule in the 20th century. These chapters will help you analyse the reasons for historical change in these countries and acquire historical perspective by comparing and contrasting each of the case studies. The European examples are in many ways very different from their African and Asian counterparts. You will not be asked to compare and contrast the developments in Africa and Asia with those in Central and Eastern Europe.

Indians celebrate the independence of their country from British rule in 1947

colonialism and decolonisation Colonialism refers to the extension of European dominance over large areas of the world. Colonies are territories established overseas from a European country's home territory. They are administered by the home territory through regional colonial officials. The relationship between the colony and the home territory is often very unbalanced, with the European power modifying the local economy and/or social structures for its own benefit. Decolonisation is the process whereby colonies acquire independence from the European colonial power. (See also page 11.)

imperialism A policy by which the power of a particular country is extended by gaining land or imposing economic or political control over other nations.

indigenous People who are born in a particular country or region.

Marxism A political ideology based on the works of Karl Marx. It centred on the belief that human societies passed through economic stages, with the basis of power being ownership of the primary means of production. The ideal final stage was a classless communist society. This model of historical development believed that socialism and then communism would evolve from advanced industrial economies like those of Britain and Germany in the late 19th and 20th centuries. The ideology was modified considerably in some of the colonial states covered in this book.

Africa and Asia – decolonisation

Three case studies have been selected from Africa and Asia – Rhodesia/Zimbabwe, India and Pakistan, and Vietnam. They were all subject to **colonialism**, but emerged as independent states after the Second World War, in a process that is often called **decolonisation**.

Each case study has been selected because of the manner of its transition from colonial rule to independence. In the late 19th century, Britain, France and other European states engaged in a 'scramble' to colonise the areas of Africa and Asia that remained independent. This 'new' **imperialism** expanded European control over these regions. More formal empires were established or consolidated, and various forms of administration were imposed on the **indigenous** populations.

By 1945, however, these colonial empires were coming under increasing pressure. Indigenous groups in the colonies had begun to form independence movements. These opposition groups were often led by Western-educated élites. The ideologies of the independence movements sometimes drew upon the intellectual bases of the European left, including the works of Karl Marx. However, **Marxism** was not a major factor in most independence movements, and only grew more significant in some states after 1945 as a result of the developing **Cold War** (see opposite).

The two world wars of the 20th century had an impact on colonial empires across the world. The rhetoric that followed the end of the First World War (1914–18) emphasised self-determination and national identity – concepts at odds with the European colonial domination then prevalent. Failure to address the demands of indigenous nationalist leaders in the decade after the war only intensified activity on the part of these independence movements to bring an end to European colonial rule.

The Second World War (1939–45) had an even more fundamental impact. The two chief colonial powers of the mid 20th century, Britain and France, suffered greatly during the war. Britain only just survived the onslaught of the Axis powers (Germany and its allies) and emerged from the conflict almost bankrupt. British possession of India had also been threatened by Japan. France suffered even more. Metropolitan France had been occupied by German forces, and its Southeast Asian colonies had been conquered by Japan. When the rhetoric of self-determination emerged again in the post-1945 period, nationalist movements realised that their colonial masters were now ill-equipped in terms of economic and military power to resist moves towards independence.

The transition to independence in these regions must also be studied against the backdrop of the Cold War between the USA, the **USSR** and their allies.

This book examines the origins of independence movements in these regions, and the methods they used to achieve their goals. It also explores the nature and success of the post-colonial states formed as a result of the collapse of the empires controlled by Britain and France.

Central and Eastern Europe – the collapse of communism

The case studies in Chapters 5 and 6 cover events in Czechoslovakia and Poland. Both were part of mainstream European cultures with developed social and economic systems. Both emerged as independent countries after the collapse of the Russian and Austro-Hungarian empires at the end of the First World War. Both were conquered by Nazi Germany either just before or in the early years of the Second World War, and suffered terrible oppression until 'liberated' by the Soviet Red Army (though many Poles would question the term 'liberated').

These chapters examine the establishment of pro-Soviet communist states, whose social and economic structures were heavily influenced by the Soviet model, but which suffered from the economic legacy of the Second World War. Both Czechoslovakia and Poland resisted the full imposition of Soviet power, but they were restricted in what they could do by the realities of the Cold War.

This book examines the movements set up to resist the centralised state control of these countries after 1945 and the eventual collapse of communist rule in the late 1980s and early 1990s. Finally, the book will evaluate the effectiveness of the post-communist successor states.

Themes

To help you prepare for your IB History exams, this book will cover the themes relating to nationalist and independence movements in Africa and Asia and post-1945 Central and Eastern European states (Topic 4 in Paper 2), as set out in the IB *History Guide*. For ease of study, this book will examine each state in terms of a series of major themes subdivided by region. For the African and Asian case studies the three major themes that will be examined are:

- the origins and rise of nationalist/independence movements
- methods of achieving independence, including the role and importance of leaders
- the formation of and challenges to post-colonial governments.

For the Central and Eastern European case studies the three major themes that will be examined are:

- the origins and growth of movements challenging Soviet or centralised control
- methods of achieving independence from Soviet or centralised control, including the role and importance of leaders, organisations and institutions
- problems and challenges facing the new post-communist states.

Separate units within Chapters 2–6 explore these themes within the context of each case study to help you focus on the key issues. This approach will enable you to compare and contrast developments in the various states, and to spot similarities and differences.

All the main events, turning points and key individuals will be covered in sufficient detail for you to be able to access the higher markbands – provided, of course, that your answers are both relevant and analytical!

Where appropriate, each chapter will contain visual and written sources, both to illustrate the events or issues under examination, and to provide material for exam-type questions. These will help you gain practice in dealing with the questions you will face in History Papers 1 and 2.

Cold War The term used to describe the tension and rivalry between the USA and the USSR between 1945 and 1991. 'Cold war' refers to relations that, although hostile, do not develop into a 'hot war' (involving actual military conflict). The term was popularised in the years 1946–47 by US journalist Walter Lippmann and US politician and businessman Bernard Baruch. With regard to our study, the USSR became a champion of independence movements, providing political, financial and military support for geopolitical and ideological reasons.

USSR The Union of Soviet Socialist Republics. The USSR was the first communist state to develop, in 1917. It emerged from the First World War with considerable influence in Europe, although it had less influence than the USA across the world in general. Unlike the USA, which was a *global* superpower, the USSR was essentially a *regional* superpower.

Fact

Both Poland and Czechoslovakia lay firmly within the Soviet bloc after the Second World War. This meant that it was difficult, if not impossible, for Western states to openly influence developments in these countries for fear of a full-scale military – perhaps nuclear – confrontation with the USSR. However, espionage, propaganda and sabotage were frequently used.

Theory of knowledge

Alongside these broad key themes, all chapters contain Theory of knowledge links to get you thinking about aspects that relate to history, which is a Group 3 subject in the IB Diploma. The Nationalist and Independence Movements topic has clear links to ideas about knowledge and history. The events discussed in this book are recent phenomena and form good case studies for understanding the nature of the historical process. Thus, the questions relating to the availability and selection of sources, and to interpretations of these sources, have clear links to the IB Theory of knowledge course.

For example, when investigating aspects of the nature of decolonisation, the function of Soviet-style communist systems within advanced and developed European structures, or the motives and influence of individuals (such as Mahatma Gandhi or Ho Chi Minh), institutions (such as ZANU-PF) or states (such as colonial powers or Cold War rivals), historians must decide which primary and secondary evidence to select and use – and which to leave out – to make their case. But in selecting what they consider to be the most important or relevant sources, and in making judgements about the value and limitations of specific sources or sets of sources, how important are these historians' personal political views? Is there such a thing as objective 'historical truth'? Or is there just a range of subjective opinions and interpretations about the past, which vary according to the political interests and leanings of individual historians?

You are therefore encouraged to read a range of books offering different interpretations of nationalist and independence movements in Africa, Asia and post-1945 Central and Eastern Europe. This will help you gain a clear understanding of the **historiography** of the events studied, as well as equipping you with the higher-level historical skills needed to gain perspective on the events of the second half of the 20th century as a whole.

historiography Differing historical debates – in particular, those historians who focus on the problems of the imperial powers, and those who emphasise the importance of developments in the various colonies, in the move to independence.

IB History and regions of the world

For the purposes of study, IB History specifies four regions of the world:

- Europe and the Middle East
- Asia and Oceania
- the Americas
- Africa.

Where relevant, you will need to be able to identify these regions and to discuss developments that took place within them. Besides the states covered in this book, you may also study other examples of nationalist and independence movements in Africa and Asia specifically identified in the IB *History Guide*. These may include the Algerian struggle against French colonial rule, led by Ahmed Ben Bella; the long war against the Portuguese in Angola, followed by a civil war; the end of colonial rule in the Belgian Congo; or the leading role played by Kwame Nkrumah in the nationalist movement in Ghana. You may also focus on other examples of post-1945 nationalist movements in Central and Eastern Europe. Examples include the Hungarian resistance to Soviet domination, or the end of communist rule in Yugoslavia and its subsequent break-up into six independent countries.

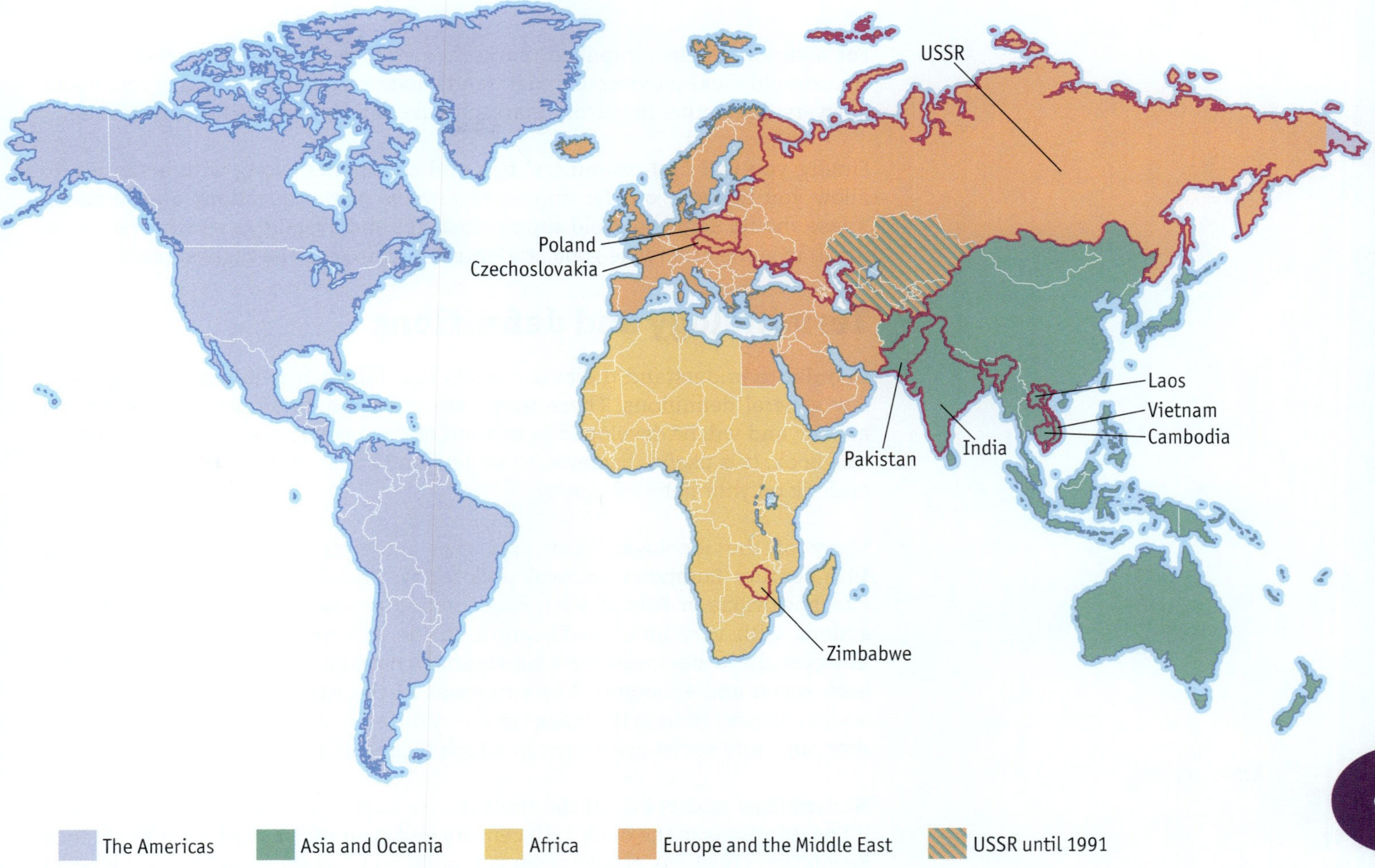

The four IB regions are shown on this map, along with some of the states covered in this book.

Remember, when answering a question that asks you to choose examples from *two* different regions, you *must* be careful – failure to comply will result in limited opportunities to score high marks.

Exam skills needed for IB History

Throughout the main chapters of this book, there are various activities and questions to help you develop the understanding and the exam skills necessary for success. Before attempting the specific exam practice questions at the end of most chapters, you might find it useful to refer to Chapter 7 *first*. This suggestion is based on the idea that if you know where you are supposed to be going (in this instance, gaining a good grade) and how to get there, you stand a better chance of reaching your destination!

Questions and markschemes

To ensure that you develop the necessary understanding and skills, each chapter contains a number of comprehension questions in the margins. In addition, three of the main Paper 1-type questions (comprehension, cross-referencing and reliability/utility) are dealt with at the end of Chapters 2–6. Help for the longer Paper 1 judgement/synthesis questions, and the Paper 2 essay questions, can be found in Chapter 7 – the final exam practice chapter.

For additional help, simplified markschemes have been put together in ways that should make it easier to understand what examiners are looking for in your answers. The actual IB History markschemes can be found on the IB website.

Finally, you will find examiners' tips and comments, along with activities, to allow you to focus on the important aspects of the questions and answers. These should help you avoid simple mistakes and oversights which, every year, result in some otherwise good students failing to gain the highest marks.

Terminology and definitions

In order to understand the case studies that follow, it is important to grasp a few general definitions. These terms are often more complex than they first appear, and will be developed in relation to the specific case studies chosen for this book. It is useful, however, to understand some of these terms before you embark on your detailed survey.

Many of the ideological concepts that underpin this study derive from 19th-century European political philosophy. In a European context, as with Czechoslovakia or Poland, such concepts influenced thinking and subsequent actions with very little modification. In the African and Asian case studies, however, these ideologies were substantially modified. The reasons for this were both social and economic. The situations in the African and Asian countries under consideration in this book were very different from the European political, economic and social conditions in which these ideologies originated.

Nationalism underpins all the movements under consideration in this book. It has its origins in the early 19th century and is, in part, a product of the French Revolution (1789–99). Nationalism is a political ideology founded on the belief that people should have political self-determination based on their nation. However, nationalism also involves issues such as a common history and shared culture and values.

SOURCE A

An extract from Johann Gottlieb Fichte's 'Thirteenth Address' in 1806. Fichte was a German nationalist writing at the time of the Napoleonic Wars.

Thus was the German nation placed – sufficiently united within itself by a common language and a common way of thinking, and sharply enough severed from the other peoples, in the middle of Europe, as a wall to divide races.

Quoted in Kelly, G. A. (ed.) 1968. Addresses to the German Nation. *New York, USA. Harper Torch. pp. 190–91.*

The problem with this ideology is that it is difficult to define 'nation'. This has been done – for example by Johann Gottlieb Fichte (see Source A) – by variously applying ethnic or cultural definitions to nationhood. In the final analysis, this definition of nation is crude in the extreme, a position outlined by historian Patrick J. Geary in his book *The Myth of Nations*. However, nationalism became a powerful social, cultural and political force in the 19th and 20th centuries. In the African and Asian case studies, nationhood was very difficult to define. All the countries in this book had problems developing a homogenous concept of nationhood because they were composed of many ethnic groups with distinct cultures and histories.

Some independence movements in Africa and Asia were heavily influenced by Marxism (see page 6). The problem was that communism was ill-suited to practical application in the agrarian societies which formed the colonial possessions under study.

Colonialism is a key term that dominates our analysis of the African and Asian case studies. In the 19th century, it developed into a form of imperialism that attempted to create more formal empires. Colonialism involved the administration of distant parts of the globe from a home country, often called the metropolitan area. Colonies took many forms, but in general terms their peoples and economies were exploited to provide resources for the colonial power. These resources were frequently turned into manufactured goods and sold back to the colonies. An example of this is British India, which supplied cotton to Britain's industries and then bought the finished products back from the colonial power.

Decolonisation is the process of transition from colonial rule to independence. This concept is at the core of many IB History questions associated with the African and Asian part of this book. Scholars debate why decolonisation occurred and the relative impact of indigenous independence movements as opposed to the economic necessities of the colonial power.

SOURCE B

John Kenneth Galbraith, an influential economic thinker during the 1960s, comments on colonialism.

The end of the colonial era is celebrated in the history books as a triumph of national aspiration in the former colonies and of benign good sense on the part of the colonial powers. Lurking beneath, as so often happens, was a strong current of economic interest – or in this case, disinterest.

Galbraith, J. K. 1994. A Journey Through Economic Time: A Firsthand View. *Boston, USA. Houghton Mifflin. p. 159.*

Neo-colonialism is a term applied to post-colonial states like those covered in the case studies that follow. It refers to the continuing economic control exerted by industrialised countries over their former colonies.

SOURCE C

Kwame Nkrumah, who became leader of the first newly independent African country, Ghana, in 1957, comments on neo-colonialism.

The result of neo-colonialism is that foreign capital is used for the exploitation rather than for the development of the less developed parts of the world.

Nkrumah, K. 1965. Neo-colonialism: The Last Stage of Imperialism. *London, UK. Thomas Nelson & Sons. p. 1.*

In your study of the post-colonial African and Asian states, you might consider whether the old colonial rulers simply changed the way they influenced events. For example, did the use of capital from the West in the form of investments and loans once more tie the new post-colonial states to their former masters?

History and changing perspectives

Historians often change their views of past events. This may occur as new primary sources come to light or simply because new perspectives emerge. An analysis of these changes (historiography) is a higher-level historical skill (see page 8).

With regard to the Central and Eastern European case studies, two developments have changed our perspective on the historical processes that saw the formation and collapse of communist states in Czechoslovakia and Poland. The first is the open access to the state archives of the communist regimes, both in these countries and in the former Soviet Union, which has come about since the fall of communism. The second is the reaction of post-communist states to the economic crisis in the first decade of the 21st century. Both these developments are ongoing at the time of writing.

In the African and Asian case studies, a broad theme is our perception of colonial empires in general. There are several different interpretations of the impact of colonialism, the move towards independence and post-colonial developments. Imperialist historians stress the positive role played by the colonial powers in bringing change, in the form of infrastructures such as railways and communications systems, political ideologies, health care, education and the concept of the nation state. They also focus on the policies of the colonial powers during the decolonisation process. Nationalist historians – whether Asian or African – often focus on the role played by leaders and nationalist groups in the move towards independence, and question the perceived benefits of colonial rule. Revisionist historians also question these benefits, viewing the colonial infrastructure as rudimentary, the services minimal and the education inappropriate. They see such moves as promoting the interests of the colonial powers, leaving many colonies unprepared for self-government and ill-equipped for independence.

Historians of the more recent 'Subaltern Studies group' focus on the role played by ordinary people in the independence struggle in India, and how they too were agents of political and social change. In this context they use the term 'subaltern' to refer to those who hold inferior positions in society in terms of race, class, gender, sexuality, ethnicity and religion. More recently this approach has been extended to historical studies of other parts of the world.

Another view, based partly on Marxist perspectives, regards the colonial empires as essentially exploitative. This perspective questions whether the process of decolonisation and subsequent independence was beneficial to the indigenous peoples of the post-colonial states. It is from this perspective that the theory of neo-colonialism (see page 12) has developed. This view is linked to the general **globalisation** of the world economy. It believes that Western states and corporations use their capital, in the form of investment, loans and even economic aid, to control and further exploit post-colonial states. From this perspective, prime minister Robert Mugabe's actions in Zimbabwe – despite the damage they have done to his country – could be seen as an attempt to fight back against this development.

globalisation The term used to describe economic and cultural developments in the later 20th century, in which the world's economies and cultures became homogenised. This has created great interdependence between all areas of the globe. Due to the Western states' superior economic capacity, globalisation may have created a new form of power for them. China, however, is fast catching up, and both China and the US, for example, might be seen as using their economic superiority to advance their geopolitical goals through the process of globalisation.

Summary

By the time you have worked through this book, you should be able to:

- show a broad understanding of the nature of decolonisation in the African and Asian states
- understand and explain the various reasons why the countries in the African and Asian case studies emerged as independent states
- analyse the effectiveness of the independent states that emerged in Africa and Asia
- understand the reasons why communism was imposed in Central and Eastern Europe
- understand the cultural context underpinning the communist Eastern bloc and the long-term tensions it created
- understand the growth of opposition to communist rule in Central and Eastern Europe
- evaluate the effectiveness of the post-communist regimes in Central and Eastern Europe
- understand and explain all the case studies in the context of the impact of the Second World War and the Cold War.

2 Zimbabwe

Introduction

Fact

Zimbabwe was the name of an African kingdom that dominated trade in the area between the 13th and 15th centuries. The capital at Great Zimbabwe was built by ancestors of the Shona people. The kingdom controlled the export of ivory and gold from the interior to the Swahili city states on the eastern coast. In the 1960s, nationalist organisations chose the name Zimbabwe as it symbolised African achievement and heritage, and had links to the pre-colonial past.

Until the Second World War, most of Africa was ruled by European colonial powers. After the war, however, the growth of African nationalism led to decolonisation and independence. In 1957, Ghana became the first independent state in sub-Saharan Africa. For most African countries the path to independence was a peaceful one, following constitutional negotiations. However, for colonies with large numbers of European settlers who were reluctant to accept majority rule, the process involved lengthy wars of liberation. The Algerians fought an eight-year war against France before becoming independent in 1962. In Kenya, a determined resistance from landless peasant farmers, called the Mau Mau uprising, forced Britain to accept the principle of black majority rule in 1963. Independence for the Belgian Congo (later called Zaire and then the Democratic Republic of Congo) was accompanied by violence and civil war, aggravated by superpower intervention. Portugal was initially determined to maintain control of its colonies, and it was only after lengthy wars of resistance to Portuguese rule that the colonies became independent in 1975. In Angola this was followed by a decades-long civil war, prolonged by Cold War politics and foreign intervention.

The last British colony to become independent was Rhodesia/Zimbabwe in 1980. Nationalist movements in Zimbabwe waged a long struggle against white rule to achieve this in the area of central southern Africa that British settlers called Rhodesia. This independence movement involved peaceful political organisations, strikes and eventually a bitter armed struggle against a white minority government that was unwilling to surrender political power and economic privilege.

A map showing the states of southern Africa as they exist in 2011

1 The origins and rise of nationalist and independence movements in Zimbabwe

Key questions

- How did Rhodesia become a British colony?
- What factors influenced the growth of opposition to white rule?
- What led to a Unilateral Declaration of Independence in 1965?

Overview

- The region that became Rhodesia was colonised by the British because of their economic interest in the area's resources.
- In 1923, Southern Rhodesia became a self-governing colony under the control of a white minority.
- The Land Apportionment Act of 1930 gave white settlers control over the best land. Africans were confined to overcrowded reserves from which their movement was strictly controlled.
- White support for a merger of Southern Rhodesia with other British colonies in central Africa was investigated by the British government's Bledisloe Commission. African opposition meant no further moves to unify the colonies were made at this time.
- After the Second World War, Britain was too weak economically to maintain its empire; Africans expected an extension of democracy to the colonies; and white settlers in southern Africa expected sympathy and support for their viewpoint.
- In 1953, Britain created the Central African Federation, joining Southern Rhodesia, Northern Rhodesia and Nyasaland.
- A strong nationalist movement emerged despite government efforts to suppress it. Several nationalist groups were formed and later banned by the government throughout the 1950s and 1960s.
- Several African leaders who later played a key role in the nationalist struggle for independence, such as Joshua Nkomo, Ndabaningi Sithole and Robert Mugabe, were involved in establishing nationalist organisations.
- Widespread protests and resistance by African nationalists in Northern Rhodesia and Nyasaland forced Britain to break up the CAF in 1963, creating the independent states of Zambia and Malawi respectively in 1964.
- The white government in Southern Rhodesia was not prepared to accept plans for majority rule. Britain was not willing to grant independence to a white minority government. Talks between the two governments reached a stalemate.
- In 1965, the right-wing Rhodesian Front government, led by Ian Smith, made a Unilateral Declaration of Independence, cutting off ties with Britain.
- The new Rhodesian state was not officially recognised, and UDI was condemned by Britain and the UN.

Timeline

1890	British South Africa Company (BSAC) begins colonising Rhodesia
1896–97	BSAC crushes uprisings by Shona and Ndebele peoples
1914–18	First World War
1923	Southern Rhodesia becomes self-governing colony
1930	Land Apportionment Act reinforces white control of land
1939	Bledisloe Commission
1939–45	Second World War
1951	Land Husbandry Act
1953	formation of Central African Federation
1957	Southern Rhodesian African National Congress (SRANC) re-launched
1959	SRANC banned
1960	formation of National Democratic Party (NDP)
1961	NDP banned
1962	formation of Zimbabwean African People's Union (ZAPU); formation of Rhodesian Front by white extremists
1963	formation of Zimbabwean African National Union (ZANU); break-up of Central African Federation
1964	Ian Smith becomes prime minister of Southern Rhodesia; ZAPU and ZANU banned
1965	Unilateral Declaration of Independence
1966	UN applies economic sanctions
1970	Smith government declares Republic of Rhodesia

How did Rhodesia become a British colony?

Zimbabwe is named after the stone ruins of Great Zimbabwe, the centre of a thriving empire that dominated the region over 500 years ago. The Shona descendants of the builders and rulers of Great Zimbabwe continued to live in the area after its decline. In the 19th century, Ndebele people from the south moved into the western part of Zimbabwe.

British interest in the area was sparked by hopes of finding gold deposits to match the substantial gold discoveries that had been made in the South African Republic. However, the British government itself did not colonise the region. In 1889, the government granted a charter to **Cecil John Rhodes** and his private company, the British South Africa Company (BSAC), to exploit the resources in the area that became known as Rhodesia.

White settlers started moving into the area in 1890, and in 1896–97 the BSAC crushed uprisings by the Ndebele and Shona people to secure white control. Using a mixture of force and diplomacy, Rhodes rapidly carved out his own empire. The white settlers and BSAC administrators used a ruthless combination of land seizure, taxation and forced labour to impose a system of harsh control over the people of Zimbabwe. By 1914, a minority of 25,000 white settlers dominated the land, which had been organised into large ranches. In the process, the local people lost their independence and freedom, as well as their land.

Terminology
African nationalists rejected the name Rhodesia because of its obvious links to imperialism and white domination. Some historians use the name Zimbabwe exclusively when discussing the history of the area. For the sake of clarity, however, this chapter uses the names by which the region was officially known at different times: Southern Rhodesia (until 1965); Rhodesia (between 1965 and 1979); Zimbabwe-Rhodesia (1979–80); and Zimbabwe (1980 onwards).

Cecil John Rhodes (1853–1902) A British businessman and politician, Rhodes established a huge commercial empire for himself in southern Africa based on mining. He was so powerful in the area that the whole region under BSAC control was named after him. Southern Rhodesia was the area between the Limpopo and Zambezi Rivers; Northern Rhodesia lay to the north.

Establishment of Southern Rhodesia as a self-governing colony, 1923

White settlers opposed continuing BSAC rule. They saw the BSAC as dominating the economy of the region for the benefit of its shareholders to the detriment of their own interests. In 1922, in a **referendum** conducted by the British government, the settlers rejected a proposal to make Rhodesia a province of South Africa. Instead, when the BSAC charter expired the following year, Southern Rhodesia became a self-governing British colony. This development placed great power in the hands of the white settlers. Britain had a supervisory role, but the white population effectively controlled the colony.

referendum The approval of a law or political action by direct public vote.

A poster released by the Empire Marketing Board in the early 1930s, showing a tobacco plantation in Southern Rhodesia

The constitution of Southern Rhodesia gave power to an elected legislative (law-making) assembly, led by a prime minister. The constitution did not specifically prohibit Africans from voting, but the franchise qualifications were so high that very few black people qualified. Thirty years later only 560 Africans, out of a population of 4 million, had the right to vote. The constitution gave Britain little control over the white government, which could effectively implement its own policies. Elsewhere in the empire – for example in Kenya – the British government had sought to protect the rights of the indigenous population. In Southern Rhodesia, however, the structure actually encouraged the domination of whites over blacks.

A key development in reinforcing white domination was the Land Apportionment Act of 1930. This formally divided the land between the indigenous population and white settlers. Although a minority, white settlers gained over half the land, while Africans were marginalised into the poorer and more arid regions, or 'reserves'. Africans could not own land outside these reserves, and had to have an official document, or 'pass', to allow them to leave in search of work in the towns. The unfair distribution of land was a deep-seated issue that would resurface again and again.

The division of the land caused a massive economic crisis for black farmers. The reserves were overcrowded, overstocked and over-grazed. In order to survive during the difficult years of the **Great Depression** in the 1930s, black farmers had to farm intensively what land they had, resulting in severe ecological damage. This led to famine and great hardship. At the same time, the white minority grew richer, increasing political tensions in the colony.

White settlers had earlier rejected a proposed union with Northern Rhodesia, but after the discovery of vast copper deposits in the north the issue resurfaced. Large numbers of white miners and farmers from Southern Rhodesia migrated to the 'Copperbelt', as it became known. Links between the two colonies had also been strengthened by the merging of their two railways into 'Rhodesia Railways'. When the imperial authorities in London proposed the formation of a 'Greater Rhodesia', to include the two Rhodesias and Nyasaland, white settlers in the three colonies supported the idea. They felt that such a union would protect their interests from African political activity. The British government appointed the Bledisloe Commission to investigate the issue. The Bledisloe Report, published in 1939, stressed the economic interdependence of the three territories, but noted the concerns of Africans that such a union would not be in their interests. Africans feared that such a move would lead to the extension of racial segregation from Southern Rhodesia to the other two territories.

SOURCE A

The African possesses a knowledge and shrewdness, in matters affecting his welfare, with which he is not always credited. It would be wrong to assume that his opposition to the amalgamation of Northern and Southern Rhodesia is based to a very large extent on ignorance or prejudice or an instinctive dread of change.

Extract from the Bledisloe Report (1939). Adapted from Blake, R. 1977. History of Rhodesia. *London, UK. Methuen Publishing. p. 226.*

Theory of knowledge

History and language

The white settlers in Rhodesia called the 1896–97 uprisings the 'Ndebele Rebellion' and the 'Shona Rebellion', but the local people themselves referred to them as the *Chimurenga*, or 'struggle'. Use this example, and others you can think of, to explain how terminology can be linked to bias in history.

Great Depression Following the 1929 Wall Street Crash (see page 66), the entire world entered a prolonged economic downturn that resulted in a contraction of economic activity and mass unemployment. This became known as the Great Depression.

Theory of knowledge

History and language

Although historians today would consider the language used in this extract from the Bledisloe Report to be patronising, it is important to take into account the time and context in which a statement was made or written. Why do you think this is? In what ways, and by whom, would this statement have seemed dangerously liberal at the time?

Question

What disadvantages did the black majority in Rhodesia face in the period before the Second World War?

The Bledisloe Report, which noted the viewpoint of the black majority, meant that African opinions were heard in London for the first time. The report caused concern amongst the more liberal civil servants in Britain, but its conclusions were totally at odds with the views of the settlers. Although the outbreak of the Second World War in 1939 postponed any further discussion about a possible merger, the idea of federation did not die.

The situation after the Second World War

The Second World War (1939–45) had a massive impact on the British Empire and the expectations of its population. Britain emerged from the conflict economically weakened, and the empire would not be able to survive in the same form as it had before the war began. By 1945, blacks and whites in southern Africa had different expectations about the future. After the horrors of Nazi race policies had been exposed, there was a worldwide condemnation of racism and a greater awareness of human rights. Furthermore, the wartime Allied leaders, Winston Churchill and Franklin D. Roosevelt, had confirmed their support for **self-determination** in the Atlantic Charter, a joint declaration of Allied war aims. Africans hoped that the end of the war would mean an end to colonialism and white domination. Whites hoped that the contribution of Rhodesian and South African troops to the war effort would win them support and sympathy. This led the white settlers in southern Africa to assume that they would not be subject to the post-war move towards decolonisation that was sweeping the British Empire. They hoped that, if independence came, it would be in the form of white-dominated states with close ties to Britain.

self-determination People's right to rule themselves. This became a key demand in Asian and African colonies after the Second World War.

The war created an economic boom in Southern Rhodesia. The growth of white commercial farming and the establishment of manufacturing industries resulted in increased demand for cheap African labour. In response to this, the government introduced the Land Husbandry Act in 1951. This act enforced a radical change in the traditional system of land tenure in the African reserves, dividing the communally owned land into individual smallholdings. Only adult males and widows living in the reserves at the time were included in the scheme.

The act was intended to force those unable to acquire land to work in the towns and on white commercial farms. The result was a huge increase in the number of landless people, many of whom moved to the towns to seek work. In the towns, social problems such as poverty and poor living conditions fuelled growing discontent. This formed the basis for the growth of African nationalism as a mass movement.

Establishment of the Central African Federation, 1953

After the war, white settlers revived the idea of a closer union of the three British colonies, wanting to create an economically powerful, white-controlled state. They put strong pressure on the British government to make the necessary constitutional changes. Africans, however, were strongly opposed to the idea and the Labour government was hesitant about proceeding. However, the election of a Conservative government in 1952 changed this. Despite continuing African protests, in 1953 Southern and Northern Rhodesia and Nyasaland were joined as the Central African Federation (CAF).

The federal parliament was made up of 35 members, of whom only six were African – two from each territory. African representative councils in Northern Rhodesia and Nyasaland selected their delegates, but the African delegates from

Southern Rhodesia were elected by white voters. Federation led to a further economic boom in Southern Rhodesia, and this assisted the government's policy of encouraging white immigration.

Federation also allowed whites to strengthen their hold on power. Originally Britain had intended that the federation would begin the transition to **majority rule**. However, this development was halted by whites in Southern Rhodesia, who had already established a self-governing state under white domination and hoped to extend this to the other two territories. In 1953, the white population in Southern Rhodesia was 150,000, out of a total population of just over 4 million, but white immigration during the 1950s pushed this number up to about 250,000. There were far fewer white settlers in Northern Rhodesia and, especially, Nyasaland.

majority rule When a government has been elected by the majority in an election in which all adults have the right to vote, regardless of race. In the context of post-colonial Africa this meant a black government. Minority rule means rule by a white minority, who dominate political power and deny others the right to vote, except perhaps in insignificant numbers. Rhodesia had a white minority government until 1979, as did apartheid South Africa until 1994.

What factors influenced the growth of opposition to white rule?

The origins of black nationalist organisations

Before the Second World War, there were no large-scale African political organisations. African dissatisfaction with colonial rule and economic exploitation was voiced mainly through societies known as Welfare Associations, which focused on issues such as voting rights for Africans, or educational and social reforms. Independent African churches also provided an outlet for discontent and defiance.

There was also support from urban workers for industrial organisations, and branches of the Industrial and Commercial Workers' Union (ICU) held mass meetings and called for improved working conditions. However, all of these were on a regional rather than a national scale. The first attempt to create a nationwide nationalist movement was the formation in 1934 of the Southern Rhodesian African National Congress (SRANC). This was cautious and conservative in its approach, and failed to gain a mass following, appealing instead to an educated élite.

Several factors hindered the development of black political organisations. Most Africans lived in the reserves or on land owned by white settlers, and it was illegal for Africans to have permanent residence in any of the urban centres. Political activity is most easily facilitated in dense population centres, not amongst farm labourers or rural dwellers dispersed across the countryside. Africans were also denied education on a large scale. African schools run by missionaries had focused initially on teaching basic literacy, as well as practical subjects such as carpentry, agriculture and domestic science.

The poor standard of education prevented the development of a large independence movement and also deprived the economy of black skilled workers and professionals. After the war, however, the number of potential leaders increased rapidly as larger numbers of Africans began to receive secondary education.

The development of nationalist movements was also negatively affected by the segregationist and repressive policies of the government, which wanted to prevent the spread of political opposition. Godfrey Huggins, prime minister of Southern Rhodesia from 1933 to 1953, and of the Central African Federation from 1953 to 1956, was a strong supporter of maintaining white domination.

A school in Rhodesia in 1959; before the Second World War few black Rhodesians received any formal education, but standards of education improved after the war

SOURCE B

Partnership between black and white is the partnership between a horse and its rider.

Godfrey Huggins. Quoted in Arnold, G. 2006. Africa: A Modern History. London, UK. Atlantic Books. p. 286.

The impact of the Second World War and the Cold War

The Second World War made a significant contribution to the growth of African nationalism. Black soldiers from Southern Rhodesia had fought with some equality alongside whites in East Africa and Burma. On their return home they found it impossible to revert to their previous subservient position. They had been part of the Allied fight for freedom, and they now wanted to know why liberation and democracy did not extend to African colonies. This new mood was reflected in the revival of the SRANC after 1945, and an increasing number

SOURCE C

We believe that the African should be given more say in the running of the country, as and when he shows ability to contribute more to the general good, but we must make it clear that even when that day comes, in a hundred or two hundred years time, he can never hope to dominate the partnership. He can achieve equal standing, but not go beyond it.

Roy Welensky, prime minister of the Central African Federation, 1956–63. Quoted in Arnold, G. 2006. Africa: A Modern History. *London, UK. Atlantic Books. p. 286.*

of strikes by workers. Despite this, the Huggins administration ignored any claims the African population made for greater rights, and continued a policy of strict social and economic segregation.

After 1945, some members of the new Labour government in Britain grew concerned about developments in the British colonies in southern Africa, and wanted to work towards a multi-racial settlement there. However, with the start of the Cold War, colonial affairs became secondary to the development of a Western alliance and containment of the perceived threat of the USSR. Indeed, the white-dominated colonies of southern Africa were seen as partners in this struggle. Thus, from 1945, the British government put little pressure on the Southern Rhodesian government to curtail its race polices. At the same time, however, Britain was concerned that continued segregationist policies would alienate the black majority and deny them any democratic route to self-determination. The British government feared that desperation might push Africans into a guerrilla war, which would lead to instability and even communist involvement in the region.

African nationalism becomes a mass movement

During the 1950s, there was increasing resistance to colonial rule all over Africa, and African nationalism became a powerful force. In South Africa, too, there was a mounting spirit of defiance towards the imposition of stricter segregation laws, while in Northern Rhodesia and Nyasaland nationalist leaders were demanding an immediate end to federation and majority rule. These developments inspired the nationalist movement in Southern Rhodesia, which was also motivated by a growing economic disparity. In 1961, for example, the average wage for black workers was less than £90 per annum, while whites earned over £1,250. There was no indication that the white minority intended to surrender their economic privileges or political control, and this intensified resistance to the white Rhodesian regime.

In 1955, a militant organisation, the City Youth League, was launched in Salisbury (Harare), and in 1957 it merged with Bulawayo-based organisations to form a re-launched SRANC, led by Joshua Nkomo. The policy of this organisation was

Activity

'The open expression of these racial views was the prelude to inevitable repression, conflict and bloodshed. In the retrospect of a later "forgive and forget" culture about imperialism it is important to recall the sheer demeaning contempt such attitudes conveyed.'
Arnold, G. 2006. *Africa: A Modern History.* London, UK. Atlantic Books. p. 286.

How do the attitudes shown in Sources B and C help to explain African opposition to the creation of the Central African Federation? Read and comment on the views of historian Guy Arnold, and explain how they relate to the sources. Suggest what he means by 'a later "forgive and forget" culture about imperialism'.

Fact

The segregationist policies applied in Southern Rhodesia were very similar to the discriminatory race policies in South Africa. After 1948, when the Afrikaner Nationalist Party was voted into power in South Africa, this policy became known as apartheid, an Afrikaans word meaning 'separateness'. In theory it segregated the white and black populations; in reality it created extreme political, social and economic inequality, with the white population benefiting disproportionately from the arrangement.

moderate, and it stressed non-racialism and the right of all – black and white – to be citizens of the country. With growing landlessness and unemployment, it rapidly grew into a mass-based organisation with support in both urban and rural areas. It was inspired by growing opposition to federation from nationalist organisations in Northern Rhodesia and Nyasaland.

However, the Southern Rhodesian government was not prepared to tolerate protests and opposition, and so in 1959 it banned the SRANC and introduced restrictions on political organisations. This move only served to intensify opposition. In 1960, the National Democratic Party (NDP) was formed, also under the leadership of Nkomo, and proposed a policy of more active resistance to white minority rule. Growing unrest and protest actions around the country led to the banning of the NDP in December 1961.

It was re-launched a week later, in January 1962, as the Zimbabwe African People's Union (ZAPU). Its programme was much more militant and it organised Land Freedom Farmers who occupied unused government or white-owned land. ZAPU also began a campaign of sabotage, targeting railway lines, electrical installations and government forests. ZAPU was banned in September 1962, but survived under the name of the People's Caretaker Council (PCC).

Question

What factors played a role in hindering the emergence of a strong national independence movement in Rhodesia/Zimbabwe?

Amongst ZAPU members there had been differences of opinion about the tactics to use to achieve majority rule. Some, including Nkomo, were prepared to compromise with Britain and the Southern Rhodesian government to negotiate a constitutional solution. Others supported more radical solutions and in 1963 they formed a separate nationalist organisation, the Zimbabwe African National Union (ZANU), which supported a policy of confrontation with the government. Its leader was Ndabaningi Sithole, and its secretary was Robert Mugabe.

A struggle began between ZAPU and ZANU to gain the support of people in the townships. Disagreements over policies and regional rivalries between the two organisations reduced their effectiveness at a crucial time in the early 1960s, when the Central African Federation was breaking up and constitutional negotiations were taking place. When Ian Smith and the right-wing Rhodesian Front Party were elected in 1964, they banned both ZANU and ZAPU/PCC.

Theory of knowledge

Historical interpretation

The Nigerian historians A. E. Afigbo and E. A. Ayandele believe that Britain's decision to break up the Federation and recognise majority rule in Northern Rhodesia and Nyasaland was influenced by British experiences during the Mau Mau uprising in Kenya and French experiences in Indochina and Algeria. They think these showed that 'attempts to suppress political ambitions of the majority in colonial countries could lead to expensive and futile wars'.

What led to a Unilateral Declaration of Independence in 1965?

The break-up of the Central African Federation

Even before the establishment of the Central African Federation, there had been strong opposition from African nationalist organisations in Northern Rhodesia and Nyasaland by those who feared the extension of white minority rule from Southern Rhodesia to the two northern territories. When Britain ignored their concerns and went ahead with the formation of the CAF in 1953, opposition intensified. Protests by the Nyasaland African Congress gained momentum after 1958, when Dr Hastings Kamuzu Banda became an outspoken critic of federation. In Northern Rhodesia, Kenneth Kaunda formed the Zambia Africa National Congress (ZANC) to step up protests and force Britain to grant independence to the territories.

The British government feared that the protests would turn into armed resistance, which would be more difficult to control and would divert Britain's military and economic resources from the Cold War. Britain also believed that governments led by Banda and Kaunda would be viable solutions to the problems in the region. Not only did these men have mass support, but they were considered to be politically moderate leaders who would block communist influence in the region.

These maps show Rhodesia/Zimbabwe at the time of the Central African Federation (above) and after the Unilateral Declaration of Independence (right)

In 1960, the British government set up a commission to review the workings of the CAF. The commission recommended that, as African opposition to it was so strong, each colony should be given the right to secede (withdraw from the federation). The government readily accepted this recommendation and on 31 December 1963 the CAF was formally dissolved. In 1964, Northern Rhodesia and Nyasaland became the independent states of Zambia and Malawi respectively, under majority rule governments.

Southern Rhodesia remained a self-governing British colony, however. The British government would not grant independence to a white minority government, and this government in turn was determined not to allow majority rule. From the perspective of white Rhodesians, Britain had ignored their concerns by creating two new black African states along their northern frontier. They believed that their future now lay in co-operation and closer links with the apartheid regime in South Africa. This reinforced the siege mentality that was deeply ingrained in the minds of white settlers, and led directly to UDI and a break with what they saw as a meddling colonial power.

The Unilateral Declaration of Independence (UDI), 1965

Since 1961, the government of Southern Rhodesia had been negotiating with the British government about full independence, but the British government insisted that certain guarantees must be made before independence could be granted. One of these was eventual progress to majority rule. As the white government's main reason for wanting independence was to maintain white supremacy, it would not agree to this. As protests and acts of resistance by black nationalist groups intensified, white Rhodesians turned to a new political party, more right-wing and racist than its predecessors – the Rhodesian Front.

Ian Smith (1919–2007) Smith was the leader of the Rhodesian Front political party. He became prime minister of Southern Rhodesia in 1964, and after UDI in 1965 he was prime minister of Rhodesia until the end of white minority rule in 1979. After independence, he remained a member of the Zimbabwean parliament until 1987.

In 1962, a Rhodesian Front government was elected to power, and in 1964 **Ian Smith** became its leader and prime minister of Southern Rhodesia. He adopted a hardline policy towards the nationalist movements, banning ZAPU and ZANU and imprisoning hundreds of their leaders, including Nkomo, Sithole and Mugabe. The government also introduced harsh security laws, including a compulsory death sentence for many political offences. Under Smith, negotiations between the British government and the white administration in Southern Rhodesia rapidly broke down, especially after the election of a Labour government in Britain in 1965. Rhodesians began to talk openly about declaring independence unilaterally.

Fact

Unilateral means 'made by one side only'. In other words, this was a one-sided decision, made by white settlers in Southern Rhodesia without the agreement of the British government, which did not recognise the legality of the declaration. The previous occasion on which British colonists had made such a move was when settlers in North America made their famous Declaration of Independence in 1776, resulting in the establishment of the United States of America.

On 11 November 1965, Smith made a Unilateral Declaration of Independence, formally severing his country's ties with Britain. In 1970, the Rhodesians took this a step further, breaking all legal ties with Britain and becoming the Republic of Rhodesia. The result of these acts was to place Rhodesia on a collision course with neighbouring African states and to intensify armed resistance to the white minority regime.

International reactions to UDI

UDI was condemned immediately by the United Nations Security Council, which called on all countries not to recognise the 'illegal racist minority regime' and to refuse to give it any assistance. UDI was also condemned by the Organisation of African Unity (OAU) and the Commonwealth. No country in the world, not even apartheid South Africa, officially recognised the Smith regime.

White voters arrive at a polling station in Salisbury, Rhodesia, in November 1964, to cast their votes in a referendum about independence

Fact

The Organisation of African Unity was established in 1963 by the 32 African states that were independent at that time. One of its aims was to eradicate colonialism in Africa, by giving support to the liberation movements fighting white minority rule in southern Africa, including ZAPU and ZANU, and putting pressure on the UN to support independence movements. Zimbabwe joined the OAU after independence in 1980. In 2002, the OAU was replaced by the African Union.

Britain regarded the declaration as illegal and moved to impose economic and diplomatic sanctions. In previous situations where the peaceful transition from colonial rule to independence had broken down, the British had been ready to use force. However, the special circumstances in Rhodesia prevented this. Firstly, Southern Rhodesia had been autonomous for almost 40 years rather than ruled directly from London. Secondly, there was a racial dimension to the decision. The presence of a large white minority in Rhodesia created fears in the British government that public opinion in Britain would not tolerate a military solution to the problem. There is even some evidence to suggest that ministers

economic sanctions Also known as trade embargoes, these ban trade with a particular country, and are used as a means of putting pressure on a country to change its policies.

feared the British army would not carry out orders directing it to fight the white settlers. As a result, the British government decided that military force would only be used if civil order collapsed in Rhodesia.

Britain decided that a combination of political and economic pressures might achieve its aims, and rallied support for **economic sanctions** at the United Nations. Over 40 countries agreed to isolate Rhodesia politically and, critically, economically. The UN passed a resolution implementing restrictions on the supply of arms, financial services and oil to Rhodesia. Later that year the embargo was extended to include a range of essential goods, and by mid 1967 the embargo was made total. At first sight these economic sanctions should have created economic collapse in Rhodesia, but they had limited impact. Instead, they helped to reinforce a siege mentality amongst whites.

There were specific problems involved in the implementation of economic sanctions against Rhodesia, which made them far less effective than they might have been. Although Britain was empowered by the UN to enforce oil sanctions, it turned a blind eye to exports into Rhodesia by British oil companies via the Mozambican port of Beira, which was connected to Rhodesia by a pipeline. Thus, Rhodesia was never really cut off from the key resource of oil. The British did not want to destroy the Rhodesian regime; rather they wanted to make life so difficult that Smith would be forced back to the negotiating table.

Another major obstacle to the successful implementation of sanctions was South Africa, which until the 1970s continued to supply goods and financial credit to another white minority regime. In addition, Portugal, a country sympathetic to the Smith regime, was in control of Mozambique until 1975. Some American and other Western companies also needed Rhodesia's valuable mineral exports, such as chromium, and continued to buy them secretly despite the sanctions.

Finally, the Rhodesians had the means to retaliate. Many neighbouring African states were linked to Rhodesia's economy and infrastructure, making them vulnerable. A good example is Zambia, which was almost totally dependent on Rhodesia for coal to power its vital copper industry, and on the Rhodesian rail routes for the export of its copper. In an effort to help Zambia break its dependence on Rhodesia and South Africa, China financed the building of a railway linking the Zambian Copperbelt with the Tanzanian port of Dar-es-Salaam, called the TanZam Railway. The rail link covered 1800 km (1100 miles) over extremely rugged terrain. It was China's most ambitious foreign aid project and built at a time when China was competing with the USA and Soviet Union for influence in Africa. Historians such as Neil Parsons believe that the real victim of sanctions was Zambia. Although the Rhodesian economy was severely damaged by sanctions, the government was in no danger of a sudden collapse.

End of unit activities

1 Create a spider diagram to illustrate the political, economic and social advantages that white settlers had in the colony of Rhodesia.

2 The historian Guy Arnold has argued that 'The history of Rhodesia is the history of Anglo-Saxon racialism in Africa. Two factors operated throughout the colonial period: white control of African education in order to limit advance and white control and demarcation of the land.' Write an argument to support this view.

3 The historian Kevin Shillington believes that the creation of the Central African Federation was designed to benefit the white settlers of Southern Rhodesia, at the expense of the black inhabitants of all three territories. Find out what you can about the Central African Federation (1953–63), and work out an argument to support or oppose this view.

4 'Britain should have played a more decisive role in the early 1960s to force the government of Southern Rhodesia to accept majority rule.'

Divide into two groups. One group should develop an argument to support this statement, and the other group an argument to oppose it.

5 Some of the African nationalist leaders who later played leading roles in the struggle for independence were Joshua Nkomo, Ndabaningi Sithole and Robert Mugabe. Find out and make brief notes on the contribution of one of these leaders in the period before UDI in 1965.

Theory of knowledge

Historical interpretation

Although the Smith regime was ultimately overthrown in 1979, it seems that economic sanctions were not a major reason for this. In a study for the Harvard Center for International Affairs, Robin Renwick, head of the Rhodesian department of the British Foreign Office, reports that between 1965 and 1974 Rhodesia's real output increased by 6% per year 'despite the depressing effect of sanctions'; the value of exports more than doubled between 1968 and 1974 and continued to rise afterwards, although much more slowly.

2 Methods of achieving independence

Timeline

1961 ZAPU formed under Joshua Nkomo

1963 ZANU formed under Ndabaningi Sithole

1964 ZAPU and ZANU banned by the government

1965 Unilateral Declaration of Independence (UDI)

1966 start of guerrilla war

1967 United Nations declares a total trade embargo on Rhodesia

1970 Land Tenure Act; Smith government declares Republic of Rhodesia

1972 Pearce Commission

1974 South Africa begins to put pressure on the Smith government

1975 Mozambique achieves independence under FRELIMO government

1976 talks between Smith and Nkomo break down; South Africa steps up pressure on Smith government; formation of Patriotic Front between ZANU and ZAPU

1977 guerrilla war intensifies

1978 Internal Settlement between Smith and 'moderate' leaders

1979 elections won by Muzorewa; establishment of Zimbabwe-Rhodesia; Internal Settlement rejected by Patriotic Front and international community; Lancaster House talks

1980 elections won by Mugabe and ZANU-PF; independence of Zimbabwe

Key questions

- What was the role of armed struggle in achieving independence?
- What other factors played a role in the success of the independence struggle?
- What part did Robert Mugabe play?

Overview

- In response to domination by the white minority government, Africans formed political organisations such as ZAPU and ZANU. When they were banned by the government in 1964, these groups resorted to an armed struggle.
- In 1966, the guerrilla movements ZIPRA and ZANLA began a 14-year war of resistance to gain majority rule in Zimbabwe.
- The independence of neighbouring Mozambique under a FRELIMO government (see page 31) in 1975 gave a boost to the Zimbabwean nationalist movement, providing economic and military support.
- In the climate of the Cold War, the West wanted to prevent the spread of communist influence in a strategically vital region, and this influenced policies towards the Smith government.
- In 1972, a settlement that would ensure the continuation of white minority control was rejected by the African majority in a report by the Pearce Commission.
- The Smith government tried to counter support for the nationalist movement by attacking guerrilla bases in neighbouring states and moving the rural population into 'protected villages'.
- South Africa played a key role in events, initially supporting the Smith regime but later increasing the pressure for reform, mainly to prevent a Marxist victory in Rhodesia, which would weaken South Africa.
- There were divisions within the nationalist movement, with leadership struggles and competition for power and influence between ZAPU and ZANU.
- As a result of pressure from Zambia and other frontline states, ZAPU and ZANU joined together in 1976 to form the Patriotic Front (PF), to strengthen the liberation movement.
- In the face of mounting military incursions and a declining economy, the Smith government concluded an 'Internal Settlement' with moderate black leaders in an effort to prevent a PF victory.
- Smith met nationalist leaders at Lancaster House in London, and the parties agreed on a settlement that was acceptable to both blacks and whites.
- Robert Mugabe played a decisive role in the nationalist struggle, and he and ZANU-PF won independent Zimbabwe's first election.

Demonstrators gather at Rhodesia House in London in protest against the British government's policies towards Rhodesia

Historical interpretation

Historian David Leaver has argued that both whites and blacks either created myths or used history to legitimise their struggles. The myth of white supremacy was based on their control of the land and the concepts behind segregation and minority rule. Black nationalists emphasised the greatness of Great Zimbabwe as a legitimate black state long before the colonists arrived. As Leaver states: 'To African nationalist movements of the 1960s and 1970s, Great Zimbabwe proved what most whites sought to deny – that blacks had, could, and would create a great nation. From the early twentieth century, there never was any doubt about the site's African origins: colonial mythmaking was believed by those who needed or wanted to believe it.'

What was the role of armed struggle in achieving independence?

ZAPU, ZANU and the move to guerrilla warfare

As seen in Unit 1, ZAPU was formed in 1961 after the National Democratic Party (NDP) had been banned. ZAPU's first president was **Joshua Nkomo** (see page 30) with the Reverend Ndabaningi Sithole as chairman and **Robert Mugabe** (see page 30) as secretary. Differences over policies and tactics, and a distrust of Nkomo's leadership, led to a split in the organisation. In 1963, Sithole and other leaders, including Mugabe, broke away to form ZANU. Even though ZAPU had embarked

Theory of knowledge

History and the manipulation of 'truth'

When the ruins of Great Zimbabwe were first seen by white explorers in the 1880s, they were reluctant to believe that their origins were African. They speculated that the builders could have been ancient Egyptians or Phoenicians or even the Queen of Sheba. Archaeologists and scientists later proved beyond doubt that the builders were the ancestors of the Shona people who lived in the area. After UDI in 1965, the Smith government tried to suppress this knowledge and perpetuated the myth that Great Zimbabwe was built by foreign invaders. Why do you think a government would encourage the spread of false historical information?

Question

Is Leaver's view convincing? As you read other case studies in this book, try to find parallels with this view of Rhodesia/Zimbabwe.

Terminology

The following acronyms are used in this unit:

ZAPU Zimbabwe African People's Union
ZANU Zimbabwe African National Union
ZIPRA Zimbabwe People's Revolutionary Army (the armed wing of ZAPU)
ZANLA Zimbabwe African National Liberation Army (the armed wing of ZANU)
ZANU-PF Zimbabwe African National Union–Patriotic Front

Joshua Nkomo (1917–99)

Nkomo was one of the founding members of ZAPU. He spent much of the 1960s and 1970s in prison. In 1974, he went to Zambia to continue the armed struggle. He was eventually eased out by Robert Mugabe and, although he held office in the independent state of Zimbabwe, by 1987 he had agreed to ZAPU being absorbed into ZANU, effectively creating a one-party state and isolating himself from mainstream politics.

Robert Mugabe (b. 1924)

Mugabe emerged as one of the primary figures in the independence movement as leader of ZANU, a splinter group of Joshua Nkomo's ZAPU. He was prime minister of Zimbabwe from 1980 to 1987, and president with special powers from 1987.

Fact

Events would prove ZANU right – it was in the countryside that the guerrillas stood the best chance of success. It was harder for the Rhodesian armed forces to maintain control over large rural areas. The presence of friendly states, especially Mozambique, along all except the southern border of Rhodesia also created safe havens for the guerrillas.

on a campaign of sabotage and the occupation of unused land, Nkomo had also been prepared to negotiate a settlement with Britain. ZANU, however, urged a policy of more active confrontation with white minority rule. There was violence between the two organisations as they fought to gain the support of the masses. In time, regional differences between them intensified. ZANU was seen to represent the interests of Shona-speakers based mainly in the eastern part of the country, and ZAPU the interests of Ndebele-speakers in the western areas.

When the Rhodesian Front government banned ZAPU and ZANU in 1964, both organisations realised that a constitutional solution was unlikely, and began an armed struggle. ZAPU formed the Zimbabwe People's Revolutionary Army (ZIPRA), and ZANU formed the Zimbabwe African National Liberation Army (ZANLA). ZAPU aligned itself with the USSR and encouraged an uprising by urban workers. Its armed wing, ZIPRA, later received Soviet support and funding. ZANU, on the other hand, aligned itself with China and attempted to mobilise the rural peasantry. It believed that the low urban density of Rhodesia, and the ease with which the authorities could monitor and control town dwellers, meant that ZAPU's strategy was doomed to failure. ZANU and its military wing ZANLA received support and training from China.

The guerrilla war begins

The first real clash between guerrilla fighters and the Rhodesian army came in April 1966, when ZANU guerrillas crossed into Rhodesia from Zambia to blow up power lines and attack white farms. They were wiped out by the Rhodesian army in what was later referred to as the battle of Sinoia. Although this event demonstrated how effective the Rhodesian armed forces were at countering insurgent activity, it also showed how vulnerable the white farming community was.

In addition, the Rhodesian government realised it would face problems in the future, if the guerrilla attacks became better organised and supported. In 1967 and 1968, the tempo increased, with attacks on urban targets such as hotels and cafés. In August 1967, a combined force of ZAPU and African National Congress guerrillas from South Africa attacked targets in Rhodesia. This force was defeated, but it drew South African forces into the conflict. For the next few years, South African paramilitary units were stationed in Rhodesia.

These early attacks showed the nationalist organisations that large-scale incursions into Rhodesia would not be successful on their own. They were inviting a devastating military response from the government, which the guerrillas could not hope to resist. However, if large areas of the countryside could be brought over to support the resistance movement, and if attacks in the cities were co-ordinated, then perhaps the government would lose control of the situation. This was the path increasingly followed by ZANU, which infiltrated Rhodesia with small numbers of guerrillas – sometimes single individuals.

ZANU and its military wing ZANLA were applying **Maoist** techniques borrowed from the Chinese. These involved creating a strong powerbase amongst the peasants, making control of the countryside impossible for the government. ZANLA even enlisted the aid of traditional leaders and local spirit mediums. The powerbase they created was initially political, but eventually it involved arming large numbers of men and women who supplemented the more formally trained ZANLA guerrillas.

External influences on the situation in Rhodesia

Unlike other parts of the continent, the colonies of southern Africa did not make the transition to independence smoothly. Portugal was fighting to retain control of Mozambique and Angola, and Namibia was under the control of South Africa. The success of the independence movement **FRELIMO** in Mozambique gave considerable encouragement to Zimbabwean nationalists. FRELIMO trained guerrilla fighters and provided safe havens for operations across the border into Rhodesia. This aid intensified after Mozambique achieved independence in 1975. The newly independent Mozambique also placed an economic embargo on trade with Rhodesia at considerable cost to its own economy.

Eventually, ZANLA guerrillas began to infiltrate Rhodesia from Mozambique's Tete province in such numbers that they posed a serious military threat to the Smith regime.

The guerrilla war in Rhodesia was also linked to the Cold War. Southern Africa supplied key minerals to the world economy, and the value of its strategic position was recognised by the USSR and China, as well as by the West. Soviet and Chinese support for ZAPU and ZANU respectively created the potential for future communist influence in the region, a situation that the West feared would be exploited by its enemies in the Cold War.

SOURCE A

Finally, the Rhodesian conflict constituted a chapter in the global Cold War, with the Soviet bloc and China supporting the two guerrilla armies and the United States and its allies backing white Rhodesia and South Africa as strategic, resource-laden bastions of anti-communism.

Mtisi, J., Nyakudya, M. and Barnes, T. 2009. 'War in Rhodesia'. In Raftopoulos, B. and Mlambo, A. Becoming Zimbabwe. *Harare, Zimbabwe. Weaver Press. p. 144.*

Attempts at a negotiated settlement

In spite of UDI, the British government continued to hold talks with Smith in an attempt to negotiate a settlement. The Rhodesian government, however, stubbornly refused to make meaningful concessions. Finally, in 1971, the two sides agreed on a proposed settlement. Although this made provision for eventual majority rule, it effectively maintained white domination for the foreseeable future. Despite this, the British government insisted that the agreement should have the support of the majority of people in Rhodesia, and in 1972 it sent the Pearce Commission to investigate. Even though ZANU and ZAPU were formally banned and their leaders in prison, there were widespread demonstrations, strikes and mass meetings showing overwhelming opposition from Africans to the proposed settlement. This was a major setback for the white minority government, which had hoped to gain international recognition of its regime.

Maoist Relating to the policies and tactics used by Chinese communist leader Mao Zedong. Working in a pre-industrial agrarian society, he modified classic Marxism to fit China's circumstances. He argued that communist activity could prepare the peasant population for a full-scale uprising against the ruling class.

FRELIMO The *Frente de Libertação de Moçambique*, or Mozambican Liberation Front. This group was formed in 1964 to fight Portuguese control in Mozambique. During the 1960s and early 1970s, Portugal waged fierce wars against resistance groups in all three of its African colonies – Mozambique, Angola and Guinea-Bissau. These resistance movements forced the Portuguese to grant independence in 1975.

SOURCE B

The whole Pearce Commission exercise proved a disaster for the Smith government. ... It showed Britain, South Africa and the world at large the depth and extent of African rejection of white minority rule in Rhodesia. It showed that the regime would be unlikely to survive for very long even if it gained legal independence. Finally it showed Africans who disliked the regime that this hatred was shared by almost every other African throughout the land. It thus played a very important part in preparing the ground for the spread of the liberation struggle.

Afigbo, A. E., et al. 1986. The Making of Modern Africa, Volume 2: The Twentieth Century. *London, UK. Longman. p. 276.*

Discussion point

Explain the similarities and differences between the significance of the Bledisloe Commission of 1939 and the Pearce Commission of 1972.

In the meantime, the Smith government had shown that it had no intention of relinquishing white control. In 1970, the Land Tenure Act replaced the Land Apportionment Act of 1930, consolidating white control over more of the land. This Act formed the basis of a new constitution, designed to maintain white supremacy, which declared Rhodesia to be a republic.

Developments in the early 1970s

Fact

The uprisings against colonial rule that had taken place in 1896–97 had been called the *Chimurenga*, which means 'struggle' in Shona. Although they had been crushed, the resistance provided inspiration to future freedom fighters. The uprising against white minority rule between 1966 and 1980 was referred to as the Second Chimurenga.

From 1972, the guerrilla war intensified. By this stage the peasants of north-eastern Rhodesia had been heavily politicised and were prepared to support guerrilla operations. ZANLA launched a series of attacks on white farmsteads which the Rhodesian security forces found difficult to contain. Even though the period of national service required by the white population was extended, the Rhodesian government simply did not have enough troops to protect the scattered white farming communities. The government therefore launched Operation Hurricane, a plan to strike the guerrilla bases in neighbouring Zambia and Mozambique. It also closed the border with Zambia to all goods except copper. These actions left no room for negotiation and served to alienate Zambia and extend the war's geographic area. The South African government was also concerned by these actions, fearing destabilisation of the whole region. The Rhodesian attempt to eliminate guerrilla bases in neighbouring countries was thus not successful.

The government next focused on the peasants, who were providing vital support for ZANLA. The government imposed collective fines on entire regions, confiscated cattle as a punishment, and closed key facilities such as shops, clinics, schools and churches. The most extreme measure was the creation of 'protected villages' – entire communities were uprooted and moved out of the war zone. This created vast unpopulated regions along the Mozambique frontier, allowing the Rhodesian military to sweep the countryside for guerrillas. Although this measure had an impact on ZANLA operations, it also alienated the rural population to such an extent that many more joined the resistance. It has been estimated that 240,000 Africans were uprooted by this scheme. Although some of the settlements to which they were relocated were a genuine improvement on their original homes, in general the new protected villages were of very low quality, and living conditions were poor. In an attempt to win support, the government offered rewards to villagers for informing on ZANLA operations. This had limited success and its effects were largely offset by the negative policy of the protected villages.

The increased tempo of the war began to have a significant effect on the white population. Rhodesia's critical shortage of troops resulted in extreme measures to fill the ranks of the army. The draft age for white settlers was extended to 38, and mixed-race Rhodesians were also conscripted. As time went on, this placed an increasing drain on the economy as more of the skilled workforce was called up for military service. The regular army was also expanded, but it was clear that a military force capable of waging a long-drawn-out war would be prohibitively expensive. ZANLA's operations, therefore, were slowly undermining the white regime.

Questions

What strategies did the Rhodesian government use in an attempt to crush the resistance movement? How successful were they?

ZANLA guerrillas in the Zambezi Valley region of Rhodesia

Theory of knowledge

History and language

An example of bias in historical terminology is the use of the word 'terrorist'. White Rhodesians referred to ZANU and ZAPU as terrorists, while the nationalist movements saw themselves as freedom fighters. What term could be used that would be more neutral than either of these?

What other factors played a role in the success of the independence struggle?

The role of South Africa and Zambia

détente An attempt by all sides in the Cold War, including China, to ease the tension and create an atmosphere of mutual tolerance and acceptance. Vorster saw parallels in its application to the affairs of southern Africa.

Portugal's withdrawal from southern Africa and the independence of Mozambique under a socialist FRELIMO government in 1975 forced the South African government to reassess the situation. The South African leader, John Vorster, realised the significance of developments in Rhodesia. He decided on a policy of **détente** – called the 'Outward Policy' – to establish better relations with the independent African states in the region.

The Outward Policy involved negotiation with neighbouring governments in an effort to secure regimes that were at least neutral to South Africa. Vorster hoped to achieve this through a combination of diplomacy and the wielding of South Africa's economic power. South Africa was the dominant economy in the region and its co-operation was essential for the economic well-being of all the southern African states.

Question

Why was the role of South Africa critical in forcing Smith's government into talks with the nationalists?

Smith's government threatened Vorster's plans for two reasons. Firstly, the actions of the Rhodesian army along its borders were causing major diplomatic problems. Secondly, it seemed to Vorster that Rhodesia's defeat was inevitable in the long term, and that the longer the guerrilla struggle went on, the more likely it was that an extreme Marxist regime would come to power in Rhodesia. This would be a direct threat to South Africa's security. It would be in South Africa's best interests if a moderate black government came to power in Rhodesia by negotiation.

frontline states These were the independent states that were geographically close to Rhodesia – Mozambique, Zambia, Botswana, Angola and Tanzania – and which were affected by the ongoing guerrilla war. Three of them shared borders with Rhodesia, and Tanzania provided the nationalist forces with support and bases. The frontline states played an influential role in urging unity among the nationalist groups and an acceptance of a negotiated settlement.

Zambia's leader, Kenneth Kaunda, also wanted the war to end as soon as possible so that Zambia could focus on its own pressing economic policies. The presence of ZANU and ZAPU leaders and their guerrilla armies was creating tensions, and they were a target for cross-border raids into Zambia by the Rhodesian security forces. By the end of 1974, Kaunda and Vorster had reached an agreement to attempt to stop the fighting in Rhodesia. As part of the process of détente, they put pressure on their respective allies. Kaunda and the leaders of the other **frontline states** urged the leaders of the nationalist organisations to negotiate. Under pressure from South Africa, Smith agreed to release ZAPU and ZANU leaders from prison. By 1975 a ceasefire of sorts was in place.

However, the ceasefire did not last and the independence struggle continued. Any chance of fruitful discussions between the two sides was prevented by Smith's refusal to make meaningful concessions. Renewed guerrilla attacks took place. The shortage of Rhodesian troops, the economic cost of the war and the strain it placed on the white minority were now becoming more obvious. Smith's confidence was severely damaged by the pressure put on him by the South African government.

Divisions among the nationalists

From the nationalist point of view, the ceasefire looked like – and was depicted as – a victory. The nationalists, however, faced problems of their own. The movement had already divided into ZANU and ZAPU; now there was infighting within ZANU's military wing, ZANLA. This was the so-called Nhari rebellion of 1975.

The Nhari rebellion was essentially a confrontation between the ZANU high command and a group of ZANLA guerrillas. The guerrillas were led by Thomas Nhari, who complained about the lack of sophisticated weapons, ammunition and supplies reaching the guerrillas while the leaders enjoyed comfortable lives in the Zambian capital, Lusaka. Eventually Nhari was arrested and executed together with 60 ZANLA fighters who had supported him.

This did not solve the divisions within ZANLA, however, and in 1975 its charismatic leader, Herbert Chitepo, was assassinated. Much later it was discovered that Chitepo's death was a result of Rhodesian covert operations, but at the time it was blamed on ZANLA infighting. The Zambians stepped in to restore order and forced the ZANLA leadership to leave for Mozambique. Zambian actions also began to starve ZANU of money. Funds for the guerrilla war went through a nationalist umbrella organisation called the African National Council, headed by Bishop Abel Muzorewa. Under Zambian pressure he withdrew funding for ZANU.

At this stage there was also a change of leadership within ZANU. Many in the organisation had come to believe that Sithole was out of touch with the fighters in the ZANLA camps in Mozambique, and he was replaced as leader of ZANU by Robert Mugabe. Sithole continued to lead a significant minority claiming to be the real ZANU. In 1975, Mugabe and a fellow ZANU leader, Edward Tekere, were under house arrest in Mozambique. This was ostensibly for their own safety, but may also have been because Mugabe was regarded with some suspicion by Mozambican leaders. These problems within ZANU shifted the power in the nationalist movement to Nkomo's ZAPU. ZAPU's military wing, ZIPRA, was almost wholly based in Zambia and received full support from Kenneth Kaunda.

This division of effort between ZAPU and ZANU weakened the effectiveness of the resistance movement. Eventually pressure from the frontline states led to the establishment of the Patriotic Front between ZAPU and ZANU in October 1976. This was not a union of the two organisations, but an agreement to work together. Although differences between the two continued – with ZANU openly critical of détente – by this time there was widespread support for both organisations throughout Zimbabwe.

Talks and negotiations, 1976

Smith and Nkomo had begun talks in March 1976. These broke down when the white government predictably failed to concede to black majority rule. Superficially, the war seemed to be going well for Smith. Fighting was limited to the frontier regions, the nationalists were split and the army was doing well. The situation was transformed, however, by events in Angola. South Africa feared that the new Angolan regime would extend its operations south into South African-controlled Namibia, where a nationalist movement called the South West African People's Organisation was struggling for independence.

South Africa feared that continuing raids by the Rhodesian army into neighbouring states would create a hostile alliance of states in southern Africa, allied to the USSR. This would obviously not be in South Africa's interests. Vorster used Rhodesia's dependence on its rail link through South Africa to put pressure on Smith to agree to a negotiated settlement. Matters came to a head in August 1976, when Rhodesian forces attacked a camp at Nyadzonya in Mozambique,

Fact

When Angola, another former Portuguese colony, gained independence in 1975, a civil war broke out between the socialist People's Movement for the Liberation of Angola (MPLA) and the National Union for the Total Independence of Angola (UNITA). Anxious to prevent an MPLA victory, South Africa invaded Angola to support UNITA, while the MPLA received substantial support from communist Cuba, including 20,000 Cuban troops. Under international pressure, South Africa withdrew its army from Angola, although its support for UNITA continued. The USA also worked to oppose an MPLA victory, although it did not send troops to Angola.

killing hundreds of people. The Rhodesian government claimed that it was a ZANLA training camp; ZANU insisted that it was a refugee camp. Whatever the truth, Vorster decided that the time had come to declare South African support for majority rule in Rhodesia, totally isolating Smith's government.

Vorster also came under pressure from the US. American foreign policy had failed to prevent a communist government coming to power in Angola and the new US secretary of state, Henry Kissinger, believed that open support for majority rule in Rhodesia would serve American interests if it prevented the nationalist movements from drawing closer to the communist bloc. He put pressure on Vorster to help deliver majority rule in Rhodesia, by promising to tone down America's anti-South Africa rhetoric. In September 1976, Vorster threatened to cut off supplies to Rhodesia if Smith failed to move to majority rule.

In addition, by this time the Zimbabwean nationalists had begun to recover and ZANLA raids from Mozambique were increasing. The combination of South African pressure and an intensification of the guerrilla war forced Smith's hand. He offered majority rule in return for the West lifting sanctions and making funds available for development. In reality, though, Smith was not prepared to accept full majority rule. Rather, he believed that some small concessions could be made to the black majority without relinquishing white control. He also believed that the nationalist movement remained so divided that it would be unable to push for full majority rule.

When the parties met in Geneva between October and December 1976, there was little prospect of a lasting settlement. The USA convinced Smith that a compromise could be reached with the nationalists. Smith, however, saw the talks as a chance to buy a two-year cessation of economic sanctions, during which time the Rhodesian security forces could destroy the guerrilla movement. The Americans had not discussed their proposals with the nationalist leadership or with the presidents of the frontline African states. The Geneva conference ended in deadlock.

Developments after 1976

After the failed talks between Smith and Nkomo in 1976, members of the guerrilla organisations and the black population in general increasingly looked to Mugabe as the nationalist leader who would succeed in gaining majority rule. His position was further strengthened when the frontline states of Zambia and Mozambique finally allied themselves to ZANU. This development proved critical in bringing down white minority rule in Rhodesia. Despite the formation of the Patriotic Front, friction within the nationalist ranks continued, but ZANU managed to strengthen its position and create a military threat that the Rhodesian government could not overcome.

Between 1977 and 1979, the guerrilla war intensified. ZIPRA forces from Zambia and Botswana, and ZANLA forces from Mozambique, launched full-scale incursions into Rhodesia. This created considerable tensions within the ruling Rhodesian Front party when extremists demanded mass conscription and a huge expansion of the army. There was even talk of a military coup against Smith. Neither came about.

Theory of knowledge

Historical interpretation

The US did not send troops to intervene in Angola, partly because 1975 was the year of America's final withdrawal from Vietnam and public opinion was opposed to further involvement in faraway wars. Nevertheless, historians have interpreted events in Angola as a defeat for American foreign policy. Afigbo *et al* refer to the 'disastrous failure of American intervention in Angola', and Mtisi, Nyakudya and Barnes refer to the 'embarrassing military approach that had been used unsuccessfully in Angola' by the US.

Question

How did the politics of the Cold War influence the Zimbabwean independence struggle?

Fact

By 1979, conscription of white Rhodesians had been extended from age 38 to 50, placing a huge strain on the economy. It also contributed to increasing numbers of whites emigrating from Rhodesia. Soon Rhodesia was conscripting black soldiers, who were obviously not committed to the fight. The protected villages scheme was extended, and by 1979 over half a million people had been relocated.

The Rhodesian security forces also stepped up their attacks on guerrilla bases outside the country. In November 1977 they launched a massive raid on Chimoio, a ZANLA camp 90 km (56 miles) inside Mozambique. Using ground troops and the entire Rhodesian air force, they killed over 1200 people. They also attacked ZIPRA camps in Zambia.

The nationalists reacted by increasing the conflict, declaring 1978 as the 'year of the people' and sending thousands of guerrillas into Rhodesia. With increasingly sophisticated weapons, including Soviet-made surface-to-air missiles, ZIPRA forces shot down two Air Rhodesia passenger planes, killing dozens of passengers. ZANLA forces blew up the oil storage tanks in an industrial area of the Rhodesian capital, Salisbury.

On the international scene, pressure on Smith's government increased. The new Democratic administration in the USA, under President Jimmy Carter, worked with the British government to create a new plan for Rhodesia. In July 1978, the US Senate voted against the lifting of sanctions. In Angola the USSR was creating a communist ally with the aid of the Cubans. South Africa was becoming ever more concerned about a total Marxist victory in the region, and from 1978 the new South African premier, P. W. Botha, put more pressure on Smith.

By 1979, the nationalist guerrillas were on the brink of victory, forcing the Smith government into a deal with moderate black leaders – those who had no military backing, and who, like Smith, were opposed to the Patriotic Front. In 1978, an 'Internal Settlement' was reached between Smith, Muzorewa, Sithole and Chief Jeremiah Chirau. They agreed to a transition to majority rule but with the white political position protected by constitutional guarantees. In 1979, elections were held in which Muzorewa's United African National Council won 67% of the vote. Muzorewa briefly became prime minister of 'Zimbabwe-Rhodesia', although whites retained control of the army, police, civil service and economy. The Patriotic Front had called on its supporters to boycott the election. It rejected the Internal Settlement and stepped up the guerrilla war.

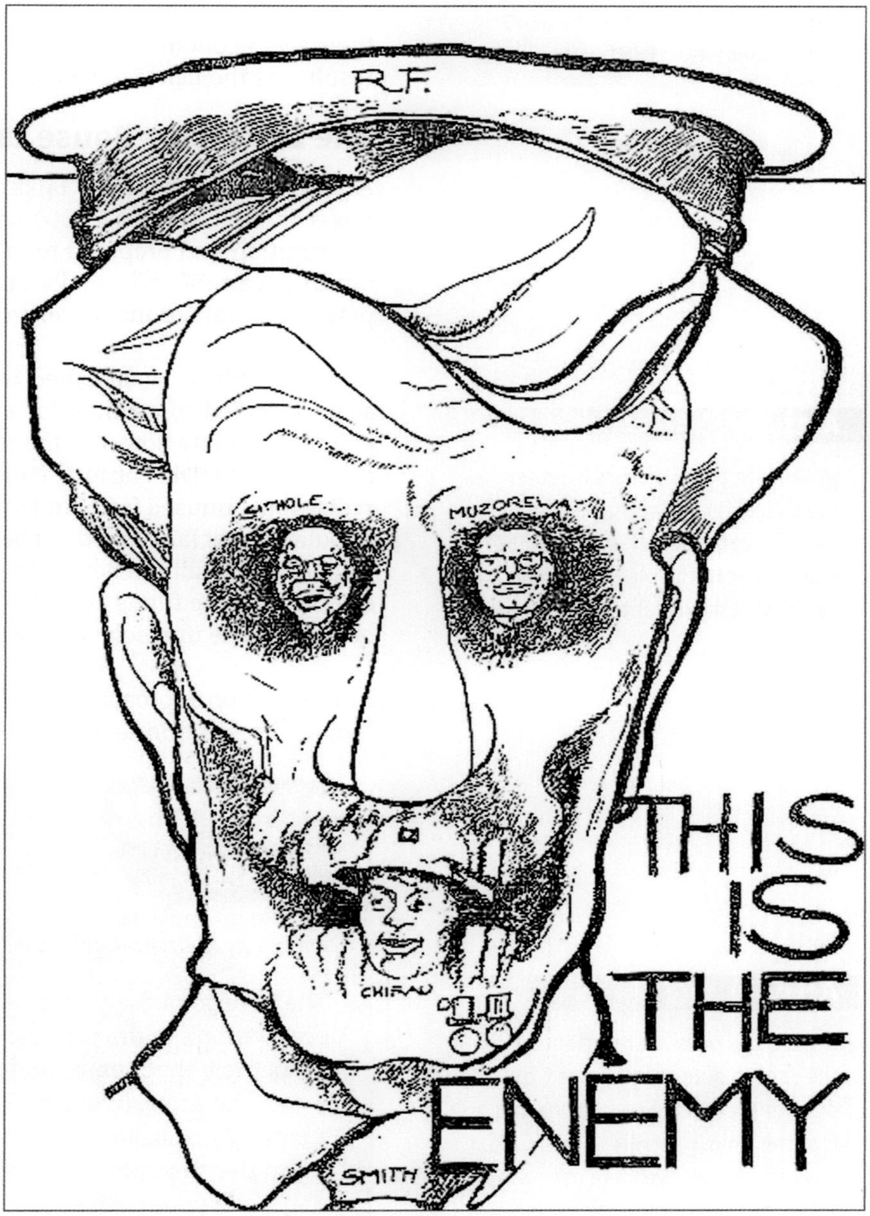

A ZANU poster deriding the Internal Settlement of 1979

Britain, the United States and the rest of the world also refused to recognise the Internal Settlement, and the frontline states, supported by the OAU, confirmed their support for the Patriotic Front. At a Commonwealth conference held in Lusaka in August 1979, African leaders put pressure on the British prime minister Margaret Thatcher, saying that it was Britain's responsibility to resolve the crisis. Nigeria, Britain's biggest trading partner in Africa, even threatened to block British investments in Nigeria. Thatcher agreed to convene a constitutional conference in London.

Question

How did a combination of internal and external pressures force the Smith government into negotiations?

At the same time, there were increasing pressures on the Rhodesian government and on the Patriotic Front. By late 1979, with over 20,000 guerrillas active within the country, Smith saw the futility of his position and agreed to negotiate a settlement. Mozambique and Zambia, both of which had suffered heavy damage as a result of raids by Rhodesian security forces, and needed peace to rebuild their own economies, put pressure on the nationalist leaders to negotiate. The result was the Lancaster House conference in 1979.

The Lancaster House talks and the election of 1980

At the Lancaster House talks in London, the parties signed a ceasefire in a war in which about 27,000 people had lost their lives. They drew up a new constitution and prepared for all-party elections in 1980. In the meantime, the Smith government formally surrendered its independence and handed over power to a transitional government under British control.

Activity

Working in pairs, discuss whether the Lancaster House agreement was of greater benefit to the white minority or to the black majority nationalist movement.

The constitution established a parliamentary democracy with 20 of the 100 seats reserved for whites for at least seven years, giving the white minority disproportionate power in the new state. The issue of land created the greatest disagreement. The Patriotic Front wanted the new government to take over and redistribute unused farmland to resettle war veterans. However, the constitution stipulated that land could not be confiscated but could only change hands on the principle of 'willing seller, willing buyer'. The British and American governments offered to make funds available to implement this, but no details were clarified or agreed. The unresolved land issue was to create problems in the future.

As the election approached, the Patriotic Front disintegrated, and ZANU and ZAPU fought the election as separate parties – ZANU-PF and PF-ZAPU respectively.

SOURCE C

Speech by Robert Mugabe pledging reconciliation, 18 April 1980.

The wrongs of the past must now stand forgiven and forgotten. If ever we look to the past, let us do so for the lesson the past has taught us, namely that oppression and racism are inequalities that must never find scope in our political and social system. It could never be a correct justification that because the whites oppressed us yesterday when they had power, the blacks must oppress them today because they have power. An evil remains an evil whether practised by white against black or black against white.

Quoted in Meredith, M. 2005. The State of Africa. *Cape Town, South Africa. Jonathan Ball Publishers. p. 328.*

Activity

Discuss the possible reactions to the speech quoted in Source C by different groups of people hearing it at the time: guerrilla soldiers who have spent many years in camps in exile; members of the Rhodesian Front; black farmers who have lost their land and been moved to protected villages; and members of the British government.

White Rhodesian (and South African) hopes of a victory by the moderates were shattered by the outcome of the election. Mugabe's ZANU-PF won 57 seats, Nkomo's PF-ZAPU won 20 seats, and the moderate Muzorewa's UNAC won only three. The 20 seats reserved for whites all went to Smith's Rhodesian Front party. All except one of PF-ZAPU's seats were won in Matabeleland in the west, and ZANU-PF won all the seats in the northern region of Mashonaland, a development 'boding ill for the post-independence period', according to historians Mtisi, Nyakudya and Barnes. On 18 April 1980, Robert Mugabe was installed as the first prime minister of independent Zimbabwe.

Fact

A song by the Jamaican reggae singer Bob Marley called 'Zimbabwe' had been an inspiration to guerrilla fighters during the nationalist struggle. Marley and his group The Wailers were invited to Zimbabwe to participate in the Independence Day celebrations in Salisbury on 18 April 1980, where they performed this song.

What part did Robert Mugabe play?

At the time of writing, Robert Mugabe is still the leader of Zimbabwe. He is of Shona origin and his ethnic background has influenced his politics. Like many other independence leaders, he received a Western education in mission schools, in his case Catholic, and qualified as a teacher after graduating from university at Fort Hare in South Africa in 1951. He also studied at Oxford University in Britain in 1952. He has two law degrees and is a Master of Science. His education brought him into contact with many future African leaders, including Julius Nyerere and Kenneth Kaunda. In the late 1950s, Mugabe taught in Ghana, where he was influenced and inspired by Kwame Nkrumah. These early years influenced his political thinking, pushing him towards the left and Marxism.

Fact

Kwame Nkrumah, the first leader of independent Ghana, was a leading supporter of Pan-Africanism. Pan-Africanists called for the liberation of Africa and promoted African unity. Ghana became an important centre of the movement, and Nkrumah an inspiration to nationalist leaders throughout Africa.

Robert Mugabe (left) with Georges Silundika (centre) and Joshua Nkomo (right) in a photograph taken around 1960

After his return to Zimbabwe in 1960, Mugabe joined the National Democratic Party, which soon developed into Nkomo's ZAPU organisation. In 1963, Mugabe left ZAPU to join Sithole's ZANU party, and in 1964 he was arrested and imprisoned for his political views. During this period he experienced at first hand the restrictions of the Rhodesian government – he was not even allowed to attend the funeral of his four-year-old son.

Mugabe's early life was thus dominated by two forces – firstly, an extensive period of education and secondly, a long period of imprisonment. It was during this latter period that he came to two conclusions about the route to majority rule. He recognised that a more conventional Soviet-style revolutionary movement would fail in the face of the poverty and lack of political consciousness of Zimbabwe's peasant class. He also saw that the white regime was so extreme in its position that considerable force would have to be applied to bring about any kind of change within the country. He concluded, therefore, that a Maoist (see page 31) approach to insurgency was necessary to politicise the mass of the black rural poor and to conceal political activity so that it could not be easily countered by the Rhodesian regime.

Mugabe's time in prison greatly increased his prestige within ZANU. He was released in 1974, after South African pressure on the Smith government to reach an agreement with the Zimbabwean independence movements. When Sithole was overthrown as leader of ZANU in 1974, Mugabe emerged to take his place. The problem Mugabe faced, though, was that he and his organisation were largely ignored by other African leaders. Thus, when he travelled to Zambia in the same year, Kaunda refused to recognise his position. At that time ZAPU was seen as the best hope for achieving independence in Zimbabwe. Mugabe had no military experience and was eyed with suspicion by other African leaders. He was a dedicated Marxist and he had an inflexible approach to the problem of gaining independence.

Mugabe consolidated his control of ZANU in 1975. This takeover was accompanied by political assassination and intimidation, which showed him that leaders had to be ruthless to achieve their goals, a view that has since dominated his political life. He then focused on defeating ZAPU to push forward his model of the fight for independence. His bid for dominance was successful, and ZANU played a vital role in the final phases of the guerrilla war. By the time of the Lancaster House negotiations, Mugabe had become a key player in events.

The Lancaster House talks demonstrated Mugabe's diplomatic skill. The events of 1979 were complex; ZAPU and ZANU were waging a guerrilla war that was wearing down the Rhodesian regime but not defeating it. Left to its own devices, there is a good argument that Ian Smith's regime would have continued the fight against the nationalist organisations. However, outside pressures in the form of the UN and South Africa had created the conditions in which Smith might be prepared to deal with Mugabe. It was at this point that the ZANU leader made two key concessions. He agreed both to the creation of a parliament in which the white population was disproportionately represented, and to place a ten-year moratorium on changes to land ownership. These concessions reassured whites and allowed them to reach an agreement which led to the formation of an independent Zimbabwe a year later. Subsequent events, however, showed that Mugabe never stopped opposing white supremacy, and that in the long term he was determined to end white dominance not only of political power, but also of the economy.

Activity

http://iwpr.net/report-news/mugabe-warrior-credentials-questioned

Read this review of a book written by Edgar Tekere, a former comrade of Mugabe's in the ZANU leadership, and later the leader of a group opposed to Mugabe. In it he critically examines how Mugabe rose to his leadership position in ZANU and then Zimbabwe.

Explain why this book is considered to be a revisionist interpretation, and what the reviewer means when he says that Tekere has 'broken one of the most sacred conventions of African liberation doctrine'.

End of unit activities

1 Draw up a table to highlight the differences between ZANU and ZAPU. Include information on leadership, support base, ideology, tactics, allies, effectiveness, and any other categories you think are important.

2 Write a report about the involvement of Mozambique and Zambia in the Zimbabwean independence struggle. Include an analysis of the negative impact that their support had on their own countries.

3 Draw a spider diagram to illustrate the factors that finally forced the Smith government to agree to black majority rule. Include the following factors plus any others you can think of:

- sanctions
- the guerrilla war
- collapsing economy
- pressure from South Africa
- impact of the Cold War
- world opinion.

4 'The key factor responsible for the attainment of majority rule in Zimbabwe was the heroism of the nationalist organisations.'

Divide the class into two groups. One group should prepare an argument to support this statement, and the other an argument to oppose it.

5 Find out what daily life was like for ordinary civilians, black and white, who lived in Rhodesia/Zimbabwe between 1965 and 1980.

6 http://news.bbc.co.uk/onthisday/hi/dates/stories/march/4/newsid_2515000/2515145.stm

Read this news report written on the day of Zimbabwe's first democratic election. Use the information here, together with information from this unit, to write a newspaper editorial commenting on the historical significance of the ZANU-PF victory in the election.

3 The formation of and challenges to Zimbabwe

Timeline

1980 Zimbabwe becomes an independent state

1982 violence breaks out between ZANU and ZAPU supporters in Matabeleland

1987 Mugabe and Nkomo sign Unity Accord; Mugabe's powers as president are significantly strengthened

1992 Land Acquisition Act

1997 Land Redistribution Act

1999 Movement for Democratic Change (MDC) formed

2000 55% of electorate rejects constitutional changes in a referendum; ZANU-PF and MDC votes evenly balanced in parliamentary elections; occupation of white farms, often accompanied by violence

2002 Mugabe re-elected

2005 ZANU-PF re-elected, followed by brutal government attacks in urban areas

2008 MDC wins majority in parliament; disputed presidential election sees Mugabe clinging to power

2009 power-sharing arrangement between ZANU-PF and the MDC formalised

Key questions

- What kind of state was established in Zimbabwe after 1980?
- What challenges did Zimbabwe face after 1987?
- What part has Robert Mugabe played since independence?

Overview

- Newly independent Zimbabwe faced many challenges in 1980, including economic reconstruction, political transformation, inequity in the ownership and control of land, and racism.
- The new government needed the co-operation of the white minority, which still controlled key areas of the economy.
- The government applied moderate economic policies and sought to retain the co-operation of white business and agriculture.
- There were significant improvements in education and health care, but these improvements were unevenly distributed, and key areas of the economy remained under foreign ownership.
- Efforts by the government to implement a programme of land reform and redistribution met with limited success.
- Rivalry and tensions between Robert Mugabe's ZANU-PF and Joshua Nkomo's PF-ZAPU surfaced once again, based on political rivalry between the two leaders and parties, as well as ethnic and regional differences between their supporters.
- In 1982, Nkomo was dismissed from the government and PF-ZAPU accused of planning a coup. The Fifth Brigade, a ruthless North Korean-trained militia, waged a war of violence and intimidation against ZAPU supporters in Matabeleland.
- The crisis ended in 1987, when Mugabe and Nkomo signed a Unity Accord, merging the two parties and increasing Mugabe's powers.
- Relations between the government and the white community deteriorated, with accusations of racism adding to tensions rooted in white economic privileges.
- After 1990, ZANU-PF consolidated its hold on power, winning all elections using violence, intimidation and vote-rigging.
- Despite the difficulties, there was opposition to Mugabe's rule, notably from the Movement for Democratic Change (MDC), which was formed in 1999 under the leadership of Morgan Tsvangirai.
- Land reform became the key issue in Zimbabwe in the late 1990s, culminating in the occupation by force of many white-owned farms by groups of landless peasants and war veterans (see page 50).
- Throughout the 1990s the economy declined, causing real hardship to the people of Zimbabwe.
- In 2008, growing support for the MDC forced Mugabe to agree to a form of power-sharing between ZANU-PF and the MDC.

What kind of state was established in Zimbabwe after 1980?

Challenges facing Zimbabwe after independence

The new state of Zimbabwe faced many challenges in 1980. The country had emerged from over 15 years of civil war, which had caused severe damage to the economy and infrastructure. The country also needed to be reintegrated into the world economy after many years of trade sanctions. The new government's main concern was economic reconstruction, but the white minority still controlled key areas of the economy so their co-operation was vital. Furthermore, the new Zimbabwe was as reliant on South Africa for economic activity as its Rhodesian predecessor had been. These factors hindered the ability of the new government to fulfil many of the wishes of its followers, especially the redistribution of land.

Another challenge was to transform the colonial state from an authoritarian white minority regime to a more democratic form of government. There was also serious inequity in ownership and control of land and resources. Whites still controlled much of the economy because, as a result of colonial land policies, they owned the bulk of the fertile agricultural land. Robert Mugabe was initially committed to gaining the confidence of the 6000 white commercial farmers who were a critical factor in the economic well-being of the country. He also attempted to reassure white-controlled businesses that the government would apply market rather than socialist solutions to the country's problems. For the white minority the new regime initially brought many advantages. Their businesses no longer had to fight against the impact of economic sanctions and they were no longer drafted into the military. There was an economic boom between 1980 and 1982, with growth at a record 24%. Whites were the major beneficiaries of this.

The government also faced the problem of nation-building in a society 'deeply divided along the lines of race, class, ethnicity, gender and geography', according to historian James Muzondidya. The government adopted as its national symbols emblems associated with the empire of Great Zimbabwe, as reminders of the pre-colonial past. The Zimbabwe bird is depicted on the flag, coat of arms and coins, and features of the ruins of Great Zimbabwe on the banknotes and coat of arms. The languages of the two main ethnic groups, Shona and Ndebele, were adopted as official languages, along with English.

The new Zimbabwean flag was filled with symbolism: the green stripes represent the land; the yellow stripes the mineral wealth; the red stripes the blood that was shed; black represents the black majority; the white triangle represents peace; the red star symbolises internationalism; and the Zimbabwe bird represents the pre-colonial history of the empire of Great Zimbabwe

Fact

As part of the process of transformation, many of the place names associated with colonial rule were replaced by African names. The capital city, which had been named Salisbury in honour of the British prime minister at the time of the takeover of the area by the British South Africa Company in 1890, was renamed Harare in 1992, after the Shona chieftain Neharawa, who had lived there with his people in pre-colonial times.

The inequality enshrined in the Lancaster House constitution, which protected the political and economic power of the white minority, was another challenge. Firstly, whites controlled 20% of the seats in parliament and were thus grossly over-represented. This concession could be reviewed after seven years. Secondly, the Lancaster constitution banned the government from forcibly seizing land for at least ten years. The government could buy land, but only at market prices, and based on a system of 'willing seller, willing buyer'. The sheer scale of such an investment meant that the nationalisation of this key resource and its redistribution to the black majority was impossible. Initially, therefore, the white minority had considerable political and economic influence.

Question

What were the economic, political and social problems facing the new government?

Continuing racism was another issue that needed to be faced. Historians Terence Ranger and Ibbo Mandaza have described the post-independence attitude of the remaining white population as a legacy of 'settler culture', based on a desire to maintain their privileged lifestyles and positions. Another historian, James Muzondidya, suggests that whites made little effort to contribute to nation-building or to rectify the racial imbalances inherited from the past. Most whites retained their privileged economic position whilst the bulk of the population lived in poverty. These unresolved issues became major problems in the 1990s.

Successes and failures of the new government

For the first decade after independence Zimbabwe followed a fairly moderate course. This was partly due to the Lancaster House constitution, which had given key concessions to the white minority. This placed a brake on radicalism in the new state, and acted as a counterbalance to the more Marxist or African nationalist policies of ZANU-PF. Initially Mugabe attempted to include whites in his government, and there were two white cabinet ministers. He also retained the white heads of the armed forces and the intelligence services, and even struck up a working relationship with Ian Smith.

Fact

There were some remarkable improvements in education. Between 1980 and 1990, the number of schools increased by 80%. Between 1979 and 1985, enrolment in primary schools rose from 82,000 to over 2.2 million, and in secondary schools from 66,000 to 482,000.

There was remarkable progress in the provision of education and health services, especially in areas neglected by the colonial administration or damaged by years of guerrilla warfare. This was helped by almost £900 million of aid that poured into Zimbabwe, especially from Scandinavian countries. Work was also done on building or repairing infrastructure, such as roads, clinics, fencing and boreholes, and in providing safe drinking water to 84% of the population. Altogether there were some notable economic and social achievements in the first few years, although many challenges remained. The economic gains were unevenly distributed and society remained very unequal, with millions of rural dwellers still desperately poor. Control over key areas of the economy remained in foreign hands, mainly British or South African-based multinational companies. In 1985, 48% of Zimbabwe's manufacturing industry was owned by foreign companies or individuals.

Question

How successful was Zimbabwe in its first decade of independence?

The new government also started on a process of land reform. This was a pressing issue: 4 million Zimbabweans lived on overcrowded communal land and black peasants had a disproportionate amount of poor land frequently threatened by drought. With British financial aid, the government began to resettle black families on formerly white-owned land that had been abandoned during the war. None of this broke the ten-year moratorium on the seizure of white land. However, progress was slow, and by 1990 only 6.5 million hectares of land had been acquired and 52,000 families resettled. In addition, much of the land that had been redistributed was in areas unsuited to agriculture.

The establishment of ZANU-PF dominance

The political situation in Zimbabwe was deeply affected by its history. For many decades the white minority had used repressive laws to crush protests, detain political opponents and silence opposition. In the liberation movement, too, there was a tradition of intolerance, where opponents were viewed as enemies and treated with a mixture of violence and intimidation, and the use of force was often seen as the only way to achieve results. These traditions continued in post-independence Zimbabwe.

Mugabe had often stated that he wanted to establish a one-party state under ZANU-PF. The chief obstacle to this was Joshua Nkomo's PF-ZAPU. Rivalry between the two nationalist movements went back a long way, but they had united to form the Patriotic Front under pressure from the frontline states in 1976. They had contested the 1980 election as separate parties but, despite ZANU-PF's convincing majority, Mugabe had included Nkomo in a coalition government. However, not long after independence, tensions and rivalries between the two parties began to surface once more. Friction surrounding the integration of the two guerrilla forces, Nkomo's ZIPRA and Mugabe's ZANLA, to form a new national army soon turned into violence.

Historical debate

Historian James Muzondidya believes that the main obstacle to successful land reform was the 'willing-seller, willing-buyer' principle in the Lancaster House constitution, which protected the interests of white commercial farmers: 'Conscious of the racial protection guaranteed by the constitution, white farmers were generally reluctant to relinquish their colonially inherited privilege.' Another view, voiced by Martin Meredith, is that ZANU-PF politicians made more effort to acquire farms for themselves than to distribute them to landless peasants, and that by 1990, 8% of commercial farmland was owned by politicians, senior civil servants and security-force officials.

ZANU-PF supporters welcome Mugabe back to Zimbabwe at the time of independence in 1980

The political conflict and personal rivalry between the two parties and their leaders also had ethnic and regional aspects. Most of PF-ZAPU's supporters were Ndebele speakers, living predominantly in Matabeleland in the western part of the country. They believed that ZANU-PF was putting the interests of the majority Shona-speakers ahead of others. In October 1980, Mugabe signed a secret agreement with the communist dictatorship in North Korea whereby the Koreans would train a Zimbabwean brigade in internal security tactics. This unit, drawn exclusively from Shona-speakers, came to be known as the Fifth Brigade.

By 1982, Mugabe felt strong enough to move against Nkomo, and he accused ZAPU of planning a military coup. Nkomo was expelled from the government and his party's property was seized, ruining the livelihoods of many ex-ZIPRA guerrillas. In the army, former ZIPRA soldiers were targeted, many were beaten up and some were killed. As a result, many former ZIPRA guerrillas fled into the bush, taking their arms with them. By late 1982, concentrations of these refugees had become a serious threat to public order in Matabeleland. The Fifth Brigade was sent in to destroy the 'dissidents', as they were labelled by Mugabe.

Question

The government called the crushing of opposition in Matabeleland the *Gukurahundi* operation, a Shona word meaning 'the rain that sweeps away the chaff'. What do you think is the symbolism implied in this term?

The Fifth Brigade attacked not only armed ex-ZIPRA soldiers, but also the civilian population. About 2000 people died within six weeks, and 20,000 between 1982 and 1987. The situation was made worse by drought and, by 1984, 400,000 people in southern Matabeleland were almost entirely dependent on relief supplies. When the Fifth Brigade stopped the movement of these supplies, the entire region was threatened with famine. In addition to the actions of the Fifth Brigade, Mugabe's secret police rounded up thousands of civilians and interned them in camps where beating and torture were routine and many died. This violence and intimidation intensified in the run-up to the 1985 election. The government used the 'Matabeleland crisis' or the 'Dissidents' war' – as the whole operation was called – as a means of ridding itself of opposition.

The violence in Matabeleland only ended when Mugabe and Nkomo signed the Unity Accord in December 1987. This formally merged ZANU and ZAPU into a single party, which retained the title of ZANU-PF. Zimbabwe was now effectively a one-party state, a situation that had been achieved by wearing down ZAPU, its officials and ex-guerrillas. At least 20,000 civilians had died as a result of this infighting.

Theory of knowledge

History and ethics

Mugabe justified the violence by accusing the opposition of plotting to overthrow the state. He claimed that it was necessary to defend the gains that the liberation movement had achieved. Can you think of other examples in history where dictators have used the notion of a threat to the security of the state to justify violence? Can violence ever be justified? Is it acceptable to use violence to save lives, or to intervene to prevent a greater evil from happening?

Nkomo became one of two vice-presidents in the new party and was given a senior post in the government, together with two other former ZAPU leaders. As Mugabe's power became more secure, he and ZANU-PF grew in confidence. On 30 December 1987, Mugabe was declared executive president by parliament, a position that merged the roles of head of state, government and the armed forces. He was also given the powers to dissolve parliament, declare martial law and hold office for an unlimited number of terms. In effect, Mugabe had become a dictator, and the key offices of state were controlled by a new élite whose members owed their positions of power to him.

The infighting between ZANU-PF and ZAPU had a negative effect on the white minority. In order to secure its victory, ZANU-PF had taken control of the state's media so it could advance its cause with propaganda. This propaganda openly referred to whites as racists and, as a result, a greater rift developed between the black and white communities. Other factors also contributed to this rift. White voters continued to support Smith and his uncompromising Rhodesian

Front, and in parliament the overrepresented white community regularly criticised the ZANU-PF government. Their continued privileged position added to the tensions, although half of the white population had emigrated within three years of independence and by 1985 only 100,000 remained. Adding to the suspicions were covert military operations by the apartheid government in South Africa in an attempt to hinder Zimbabwe's development. During 1987, the reservation of 20 seats for white voters was abolished (as had been decided in the Lancaster House constitution) and so they lost their overrepresentation in parliament.

Question

How did the ZANU-PF government use violence as a means of consolidating its power?

What challenges did Zimbabwe face after 1987?

Political developments: the move to authoritarian rule

After 1987, ZANU-PF strengthened its hold on power, and in the 1990 election it won 117 of the 120 seats. However, there were signs of discontent with the state of affairs. Edgar Tekere, a former ZANU leader and member of Mugabe's government, broke away and formed the Zimbabwe Unity Movement (ZUM). Tekere ran unsuccessfully against Mugabe in the 1990 presidential election, but ZUM won 20% of the votes in the parliamentary elections. Anti-government protests by students at the University of Zimbabwe led to its closure by the government for six months in 1990–91. When the Zimbabwe Congress of Trade Unions (ZCTU) sympathised with the students, its leader Morgan Tsvangirai was arrested and detained for six weeks.

Despite growing dissatisfaction with the government, ZANU-PF won the 1995 elections with a convincing 82% of the votes cast. However, eight opposition groups boycotted the elections, which were marred by a great deal of violence. In presidential elections held in 1996, Mugabe was re-elected, winning nearly 93% of the votes against his two opponents – Abel Muzorewa and Ndabaningi Sithole – in an election in which fewer than 32% of the electorate voted.

As the state of the economy deteriorated in the late 1990s, there was increasing criticism of government policies. Government actions against its critics, including newspaper editors, led to a confrontation between the government and members of the judiciary, who tried to uphold the rule of law. The government's response was to appoint a Constitutional Commission to amend the constitution, and Mugabe announced that a referendum would be held to approve its findings.

As concerns mounted, a new political movement was formed in 1999. This was the Movement for Democratic Change (MDC), a coalition of civic groups, churches, lawyers and trade unionists opposed to ZANU-PF. It was led by Gibson Sibanda, the ZCTU chairman, and Morgan Tsvangirai.

The referendum on the constitutional amendments was held in February 2000. The 55% 'No' vote showed the strength of opposition to Mugabe's government, which proceeded to launch a campaign of intimidation against its opponents. The parliamentary elections later that year were characterised by yet more violence. However, despite government attempts to intimidate voters, the MDC attracted large crowds to its meetings and managed to win 47.06% of the votes. ZANU-PF won 48.45%. Fearing the strength of the opposition, the government constantly harassed MDC leader Tsvangirai. It also acted against independent

Questions

Mugabe referred to the 2002 election as the 'Third Chimurenga', or struggle. The first one had been the uprising against the imposition of colonial rule in 1896–97; the second the guerrilla war against the Rhodesian Front government between 1966 and 1980. What is the significance of the use of the term in the context of the 2002 election? What propaganda function would it serve?

newspapers that were critical of its policies, threatening to silence them. The printing presses of one such newspaper, the *Daily News*, were blown up. During 2001, the government moved against the judiciary, which had until then managed to retain a degree of independence. The chief justice was forced out of office and two other judges retired early, leaving the Supreme Court with a ZANU-PF majority in favour of government actions.

In the 2002 presidential elections Tsvangirai stood against Mugabe. The election was marred by further violence and intimidation, as well as serious irregularities. For example, a severe shortage of ballot boxes in urban constituencies – the MDC stronghold – meant that only 28% of registered voters were able to cast their votes by the end of the second day of polling. After two re-counts, the official result gave Mugabe 56% of the vote to Tsvangirai's 42%. A new and sinister development in the 2002 election was a threat by the army to step in if ZANU-PF lost. After the election, government-sanctioned violence continued in the constituencies that had supported the MDC.

SOURCE A

I don't think that anyone could fail to notice how central to ZANU-PF's [election] campaign was a particular version of history. I spent four days watching Zimbabwe television which presented nothing but one 'historical' programme after another. Television and newspapers insisted on an increasingly simple and monolithic history. Television constantly repeated documentaries about the guerrilla war and colonial brutalities. The newspapers regularly carried articles on slavery, colonial exploitation and the liberation struggle. I recognised the outlines of many of my own books but boiled down in the service of ZANU-PF.

Extract from 'The Zimbabwe Elections: A Personal Experience', an article written by Terence Ranger, a leading historian of Zimbabwe, at the time of the 2002 presidential election. Quoted on http://africalegalbrief.com.

Question

How might the influences referred to in Source A affect our ability to find historical truth?

The 2005 parliamentary elections were characterised by vote-rigging on a massive scale, which gave ZANU-PF a comfortable majority. However, the MDC retained the support of all the main towns. As punishment for this – and in a brutal display of state-sanctioned violence – Mugabe's police and youth militia attacked the poor inhabitants of informal settlements on the fringes of the towns. Houses were bulldozed, markets destroyed, the goods sold by street vendors confiscated or burnt, and people left to fend for themselves. The operation was known as *Murambatsvina*, a Shona word meaning 'drive out the rubbish'. A UN investigation estimated that 700,000 lost their homes and livelihoods, and that another 2.4 million people were affected indirectly. According to historian Martin Meredith, the purpose of the operation was to make clear the fate of anyone who voted against Mugabe. In spite of this the MDC won a majority in the 2008 elections, and Tsvangirai won the first round of the presidential election. However, a re-run of this election was 'won' by Mugabe, after some of the worst political violence since the Matabeleland campaign in the 1980s. After this, Mugabe reluctantly agreed to a form of power-sharing with the MDC in an 'inclusive government'.

Children watch a stall burning during the violent government attacks in 2005 known as Operation Murambatsvina, which the government claimed was designed to clear Zimbabwe's slums

International observers had watched political developments in Zimbabwe with grave concern. Western countries suspended aid and the European Union applied 'smart sanctions' against Mugabe and other top ZANU-PF leaders, prohibiting travel and freezing overseas bank accounts.

African leaders attempted to exert pressure on Mugabe in different ways. For example, President Obasanjo of Nigeria tried to persuade him to observe the rule of law. In 1994, when a democratically elected government replaced the apartheid regime in South Africa, Zimbabwe finally had a sympathetic state on its southern border. But in 2000, former president Nelson Mandela publicly criticised Mugabe's use of violence and the erosion of the rule of law. Archbishop Desmond Tutu of Cape Town warned that Zimbabwe was sliding towards dictatorship.

However, other South African leaders – notably president Thabo Mbeki – did not voice open criticism of the Mugabe regime, and were themselves criticised for their apparent support of it.

Activity

Use the information in this section to explain why Zimbabwe can be considered an example of an authoritarian state, but not a one-party state.

The issue of land

Although some progress had been made on the land issue in the first decade of independence, it was not nearly enough to tackle the inherited problem, which was aggravated by population growth in rural areas. The fact that 4500 white farmers owned 11 million hectares of the best farmland, while more than a million black farmers shared 16 million hectares, was an issue that obviously had to be addressed. This fact, together with years of reluctance on the part of white farmers to compromise on the issue of land, became the main political prop of Mugabe's regime. He was able to use the land issue as a political weapon to keep himself in power – with disastrous economic consequences.

The Lancaster House provisions protecting the white ownership of land and guaranteeing full compensation for it expired after ten years. In 1992, they were replaced by the Land Acquisition Act. This gave the government the right to purchase half of the land still owned by white farmers for the resettlement of small-scale black farmers. Widespread criticism erupted when it emerged that, rather than peasant farmers, the political élite loyal to Mugabe was acquiring the leases to some of the farms. Mugabe stepped in to defuse the situation. He announced an investigation into the whole system of land tenure and requested financial assistance from Britain to pay for the purchase of land. Britain had already provided £44 million for land resettlement – a figure that fell far short of the funds needed to effect any meaningful redistribution of land – and cut off any further support.

In 1997, the Land Redistribution Act came into effect. It listed 1503 white farms for compulsory purchase and reallocation, including some of the largest and most productive commercial farms in the country. War veterans began to invade white-owned farms and threaten farmers and their workers with violence. Over the next few years the war veterans became increasingly hostile. Historian Guy Arnold poses the question of whether Mugabe controlled the war veterans or whether he was in fact their prisoner: 'He had unleashed a demand and with it a sense of grievance that could not be bottled up or contained.'

In 1998, a conference of leading aid donors to Zimbabwe, including Britain and the World Bank, met in Harare to discuss an orderly system of land reform. They approved the principle of land redistribution provided that it was fairly applied and that it benefited the poor. But there was no real follow-up to this meeting and in November 1998 the government announced the seizure of 841 white-owned farms without compensation. This led to the cancellation of donor aid. In 2000, Mugabe blamed the government's defeat in the referendum on white farmers and stepped up his campaign to force them off the land. The government condoned the often violent invasion of farms by landless peasants, many of whom claimed to be war veterans. By the middle of 2001, 95% of all white farms had been occupied or listed for resettlement.

These events affected not only the white farmers themselves but also their farm workers. Many were assaulted and about 20,000 were evicted from the farms where they had lived all their lives. The land seizures were not accompanied by back-up services to help small farmers. Large tobacco and dairy farms were often dismantled in a piecemeal manner and handed over to small peasant farmers, many of whom lacked experience of commercial farming. Once again, claims were made that many of the most productive farms were not distributed among small farmers but in fact went to high-ranking politicians and ZANU-PF supporters. In this way, the redistribution of land – although welcomed with

Fact

When landless peasants invaded and occupied white-owned farms, many of them claimed to be 'war veterans' of the independence struggle in the 1970s. Many guerrilla fighters had left school early to join up, had little education and few skills, and had struggled to survive after independence. Initially loyal supporters of Mugabe, they began to protest in the late 1990s at the government's apparent indifference to their situation. Critics of Mugabe believed that condoning the land invasions was his government's way of attempting to solve this issue.

great joy by the bulk of Zimbabwe's people and in many ways a fair outcome after years of injustice – had a catastrophic effect on agricultural production and contributed to the collapse of the economy.

Question

Why was land such an emotive issue in Zimbabwe?

Economic decline and collapse

Throughout the late 1990s, the unresolved challenges and political extremism in Zimbabwe resulted in the country's economic collapse. The health and education systems – real achievements of the new government in the 1980s – started to collapse as funds dried up. In 1991, after the fall of communist governments in Eastern Europe and the collapse of the USSR, the Zimbabwean government adopted an economic structural adjustment programme, with support from the World Bank and the International Monetary Fund. Government rhetoric in support of communist economic policies was replaced by more market-related terminology such as 'indigenous capitalism', and in 1996 ZANU-PF formally announced that it had abandoned Marxism–Leninism.

Rising unemployment and dissatisfaction with working conditions led to widespread industrial unrest and strikes in 1994 and 1996. As the economic situation deteriorated, there were accusations of corruption against senior officials. There was also criticism of the government for its misuse of funds to benefit senior politicians at a time when the population as a whole was suffering. Towards the end of 1997, the Zimbabwean currency collapsed after a government decision to compensate ex-guerrilla soldiers for their role in the independence struggle.

By 1998, the economy was in crisis and ZCTU organised a two-day general strike, which was widely supported. The economic situation deteriorated even further when the Zimbabwean government decided to provide military aid to Congolese president Laurent Kabila in a civil war in the Democratic Republic of Congo. As the defence spending escalated to support this, Zimbabwe saw increasing unemployment, inflation at 70% and shortages of fuel and other commodities. The effects of AIDS added to the problems facing Zimbabwe – by 1999, 1700 people a week were dying as a result of the disease.

From 2000, the economy declined even further, with shortages of petrol, electricity and other commodities, rising food prices and a collapsing currency. The military venture in the DRC continued to drain the economy, and income from tourism dropped drastically as visitors stayed away, scared by the political violence and instability. Foreign investment dried up as banks and companies feared risking money in a politically and economically unstable environment.

A Zimbabwean banknote to the value of one hundred million dollars, issued in 2008; even higher values were issued later as Zimbabwe tried to control inflation

Question

What factors contributed to the ongoing political and economic crises in Zimbabwe?

The disruption to agriculture caused by the land invasions resulted in food shortages and starvation, with millions of people living in desperate poverty. With skyrocketing unemployment, town dwellers in particular found themselves badly hit by the economic problems. By the end of 2002, an estimated 3 million Zimbabweans had fled as refugees or illegal immigrants to neighbouring countries, especially South Africa, and more were to follow in the next few years as the economy declined further and Mugabe clung to power despite mounting opposition.

By 2010, there was an uneasy balance between Mugabe and Tsvangirai as a result of a political agreement to have a form of power-sharing in an inclusive government. Although the violence had substantially reduced, Zimbabwe still faced enormous economic challenges.

What part has Robert Mugabe played since independence?

During his 30-year rule, Mugabe became more dictatorial and more isolated even from ZANU-PF. His position within a ring of close confidantes made it difficult for him to fully appreciate the extent of the economic crisis. Furthermore, the power, wealth and position of the political élite depended on the patronage of Mugabe, so few of them were willing to challenge him. In addition to this, a cult of personality had been established that made it difficult for him to reverse his earlier policies and be seen to be wrong. This restricted the ability of his regime to implement 'sensible' policies to solve the economic problems.

Robert Mugabe reviews troops on parade during the 28th anniversary celebrations of Zimbabwe's independence in 2008

It is possible to argue that Mugabe was determined to hold on to power at all costs. Proof of this may lie in the political and economic crises Zimbabwe still faces in the 21st century. Mugabe may be determined to socially engineer Zimbabwe to become a peasant republic. On the other hand, he may simply be rewarding his followers with land, or buying political support. An extreme view is that he has little choice in the matter and that he is a figurehead for a ZANU-PF élite so embroiled in corruption that they cannot let go of power. Some historians, such as Guy Arnold, believe that the reasons for ongoing support for Mugabe have their roots in Zimbabwe's colonial past (see Source B).

SOURCE B

The Zimbabwe crisis at the end of the century raised many questions that were not addressed in the West. It was, of course, about a dictatorial ruler using every weapon at his disposal to hold onto power: these included violence and intimidation of his opponents, altering the constitution or ignoring it; destroying the independent judiciary; and seeking popular support by deploying as weapons the two highly emotive issues of land redistribution and the control of land by the white farmers. But Mugabe was also using as a weapon the deep underlying resentments of past colonialism and the ingrained bitterness resulting from a century of the racial arrogance and contempt that had been second nature to the majority of the white settlers.

Arnold, G. 2006. Africa: A Modern History. *London, UK. Atlantic Books. p. 904.*

Discussion point

How accurate do you think Guy Arnold's assessment of Mugabe's rule is? Refer to the post-colonial history of Zimbabwe in your discussion.

Of all the nationalist leaders in this book, Mugabe is the most difficult to analyse. It is clear that he is intelligent and well-educated, and it is easy to understand how he formed his political views – not only about the best road to independence but also about the form of a post-colonial Zimbabwe. He is clearly both a ruthless and a sophisticated political operator. The manner in which he eliminated potential rivals and opposition proves the former; his subtle handling of the white minority at the Lancaster House talks and in the first decade of his premiership suggests the latter. He clearly was an accomplished leader in the 1980s, a decade that saw Zimbabwe prosper. His role in his country's subsequent problems is far more difficult to establish.

Activity

The role of Mugabe is at the core of this unit. Did he have an elaborate plan to portray himself as a moderate before embarking on more radical policies? Or were his actions logical and just all along, intending to redistribute the wealth of the country to the black majority? Was Mugabe simply a pawn, used as a front to cover the activities of a clique of ZANU-PF members who used their position to their own benefit? In this view, Mugabe could not stand down or act against their wishes for fear of the political consequences. In groups, discuss these views of Mugabe's role.

End of unit activities

1 Draw up a table to summarise the challenges facing Zimbabwe after independence, how the government tried to deal with them, and what the results were.

2 http://www.independent.co.uk/news/world/africa/zimbabwes-last-white-ruler-the-man-who-defied-the-world-758891.html

Read the article on this website, written at the time of Ian Smith's death in 2007. Explain why the writer argues that Smith was a good role model for Robert Mugabe. Comment on the view expressed in the concluding paragraph that 'in struggling so long to ensure that whites in Zimbabwe clung on to everything, Smith finally ensured that they lost everything'.

3 Find out what you can about the Movement for Democratic Change (MDC) and its leader Morgan Tsvangirai.

4 Joshua Nkomo, the former leader of ZAPU and vice-president under Mugabe, died in 1999. Work out a list of questions you would like to have asked him before his death, and compose the answers you think he may have given. You can start by reading the information about him on this website:

http://news.bbc.co.uk/2/hi/africa/382848.stm

5 'The problems of post-independence Zimbabwe can undoubtedly be attributed to the legacy of colonial and white supremacist rule.'

Divide the class into two groups. One group should work out an argument to support the statement above and the other an argument to oppose it.

6 Write two speeches, one criticising and one defending the developments in Zimbabwe since 1980. One should be written from the perspective of a white farmer who has recently lost his land, the other from a ZANU-PF veteran who has recently acquired land.

End of chapter activities

Paper 1 exam practice

Question

According to Source A below, what was the Soviet government's attitude to UDI?
[2 marks]

Skill

Comprehension of a source

SOURCE A

The racialist regime in Southern Rhodesia ... constitutes a hotbed of danger for all other African peoples, including those which have already freed themselves from colonial oppression. It is a bayonet pointed at the heart of liberated Africa, a constant threat to peace on the African continent and a threat to world peace. The Soviet government, guided by its principled stand in questions of abolishing colonialism, strongly condemns the new crime against the peoples of Africa and declares that it does not recognise the racialist regime which has usurped power in Southern Rhodesia. The Soviet Union fully supports the decisions adopted by the United Nations Security Council and General Assembly on the situation in Southern Rhodesia and will carry them out unswervingly.

Extract from a Soviet government statement referring to UDI. From Soviet News, *No. 5206. 16 November 1965. p. 70.*

Examiner's tips

Comprehension questions are the most straightforward questions you will face in Paper 1. They simply require you to understand a source and extract two or three relevant points that relate to the particular question.

As only 2 marks are available for this question, make sure you don't waste valuable exam time that should be spent on the higher-scoring questions by writing a long answer here. Just write a couple of short sentences, giving the necessary information to show you have understood the source. Try to give one piece of information for each of the marks available for the question.

Common mistakes

When asked to show your comprehension/understanding of a particular source, make sure you don't comment on the *wrong* source! Mistakes like this are made every year. Remember, every mark is important for your final grade.

Simplified markscheme

For **each item of relevant/correct information** identified, award **1 mark** – up to a **maximum of 2 marks**.

Student answer

According to Source A, the Soviet government was against UDI, and so it 'strongly condemns' what it saw as a 'new crime against the peoples of Africa'.

Examiner's comments

The candidate has selected **one** relevant and explicit piece of information from the source – this is enough to gain 1 mark. However, as no other reason/information has been identified, this candidate fails to gain the other mark available for the question.

Activity

Look again at the source and the student answer above. Now try to identify **one** other piece of information from the source, and so obtain the other mark available for this question.

Summary activity

Copy this diagram and, using the information in this chapter, make point form notes under each heading.

Zimbabwe: the road to independence

Southern Rhodesia until 1965

- White political control
- Central African Federation
- Land issues
- Nationalist organisations

Rhodesia 1965–79

- UDI
- ZAPU
- ZANU
- Guerrilla war
- Economic sanctions
- External factors

Zimbabwe 1980 onwards

- 1980 election
- Authoritarian rule
- Opposition to Mugabe
- Violence in Matabeleland
- Land issues
- Economic decline

Paper 2 practice questions

1 To what extent was armed struggle the main reason for the eventual independence of Zimbabwe in 1980?

2 Examine the political problems faced by Rhodesia/Zimbabwe in the second half of the 20th century.

3 'New states found it impossible to implement democracy.' To what extent do you agree with this verdict in a Zimbabwean context?

4 Account for the successes and failures of Robert Mugabe as ruler of a newly independent Zimbabwe.

5 For what reasons, and with what results, did colonial control weaken in Rhodesia/Zimbabwe?

6 To what extent did Zimbabwe succeed in dealing with the problems presented by independence?

Further reading

Try reading the relevant chapters/sections of the following books:

Arnold, Guy. 2006. *Africa: A Modern History*. London, UK. Atlantic Books.

Curtin, P., Feierman, L. T. and Vansina, J. 1995. *African History from the Earliest Times to Independence. 2nd Edn*. London, UK and New York, USA. Longman.

Dowden, Richard. 2008. *Africa: Altered States, Ordinary Miracles*. London, UK. Portobello Books.

Hudson, Miles. 1981. *Triumph or Tragedy? Rhodesia to Zimbabwe*. London, UK. Hamish Hamilton.

Meredith, Martin. 2005. *The State of Africa*. London, UK. Free Press.

Moorcraft, Paul and McLaughlin, Peter. 2008. *The Rhodesian War: A Military History*. Barnsley, UK. Pen and Sword Books.

Nugent, Paul. 2004. *Africa Since Independence*. Basingstoke, UK. Palgrave Macmillan.

Raftopoulos, Brian and Mlambo, Alois. 2009. *Becoming Zimbabwe*. Harare, Zimbabwe. Weaver Press.

Verrier, Anthony. 1986. *The Road to Zimbabwe 1890–1980*. London, UK. Jonathan Cape.

3 India and Pakistan

Introduction

During the 19th century, when most of Africa and much of Asia were colonised by European powers, a large area of South Asia became the British colony of India. In all the colonial empires, resistance to the imposition of foreign rule took many forms, ranging from uprisings and armed rebellion to acts of defiance or the creation of anti-colonial cultural forms. In India after the First World War, a strong nationalist movement developed, determined to end British rule. This was finally achieved after the Second World War, when India and Pakistan became independent countries. The success of the Indian nationalist movement inspired similar movements in other Asian and African colonies.

India emerged as a stable democracy, but Pakistan was not as successful in its transition to independence, lacking many of the advantages held by India. India has since developed into the world's largest democracy, and, with China, is well placed to emerge as one of the most powerful and influential states in the 21st century. Pakistan, on the other hand, still faces considerable political, social and economic problems.

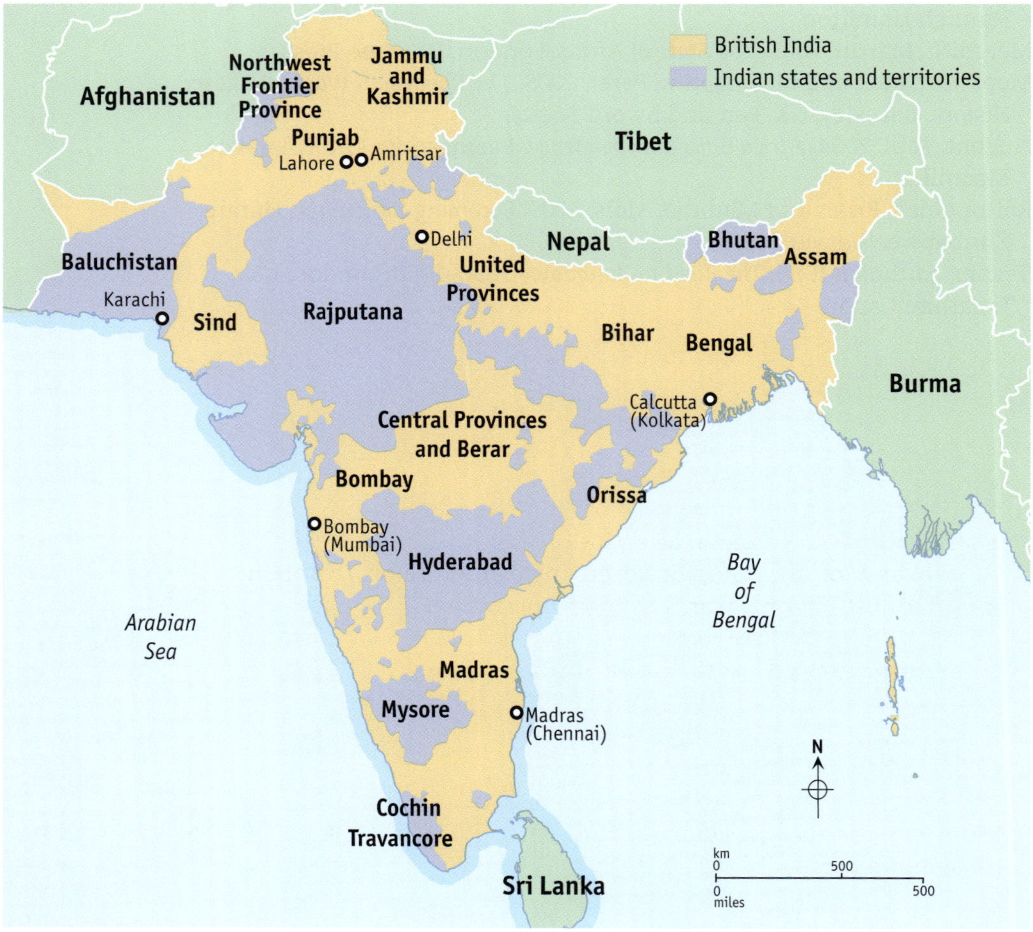

Map showing pre-independence India, before its partition into India and Pakistan in 1947

1 The origins and rise of nationalist and independence movements in the Indian subcontinent

Key questions

- How did India develop as a British colony?
- What factors influenced the rise of nationalism?

Overview

- India's complex cultural history is critical to understanding the development of the Indian nationalist movement and the progress towards independence from colonial rule.
- Until 1947, India was a British colony. Colonial rule was efficient but authoritarian, and Indians themselves had no meaningful representation.
- Britain consciously sought to emphasise religious and other differences among the people of India, applying a policy of 'divide and rule'.
- Britain derived great economic benefits from India, including raw materials. Indian soldiers fought Britain's colonial wars, and indentured workers from India provided labour in British colonies in Africa, the Caribbean and other parts of Asia.
- In 1885, the first nationalist organisation was formed – the Indian National Congress. At first, this represented the educated élite and called for greater representation for Indians in government, rather than independence from British rule.
- A separate organisation, the Muslim League (1906), sought to protect and advance the interests of Muslims, who were a minority in a predominantly Hindu country.
- A decision by the British to partition the province of Bengal in 1905 resulted in widespread protests. Britain suppressed the protests, but also granted concessions, including giving Indians limited representation in government.
- Indians played a key role in supporting Britain during the First World War. In return, they hoped for self-rule after the war. India's considerable contribution to Britain's victory over Germany demonstrated its potential as an independent state.
- At the end of the war, however, instead of reform, Britain introduced stricter measures to crush opposition.
- A protest against these measures at Amritsar in 1919 had tragic consequences, when soldiers shot and killed nearly 400 unarmed civilians, and wounded over 1000. The Amritsar Massacre was a turning point in Anglo-Indian relations and in the development of the Indian nationalist movement.
- The announcement of further reforms by the British government failed to satisfy the demands of the growing nationalist movement, especially during the crisis of the Great Depression.

Timeline

1857–58 Indian uprising

1858 British government takes over control from the East India Company

1885 Indian National Congress (INC) formed

1905 first partition of Bengal

1906 formation of the Muslim League

1909 Morley reforms make concessions to the nationalists

1914–18 First World War

1919 Amritsar Massacre; Government of India Act introduces limited reform

1929 Wall Street Crash leads to start of Great Depression

How did India develop as a British colony?

India before the British

The area of Asia in which India, Pakistan and Bangladesh are situated today is often referred to as the 'subcontinent' or South Asia. Over the centuries, many different people moved into this region, bringing with them their languages, traditions and religions. As a result, the area contains a rich mixture of people and cultures. At first the main religion was Hinduism, and Hindu princes ruled most of the region. Later, Muslim invaders brought Islam to the subcontinent and established the powerful Mughal Empire, which lasted for over three centuries (1526–1858). Although the rulers of the empire were Muslim, most of the local leaders and the general population remained Hindu. The Sikhs were a much smaller, but significant, religious group.

Theory of knowledge

History and language

Indian nationalists regarded the uprising as the First War of Independence. The British, however, referred to it as the Indian Mutiny, because it started among *sepoys* – Indian soldiers serving in the British army. The uprising had broad-based support, however, from a wide range of Indians, including peasants, workers, landlords and princes. As a result, historians now describe it as the Indian Revolt. Use this example, and others you can think of, to explain how terminology can reflect bias in history.

British rule in India

British interest in India began when the English East India Company (EIC) set up trading posts along the coast from the beginning of the 17th century. EIC rule gradually expanded into the interior, and by the middle of the 19th century the company controlled large parts of India. Although there was still a Mughal emperor, he had no real power. However, an uprising against EIC control in 1857–58 resulted in the intervention of the British government, which sent troops to crush the uprising and take over control from the EIC.

The Mughal emperor had supported the uprising, and after its failure he was removed from power and sent into exile. India became part of the British Empire. Large parts of the country were placed under direct British administration, but some areas remained under the control of hereditary Indian rulers, with whom the British signed treaties that recognised their autonomy over local affairs. There were over 500 of these 'princely states', as they were called. India was ruled by a **viceroy** and an administration of 5000 officials sent from London, who provided efficient, but authoritarian, government. Indians themselves had no meaningful representation in this government, although they formed the bulk of the staff in the Indian Civil Service. British control over 300 million Indians was enforced by a large army, staffed by British officers and Indian troops. The administration and the army were financed out of taxes paid by Indians.

viceroy The viceroy was the highest official in the colonial administration, who ruled India on behalf of the British monarch. Although there was a great deal of status, material comfort and wealth attached to the position, the viceroy had limited power to influence policy, which was decided by the British government in London and implemented by the secretary of state for India.

The British brought certain benefits to India. These included an efficient administration and judicial system, a good railway network and Western education for some. However, British rule was always based on an assumption of superiority, as the statement in Source A by a British official, quoted by historian Lawrence James, shows.

Question

How can the ideas expressed in Source A be considered a form of 'cultural imperialism'?

SOURCE A

We must rule our Asiatic subjects with strict and generous justice, wisely and beneficently, as their natural superiors, by virtue of our purer religion, our sterner energies, our subtler intellect, our more creative faculties, our more commanding and indomitable will.

James, L. 1997. Raj: The Making and Unmaking of British India. *London, UK. Abacus. p. 297.*

The British believed that government should be firm and vigilant against the rise of any resistance to their rule. Above all, they wanted to prevent the formation of a united opposition movement. To this end, they stressed differences between people – significantly differences of religion, and also of caste. They regarded caste as a form of fixed identity, instead of something that had developed and changed over time. According to the historian Thomas Metcalf, the British saw caste as a 'concrete, measurable "thing" that could be fitted into a hierarchy able to be ascertained and quantified in reports and surveys'. The result of this colonial policy was to create and intensify existing differences in Indian society (see Source B).

Fact

The caste system in India developed about 2500 years ago. It divided society into a hierarchy of levels called castes. Status, occupation, rights, privileges and opportunities in life were all determined by the caste into which one was born. The caste system is usually associated with Hindu tradition but, according to historian Mridula Mukherjee, it was prevalent among Sikhs, Christians and Muslims, too.

SOURCE B

Having unified India, the British set into motion contrary forces. Fearing the unity of the Indian people to which their own rule had contributed, they followed the classic imperial policy of divide and rule. The diverse and divisive features of Indian society and polity were heightened to promote cleavages among the people and to turn province against province, caste against caste, class against class, Hindus against Muslims, and the princes and landlords against the nationalist movement.

Chandra, B., Mukherjee, M. and Mukherjee, A. 2000. India after Independence: 1947–2000. *London, UK. Penguin. p. 18.*

Questions

What is meant by a policy of 'divide and rule'? How and why did the British use this policy in India? How could a nationalist movement overcome such tactics?

Britain derived great economic benefits from its Indian empire. Money, collected from peasants in the form of taxes, was transferred to London to fund the British government's purchase of EIC shares, finance capital investments (especially railways), and provide funds for the administration of India. Critics felt that the money could have been better used for internal investments in India itself. Britain also benefited from the balance of trade with India, which supplied raw materials – mainly cotton, jute, indigo, rice and tea – to British factories. In return India bought manufactured goods such as textiles, iron and steel goods and machinery, and by 1914 was the biggest export market for British goods. As a result, India under colonial rule was no longer an exporter of cloth to European markets. Instead it produced raw cotton that was manufactured into cloth in British factories and re-exported to Asia. In this way, colonial rule 'de-industrialised' India. Another disadvantage for India was that land formerly used to grow grains for staple foods was now used for commercial cash-crop production, making peasants dependent on foods grown elsewhere.

India also served Britain's political and economic interests in other parts of the empire. Indian soldiers, paid for by Indian tax payers, were used to protect trade routes and serve British interests in China, East Africa and the Middle East. India also served as a source of indentured labourers for British colonies in the West Indies, Africa and other parts of Asia. By 1920, however, the system of indenture was stopped, partly as a result of criticism from Indian nationalists, who saw it as one of 'imperial exploitation that brought shame to India', according to Barbara and Thomas Metcalf. These historians also note that the plight of **diaspora** Indians was a 'critical stimulus to Indian nationalism'.

diaspora A 'diaspora' refers to a scattering of people around the world, away from their country or continent of origin. Partly as a result of the system of indentured labour, there are substantial Indian minorities living in other parts of the world today. One such Indian community is in South Africa, where Mohandas Gandhi, later to become the dominant figure in the Indian nationalist movement, spent 20 years and developed his political ideas.

What factors influenced the rise of nationalism?

Anti-colonialism and early nationalism

After the harsh suppression of the 1857–58 uprising, British power in India seemed to be secure. However, Indians resented the harsh realities of colonial control and the superior attitudes of the colonising power towards them. This view was later explained by Jawaharlal Nehru, who became a leading figure in the nationalist movement against British rule (see Source C).

SOURCE C

We in India have known racialism in all its forms since the beginning of British rule. The whole ideology of this rule was that of the master race, and the structure of government was based upon it; indeed the idea of the master race is inherent in imperialism. There was no subterfuge [nothing hidden] about it; it was proclaimed in unambiguous language by those in authority. More powerful than words was the practice that accompanied them and, generation after generation and year after year, India as a nation and Indians as individuals were subjected to insult, humiliation, and contemptuous treatment. The English were an imperial race, we were told, with the god-given right to govern us and keep us in subjection. As an Indian I am ashamed to write all this, for the memory of it hurts, and what hurts still more is that we submitted for so long to this degradation. I would have preferred any kind of resistance to this, whatever the consequences, rather than that our people should endure this treatment.

Nehru, J. 1946. The Discovery of India. London, UK. Meridian Books.

Activity

Compare and contrast the views expressed in Sources A (page 60) and C. Explain how colonial attitudes helped to stir feelings of nationalism and resistance in India.

The establishment of the Indian National Congress

Towards the end of the 19th century, there was a growing feeling among educated Indians that there should be more Indian representation in government. In 1885, they formed a nationalist organisation called the Indian National Congress (INC). In its early stages, the Congress represented the interests of the wealthy middle class and it did not have mass support. Most of the founding members were graduates and all spoke English. They saw themselves as a bridge between the Indian masses and the colonial power. As a result, the existence of the Congress tended to limit the development of more radical nationalist groups.

The élitist nature of the early Congress made it very conservative in its goals, and it used petitions to try to achieve them. It did not question the continuation of British rule, but called rather for greater Indian representation in the legislative councils, easier access to the Indian Civil Service and less expenditure on the army. Most of its membership was Hindu, although it also had Muslim members. Right from the start, Congress leaders made explicit efforts to draw Muslims into their meetings, and members of the organisation believed that the interests of caste or religious affiliation should be secondary to the needs of the Indian nation as a whole.

However, in 1906, Muslims established their own political organisation, the Muslim League, believing that this was the only way to protect the interests of the Muslim minority. At first the League was dominated by a similar middle- and upper-class leadership to the Congress.

Question

What was the nature of the early nationalist movement in India?

Conflict in Bengal

Serious nationalist opposition to colonial rule in India started when the British decided to partition the province of Bengal in north-eastern India. Bengal had been the first region to come under British control, and its main city, Calcutta, was the capital of British India. The province had a population of over 80 million people, the majority of whom were Bengali-speaking Hindus. In 1905, the British viceroy announced that the province would be divided into two, in order to provide more efficient administration. This partition created an eastern province with a Muslim majority, and a western part in which Bihari- and Oriya-speaking Hindus were in the majority. Bengali-speaking Hindus saw the partition as a threat to their position in the region and a deliberate attempt by Britain to weaken Bengali nationalism.

Fact

In recent years, many place names in India have been changed. In this chapter, we have used the names that were in use at the time of the historical events discussed. Among other changes, Calcutta is now Kolkata and Bombay is now Mumbai.

The partition prompted Congress into action. An anti-partition movement expressed its opposition using petitions, protests in the press, and rallies. When these failed, protestors organised a boycott of British goods. They made public bonfires of manufactured goods from Britain and urged Indians to use local products instead. This boycott proved to be very effective. British imports into India dropped by 25%, and the economy of some areas – such as the city of Bombay on the west coast – expanded as Indian industries developed to take advantage of the gap. The British authorities reacted to the anti-partition protests with mass arrests, which had limited impact. The events had significant results: Congress realised the political power of an economic boycott, and nationalists in other parts of India were united in support for the Bengali cause.

The confrontation over Bengal radicalised parts of the Congress and a revolutionary wing, called the New Party, emerged. This faction was especially strong in Calcutta, Poona and Lahore. This development was significant because it seemed that the more moderate leaders were being marginalised in favour of radicals such as **Bal Gangadhar Tilak**, who urged more active opposition to British rule. Another more radical group favoured assassination and sabotage as forms of protest against colonial policies and actions.

Bal Gangadhar Tilak (1856–1920) Tilak was the first leader of the Indian National Congress to gain popular support. He demanded self-rule – or *swaraj* – from the British, who saw him as a dangerous troublemaker, and in 1908 sentenced him to prison for sedition (treason). He was released in 1914.

SOURCE D

Extract from Tilak's address to the Indian National Congress, 1907.

We have a stronger weapon, a political weapon, in boycott. We have perceived one fact; that the whole of this administration, which is carried on by a handful of Englishmen, is carried on with our assistance. We are all in subordinate service. This whole government is carried on with our assistance and they try to keep us in ignorance of our power of cooperation between ourselves by which that which is in our own hands at present can be claimed by us and administered by us. The point is to have the entire control in our hands.

Quoted in De Bary, W. T. Sources of Indian Tradition. *1958. New York, USA. Columbia University Press. pp. 719–20.*

Question

In what ways is Tilak's address critical of Indians themselves, rather than of the British?

Muslims in Bengal became increasingly unnerved by the developments, and by the appeals to Hindu nationalism made by some anti-partition protestors. Support for the Muslim League increased as the Islamic minority sought to safeguard its own interests. Representatives met with the viceroy and stressed the view that Muslims were a distinct community which needed separate representation for its own protection.

The strength of opposition to the partition of Bengal forced Britain to reassess its policies in India. At first it tried to crush the protests, and by 1909 large numbers of Bengalis were in prison and the situation seemed to be running out of control. Then, in a change of policy, the secretary of state for India, John Morley, decided that concessions should be made to the nationalists so that Britain could maintain its control of the subcontinent. These reforms gave Indians some representation in government, and in 1910 elections were held for the central and provincial legislative councils. Muslims were given separate representation – separate electorates and reserved seats – in a move that shaped future political developments. Indians now had the power to question the decisions of colonial officials and debate the budget for the country.

Question

What did the Indian nationalists and the British government each gain as a result of the 1909 changes?

In an elaborate ceremony incorporating many features of the Mughal past, the British king George V was crowned emperor of India in 1911

In addition to this, Bengal was reunited and the capital of India was moved from Calcutta, the site of anti-British activism, to the city of Delhi, which had been the capital of the Mughal empire. This move pleased Muslims. The Morley reforms cooled the situation in the subcontinent and restored the more moderate elements of Congress to power.

The impact of the First World War

The First World War was essentially a conflict between European powers, but it involved their overseas empires as well. When war broke out in 1914, Britain expected support from its colonies, and India supplied large numbers of soldiers and huge amounts of resources to the cause. Some nationalists viewed the war as an opportunity to press for greater independence, but most Indians, including radicals like Tilak, urged support for Britain's war effort.

However, as the war dragged on dissatisfaction grew, partly due to heavy wartime taxation and increased efforts at recruitment. The war also caused a conflict of loyalties for Muslims in India, because the Ottoman Empire – the world's leading Islamic power – had an alliance with Germany. By the end of the war it had become obvious to many Indians just how dependent Britain had been on their help to secure victory over Germany. Indian soldiers returning from Western Europe passed on their experience of the high living standards and wealth of even the poorest classes in Britain and France when compared to the people of India. Indians hoped that their sacrifices in the war would result in reforms that would give them greater representation in government.

In this way, the experiences of the war heightened nationalist sentiments and many hoped that the British would soon allow India a greater degree of independence. Indeed, in 1917 the British government announced its intention to encourage 'the gradual development of self-governing institutions' in India. The proposals, however, were rejected by both Congress and the Muslim League as not going far enough. Then, in 1918, instead of reform a series of harsh repressive measures was introduced to crush opposition. The anger at this situation was compounded by the effects of the worldwide 1918 influenza epidemic, which killed 12 million Indians.

Fact

One and a half million Indians volunteered to serve in the British army during the First World War – the largest volunteer army in history. They fought on the Western Front, in Gallipoli, Palestine and North and East Africa. Indian troops won 13,000 medals for bravery, including 12 Victoria Crosses. About 65,000 Indian soldiers were killed in the war, and an equal number wounded.

The Amritsar Massacre

There were protests all over India against the new measures. A new form of protest was a nationwide *hartal*, or work stoppage, as well as large marches in major cities. Ignoring a ban on public meetings, a crowd of 5000 gathered at Amritsar, where the British officer in charge, General Reginald Dyer, ordered his troops to open fire on the unarmed protestors. The soldiers killed 379 people and wounded over 1000 more in ten minutes. Many of those killed were women and children who had been trapped because soldiers had blocked the exits. Indians were shocked at the news of the massacre, and more especially by British reactions to it.

The British government ordered an inquiry into the incident and Dyer was forced to resign from the army, but some British officials expressed approval of his actions, some settlers in India regarded him as a saviour, and he was welcomed back in England as a hero.

Fact

Indian national pride was strengthened when Rabindranath Tagore (1861–1941), a Bengali poet, novelist, musician and playwright, was awarded the Nobel Prize for Literature in 1912, becoming the first Asian Nobel laureate. He was later knighted by the British king, but returned his knighthood in protest after the massacre of hundreds of unarmed civilians in 1919 by British troops at Amritsar (see left).

An illustration from a German satirical magazine, 21 February 1929, showing British general Reginald Dyer surveying the aftermath of the massacre at Amritsar

Question

Why is the Amritsar Massacre considered to be a turning point in the development of the Indian nationalist movement?

After the massacre, many more people began to support Congress and its call for an end to British rule. Among the new supporters were moderate members of the Indian élite who until that point had considered themselves to be loyal British subjects. One of the Congress leaders who was outspoken in his condemnation of the Amritsar Massacre was Mohandas Gandhi. From this point, Gandhi emerged as the dominant figure in the nationalist movement (you will learn more about him in the next unit).

Developments after the First World War

During the First World War, key industries in India, such as cotton textiles and iron and steel, experienced a boom as manufacturers took advantage of the increased demands caused by the war. Agriculture, however, remained the dominant sector of the economy, and it faced increasing problems after the war. Food production could not keep up with the high population growth rate. In addition, India was badly affected by the Depression, which followed the **Wall Street Crash** in 1929. Overseas markets for India's exports declined, and the value of export crops dropped substantially. This forced Indian peasants to borrow to survive and, when debt became unmanageable, millions were thrown off the land, creating masses of rural unemployed. As a result millions of peasants migrated to the cities in search of work, adding to the numbers of urban unemployed. The impact of the Depression on India was one of the causes of civil unrest in the 1930s, as dissatisfied and unemployed people joined the nationalist movement.

Wall Street Crash The collapse of the New York stock exchange in 1929 caused a banking and economic crisis in the United States and spread to the rest of the world. It resulted in the Great Depression, which lasted for much of the 1930s.

There were also constitutional developments after the war. In 1919, the British parliament passed the Government of India Act, which was regarded as a first step in the progress towards self-government for India. Although the central government in Delhi remained under British control, certain responsibilities in the provinces – such as agriculture, education and health – were given to Indian ministers. Crucially, though, the British retained control of the police and the justice system. About 10% of the adult male population was given the right to vote for provincial legislatures. However, these tentative steps towards reform were soon overshadowed by the growth of a mass-based nationalist movement.

End of unit activities

1 Draw a spider diagram to show how the British administration of India worked.

2 'The British derived more benefits from India than Indians did from Britain.'

Divide into two groups. One group should prepare an argument to support the statement above, and the other group should prepare an argument to oppose it.

3 http://www.bbc.co.uk/history/worldwars/wwone/india_wwone_01.shtml Find out what you can about the experiences of Indian soldiers during the First World War by looking at this website. Explain how their exposure to new ideas, customs and perspectives might have affected them on their return to India after the war.

4 Draw up a table to contrast the Indian National Congress and the Muslim League, using the following categories: support base; political outlook; attitude towards the British; political aims.

5 In class, divide into small groups. Each group should prepare ten cards, each with a question based on this unit, that requires a single relevant fact as an answer. Each group exchanges cards with another group. The answers can be scored as a fun quiz activity. This is an example:

> *What global event in 1929 had an impact on the Indian economy?*
> Answer: *Wall Street Crash*

As an extension activity, after discussion, each group should write a short paragraph for each card. The paragraph should explain how each fact fits into the general historical process studied in this unit, showing how it relates to the Indian independence movement. This is an example:

> *The Wall Street Crash created unemployment in India, both rural and urban, as markets shrank. The crisis in the global economy hindered India's ability to trade its way out of the crisis. Poverty and unemployment created political unrest and strengthened calls for independence.*

2 Methods of achieving independence in the Indian subcontinent

Timeline

1920–22 Gandhi's first non-co-operation campaign begins

1929 Congress demands complete independence for India

1930 Salt March

1935 Government of India Act

1937 Congress wins elections for provincial legislatures

1939 Second World War begins

1942 British government sends Cripps mission to negotiate with Indian leaders; 'Quit India' resolution by Congress

1943 Bose forms Indian National Army under Japanese command

1945 Second World War ends

Key questions

- What was the nature of resistance to British rule in the 1920s?
- How did resistance develop into a mass-based nationalist movement in the 1930s?
- What was the impact of the Second World War on the nationalist movement?
- What part did Jinnah play in the struggle for independence?
- What was Gandhi's contribution to the independence movement?

Overview

- Mohandas Gandhi and his philosophy of *satyagraha*, or non-violent resistance, was at the core of the Indian independence movement. His campaigns of non-co-operation transformed the Indian National Congress into a mass-based nationalist organisation.
- During the 1920s there was a rise in tension between religious communities, partly as a result of the emergence of *Hindutwa*, a Hindu cultural and nationalist movement.
- Indian nationalists were frustrated by the slow pace of constitutional reform, and in 1929 Congress demanded complete independence.
- The 1930 Salt March gained worldwide attention and forced Britain to start negotiations with the nationalists at a series of Round Table conferences in London.
- There were increasing political tensions in the 1930s, and the Muslim League made calls for the recognition of their identity as a separate nation.
- Constitutional reforms in the 1935 Government of India Act made provision for provincial elections in 1937, which Congress won.
- After its failure to win support in these elections, the Muslim League tried to rally Muslim support for a separate future state, to be called Pakistan.
- In 1939, there was a split between left and right wings in the Congress movement, and the more radical Subhas Chandra Bose left to form the Forward Bloc Party.
- The outbreak of the Second World War forced Britain to re-evaluate its policies towards India, and it offered independence once the war was over. However, Congress adopted the 'Quit India' resolution and continued its campaign of non-co-operation to force Britain to leave immediately.
- The Muslim League co-operated with Britain during the war and was consequently in a stronger position at the end of the conflict, when negotiations about independence began.
- India played a significant role in the Allied war effort, and by the end of the war was economically stronger. By contrast, Britain emerged from the war in a weak position and was ready to negotiate the end of its Indian empire.

What was the nature of resistance to British rule in the 1920s?

The person who transformed the Indian National Congress into a mass nationalist movement after the First World War was Mohandas Gandhi. Until then, support for Congress had come from the Indian élite, so, for the movement to succeed in challenging British rule in India, it needed to expand its appeal. This was Gandhi's great achievement.

Gandhi and *satyagraha*

Gandhi championed a form of non-violent resistance, or civil disobedience, to colonial rule that stemmed from an Indian concept called *satyagraha*, or 'soul force'. It was based on the belief that ordinary people can bring about political change by using peaceful means to fight for justice.

SOURCE A

Gandhi describes the concept of satyagraha.

Soul force, or the power of truth, is reached by the infliction of suffering, not on your opponent, but on yourself. Rivers of blood may have to flow before we gain our freedom, but it must be our blood. ... The government of the day has passed a law which I do not like. If, by using violence, I force the government to change the law, I am using what may be called body-force. If I do not obey the law, and accept the penalty for breaking it, I use soul force. It involves sacrificing yourself.

Quoted in Bottaro, J. and Calland, R. 2001. Successful Human and Social Sciences Grade 9. *Cape Town, South Africa. Oxford University Press. p. 45.*

Theory of knowledge

History and ethics

Gandhi believed that the authorities could be forced to give in, by the firm yet peaceful demonstration of the justice of a cause. How could *satyagraha* be an effective moral force to bring about political change? Can you think of other contexts in 20th-century history where non-violent resistance has been used effectively?

Satyagraha involved a campaign of non-co-operation with the British administration, boycotts of British schools, universities and law courts and, critically, boycotts – called *hartal* – of British goods. Gandhi consciously rejected Western values and adopted the dress and lifestyle of a simple peasant. He established an *ashram*, or community, committed to non-violence and self-sufficiency using traditional methods. This appeal to traditional cultural values allowed him to connect to the mass of the Indian peasantry. He also identified with the problems of specific groups, earning their respect and support: tenant farmers exploited by landlords, industrial workers involved in disputes with factory owners, and poor farmers unable to pay taxes after bad harvests.

This non-violent opposition stemmed in part from the fact that armed resistance was simply not an option given the military power of the British. *Satyagraha* would exploit Britain's greatest weakness in India – the British economy's reliance on the subcontinent. Simply boycotting British goods would have a massive effect on the colonial power's ability to trade successfully, and non-co-operation in the form of strikes would severely damage British-owned companies. Non-violent resistance also suited the Indian élite, who feared that an armed struggle would destabilise India so much that potentially radical groups and individuals might gain a foothold and threaten their position in Indian society.

Khalifat Caliph is a Muslim term for a supreme political and spiritual leader in the Muslim world. The Khalifat movement among Muslims in India wanted to protect the Ottoman Empire by putting pressure on the British. When the Ottoman Empire was broken up after the First World War, and Turkey became a secular state, the movement lost its primary goal and became part of the wider nationalist movement in India.

Gandhi changed Congress from a narrow, élite organisation into a mass nationalist movement that incorporated all sectors of Indian society. This inclusiveness was not only based on class, but also crossed ethnic and religious lines. After the First World War, one of Gandhi's strongest sources of support was the **Khalifat** movement, led by the brothers Mohammed and Shaukat Ali. Historians Sugata Bose and Ayesha Jalal describe the 'courageous display of unity among Hindus, Muslims and Sikhs' that existed at this period. Although the British tried to crush resistance by implementing harsh laws and jailing Gandhi and other leaders, the movement gained increasing support.

The non-co-operation campaign, 1920–22

In 1920, Congress formally agreed to support Gandhi's plan for a campaign of non-co-operation, which now included a call for *swaraj* (self-government) as well, through legitimate and peaceful means. The boycott of British goods and institutions had some success. The British reacted to the campaign by arresting 20,000 protesters, but this only prompted further resistance. However, when protests got out of control and protesters turned to violence, Gandhi called off the campaign. A month later, Gandhi was arrested and sentenced to six years in prison. Although he was released after two years for health reasons, he abstained from direct political activity until 1929. During this period he abandoned any political action and withdrew to fast and to meditate. He called for a 'constructive programme' of local hand-weaving industries and social programmes to promote self-reliance.

Gandhi at his spinning wheel; his promotion of spinning had symbolic significance rather than practical use – hand-woven cloth symbolised a rejection of foreign manufactured goods and the promotion of self-reliance; the spinning wheel became the symbol of the Indian nationalist movement

Fact

Traditionally, the 'Untouchables', the lowest category in the caste system, suffered many forms of discrimination. They could not own land, enter temples, or use common resources such as village wells or roads. They performed all the menial work, such as carrying water, tanning leather and working the land, usually as sharecroppers. The British colonial administration referred to them as the 'depressed classes'. Gandhi fought for their rights and called them *Harijans*, or children of God.

During this period, Gandhi fought for greater rights for the 'Untouchables' and managed to negotiate some reforms to the caste system in the province of Travancore, allowing freedom of movement. By championing their cause, Gandhi encouraged social integration and, critically, sent out a significant signal that post-colonial India would be a modern state based on the values of social equality for all.

Communal tensions

A feature of the early non-co-operation campaign had been the unity between Hindus and Muslims. For example, the Khalifat leader Mohammed Ali had served as president of Congress as well. However, a disturbing development in the mid 1920s was the growth of tension and violence between religious communities. This was partly due to the emergence of a politicised form of Hinduism, called *Hindutwa*, which promoted an anti-Muslim message.

The 1920s also saw a strengthening of the Muslim League, as the Khalifat movement declined with the collapse of the Ottoman Empire. Mohammed Ali Jinnah, the leader of the League, offered to co-operate with Congress to draw up proposals for constitutional reform, in return for safeguards for the Muslim minority. But, under pressure from Hindu nationalists, Congress rejected this offer. Tensions between the two communities were heightened in some regions by economic factors. In many – but certainly not all – provinces, many of the landlords and traders were Hindu, while the Muslims were peasant farmers or poor workers.

Fact

Hindutwa, or the promotion of Hindu values and the creation of a state modelled on Hindu beliefs and culture, was the aim of a militant Hindu nationalist group, the Rashtriya Swayamsevak Sangh (RSS), which was formed in 1925. It was a member of the RSS who later assassinated Gandhi because of his tolerant attitude towards Muslims. The ideas of *Hindutwa* re-emerged as a powerful political force in Indian politics in the 1980s, in the Bharatiya Janata Party (BJP), the political group associated with Hindu nationalism.

Question

Explain the dilemma facing Muslims in India during the 1920s.

SOURCE B

Mohammed Ali, commenting on the conflicting sense of identity facing Muslims in India in the 1920s.

I have a culture, a polity, an outlook on life – a complete synthesis which is Muslim. Where God commands I am a Muslim first, a Muslim second, and a Muslim last, and nothing but a Muslim. ... But where India is concerned, where India's freedom is concerned, where the welfare of India is concerned, I am an Indian first, an Indian second, an Indian last, and nothing but an Indian.

Quoted in Bose, S. and Jalal, A. 1996. Modern South Asia. *London, UK. Routledge. p. 143.*

Motilal Nehru (1861–1931)

Nehru was an early leader of the Indian nationalist movement, a leader of the Indian National Congress, and founder of the influential Nehru–Gandhi family. His son, Jawaharlal Nehru, was independent India's first prime minister (1947–64); his granddaughter, Indira Gandhi, was prime minister from 1966 to 1977 and from 1980 to 1984; and his great grandson, Rajiv Gandhi, was prime minister from 1984 to 1989.

Political and constitutional developments

In 1927, the British government appointed the Simon Commission to make recommendations for constitutional reform in India. However, no Indians were included in the commission so the nationalists rejected it. In the same year, **Motilal Nehru** drafted a proposed constitution that called for **dominion status** and full self-government. Younger and more radical members of Congress, such as Subhas Chandra Bose and Jawaharlal Nehru, went even further and called for complete self-government outside the British Empire. At the same time, Jinnah and the Muslim League were insisting that Muslims should be given separate representation to protect their position as a minority.

dominion status This gave colonies autonomy to run their own affairs. They were linked to Britain as members of the empire but not ruled by Britain. Australia, New Zealand, South Africa and Canada had dominion status; British colonies in Asia and other parts of Africa did not.

During 1928, there were radical protests by students and urban youth and a series of strikes by workers in Bombay, backed by the Communist Party of India. The British authorities responded by charging 31 trade union leaders with planning to overthrow the government, although they were eventually freed after their trials collapsed. When the British ignored the demand for dominion status and made vague statements about future constitutional developments, impatience at the slow pace of reform increased.

At the 1929 session of Congress, Gandhi backed the demand for *purna svaraj*, or complete independence. The failure of the colonial power to establish dialogue with the nationalists had pushed Congress into radical action. Even Gandhi had, to a degree, become more radical as a result of the stagnation of British policy in the 1920s.

How did resistance develop into a mass-based nationalist movement in the 1930s?

The Salt March, 1930

Gandhi chose to make salt the issue upon which he would base his second great *satyagraha* campaign. Salt was a vital commodity in India, a basic life-sustaining resource. Not only did the British tax it heavily but its production was a state monopoly – it was illegal for ordinary Indians to manufacture or sell salt. In March 1930, Gandhi began a march of nearly 400 km (250 miles) to the coast. Crowds gathered to support him and the event received media coverage all over the world. When Gandhi arrived at the sea, he picked up a lump of natural salt, symbolically breaking the law. The authorities made no attempt to stop this act, so powerful was the message that the protest action sent out to millions of Indians, and to people around the world. Soon the protests spread, and thousands of people began to break the salt laws. Eventually, the authorities reacted by imprisoning thousands of protesters, including Gandhi. His arrest prompted nationwide strikes and rioting in the larger urban centres. By the end of 1930, 100,000 people had been arrested and 100 killed by the police.

Eventually the British decided on negotiation, and a Round Table conference was held in London. However, without any representatives from Congress – which boycotted the meeting – little progress was made. In 1931, Irwin, the viceroy of India, released Gandhi and began talks with him in Delhi. Given Irwin's previous opposition to reform in India, this shows just how seriously the British viewed the situation. Irwin and Gandhi reached an agreement: Gandhi called off the civil disobedience campaign and, in return, the British recognised the development of an indigenous Indian manufacturing economy and invited Gandhi to London for a second round of talks. The second Round Table conference in London did little to advance India's cause, and on his return to India Gandhi called for a renewal of civil disobedience.

Increasing political tension

In 1932, Gandhi was arrested and imprisoned once again, leading to widespread resistance to the colonial power. Peasants refused to pay taxes and support for the boycott of British goods increased. During this period another 80,000 Indians were imprisoned. As well as repression, Britain also resorted to 'political engineering to divide and deflect the nationalist challenge', according to Bose and Jalal. This took the form of the Communal Award, a voting formula that confirmed separate electorates for religious minorities, such as Muslims

A significant feature of the salt campaign was the involvement of large numbers of women as marchers and speakers

and Sikhs, and also for the 'depressed castes' (the Untouchables). Gandhi viewed this development as a serious challenge to the unity of the nationalist movement, and threatened to fast to death in his prison cell. The fast had a wide impact on public opinion and eventually led to an agreement between Gandhi and Dr B. R. Ambedkar, the leader of the Untouchables, that a separate electorate would be abandoned in favour of a larger number of reserved seats. Some more traditionalist Congress members were troubled by Gandhi's pact with Ambedkar and his championing of the depressed castes.

Historical debate

There are different interpretations of modern Indian history. Imperialist historians focus on the role of the British in the progress towards independence. Indian nationalist historians focus on the role played by Indian leaders such as Gandhi and Nehru in the independence movement. Historians of the more recent 'Subaltern Studies' group focus on the role played by ordinary people in this struggle, and how they too were agents of political and social change. The word 'subaltern' is a military term meaning someone of inferior rank, but in this context it is used to refer to anyone who holds an inferior position in society in terms of race, class, gender, sexuality, ethnicity or religion.

Activity

In pairs create a chart. On one side list Gandhi's actions and policies, on the other rate their effectiveness in bringing about an end to British domination in India from 1 (very ineffective) to 5 (very effective).

Around this time, the Muslim League began calling for a separate Muslim state as part of the process of decolonisation. During the First World War, the League and Congress had made an agreement, the Lucknow Pact, to co-operate in striving for independence. However, this agreement had later collapsed and the two organisations became alienated from one another. After the failure of the Round Table talks in 1930, the League drafted its first demands for an independent Muslim state, which it called Pakistan. The name means 'land of the pure' in the Urdu language, and was made up from the initial letters of the Muslim-majority provinces of **P**unjab, the **A**fghan frontier, **K**ashmir and **S**ind. The aspirations of the League were further reinforced in 1932 with the British government's announcement of the Communal Award.

Constitutional developments

In 1935, the British parliament passed the Government of India Act, a new set of constitutional reforms which gave more control in the provinces to elected Indian ministers. However, the act ensured that Britain retained control through emergency powers, which could be imposed whenever it was deemed necessary. Indian leaders condemned the proposals as too little too late. Nehru called the act a 'charter of slavery'; Bose dismissed it as a scheme 'not for self-government, but for maintaining British rule'; and Jinnah described it as 'most reactionary, retrograde, injurious and fatal to the interest of British India *vis-a-vis* the Indian states'.

Nevertheless, Congress and the League decided to participate in the provincial elections held in 1937. The right to vote was based on a property qualification, and so was limited to 35 million of the wealthier part of the Indian population, including women. In the elections, Congress emerged as by far the most influential political force, gaining a landslide victory with 70% of the popular vote. In stark contrast, the Muslim League did not do well in the elections, winning barely 5% of the total Muslim vote.

Growing divisions

Although the Muslim League had fared badly in the elections, Jinnah hoped that the League could form part of coalition governments in the provinces that had large Muslim minorities. Having won the elections so convincingly, however, Congress was not prepared to compromise with the League in this way. It turned down Jinnah's offer of co-operation, although it did appoint some of its own Muslim members to provincial governments. Historians such as Barbara and Thomas Metcalf refer to the attitude and actions of Congress towards the League at this time as arrogant and 'high-handed', and say that they caused the League to strengthen its efforts to gain a mass following. In some provinces, Muslim leaders complained of favouritism towards Hindus, and the promotion of Hindu symbols and the Hindi language, although this was never Congress policy. Using the slogan 'Islam in danger' as a rallying call, Jinnah tried to build up his power base by uniting all Muslims within the League. Support for the idea that India's Muslims were a distinct nation entitled to a separate state gained ground, especially as the election results had revealed the electoral dangers that Muslims faced as part of a single state. However, some Muslims continued to support the goal of a united India, as the statement by Maulana Azad, president of Congress in 1940, shows (Source C).

SOURCE C

Statement by Maulana Azad, president of the Indian National Congress, 1940.

I am proud of being an Indian. I am proud of the indivisible unity that is Indian nationality. ... Islam has now as great a claim on the soil of India as Hinduism. If Hinduism has been the religion of the people here for several thousands of years, Islam has also been their religion for a thousand years. Just as a Hindu can say with pride that he is an Indian and follows Hinduism, so also we can say with equal pride that we are Indians and follow Islam.

Quoted in Metcalf, B. and Metcalf, T. 2006. A Concise History of Modern India. *Cambridge, UK. Cambridge University Press. p. 198.*

Questions

Compare and contrast the views expressed in Source B (page 71) and C (opposite). How might Jinnah have responded to this statement by Maulana Azad? What response would a supporter of *Hindutwa* make to it?

By the late 1930s there was growing conflict between the left and right wings within Congress itself. The most prominent leaders in the left wing were **Jawaharlal Nehru** and **Subhas Chandra Bose** They were impatient with the cautious and conservative approach advocated by Gandhi and others. Gandhi tried to heal the rift by ensuring that first Nehru (in 1936–37) and then Bose (in 1938) served as president of Congress.

Jawaharlal Nehru (1889–1964) Nehru played a key role in the Indian nationalist movement, as a leader of the Indian National Congress and as the recognised heir of Gandhi. A strong supporter of democracy and secularism, he advocated socialist central planning to promote economic development in India. He served as India's first prime minister, leading the Congress Party to victory in India's first three general elections. He died of a heart attack while still in office.

Subhas Chandra Bose (1897–1945) Bose was an Indian nationalist leader who supported radical social and economic policies and a more militant nationalism. He believed that a non-violent approach to British rule would not be effective and advocated violent resistance. He later formed the Indian National Army to fight the British during the Second World War.

In 1939, Bose was re-elected as president of Congress in the first contested election in the history of the movement. He was supported by the youth, trade union and peasant wings of the party. It seemed that elements within Congress had run out of patience and were moving towards support for a more radical revolutionary – and potentially violent – solution to British domination of India.

However, Bose's re-election was opposed by Gandhi and many of the most powerful figures in Congress, and the election threatened to split the party in two, weakening the nationalist movement. When Bose realised he would not have the co-operation of the moderates in Congress, he left to form the revolutionary Forward Bloc Party. These developments showed that, despite the emergence of radical forces, the moderates managed to maintain control of the nationalist movement.

On the eve of the Second World War, the situation in India was a complex one for Britain. On the one hand, the lack of unity amongst the nationalists seemed to serve Britain's interests. On the other hand, the growing tensions and divisions had the potential to cause unrest that would be difficult to contain. The outbreak of war in 1939 meant a postponement of the further constitutional reforms laid out in the 1935 Government of India Act.

Question

What caused the split in the Indian National Congress in 1939?

What was the impact of the Second World War on the nationalist movement?

The effects of the war on India

When the Second World War started in 1939, the British viceroy committed India to fight on the Allied side against Germany without consulting the Indian legislative council. This act was legal and constitutional, but it emphasised India's subservience to the colonial power. This strengthened the resolve of the nationalist movement to continue the independence struggle. In December 1941, Japan entered the war on Germany's side with a series of successful military strikes across East Asia. The Japanese rapidly overran European colonies in Indochina, the Malayan peninsula and Burma, bringing their armies to the border of India, and severely denting Britain's military and imperial prestige.

Sikh soldiers serving alongside the British 8th Army in Italy during the Second World War

The war created political opportunities for the Indian nationalists. The British simply did not have the resources to suppress a potential nationalist rising in India while they were fighting the war. Consequently, Britain decided to make political concessions to Congress and the Muslim League. In the face of it this seemed a wise decision – after all, neither Indian independence party was radical, nor were they champions of armed resistance. The problem was that the British were not prepared to make *significant* concessions. In 1941, the British prime minister, Winston Churchill, committed Britain to the Atlantic Charter, a document that supported the right of all peoples to political self-determination. However, shortly afterwards, Churchill told the British parliament that this provision did not apply to India. It was clear that the British position on India had changed little by 1941. Indian nationalists were outraged by this turn of events.

By 1942, however, Japan's sweeping victories in Asia forced Churchill to change his position. He recognised the urgent need to gain the support of Indian leaders in fighting Japan. In March 1942, he sent Stafford Cripps, a member of the British government, to India to negotiate with the nationalist leaders. Cripps made the commitment to grant India independence but only after the war was over. In return, Congress was to commit itself fully to the British war effort.

Congress and the 'Quit India' campaign

Congress rejected the offer. It accepted that, in the long term, a Japanese victory in Asia would simply replace one form of colonial domination with another; however, the postponement of independence seemed unreasonable. As a result, Congress began to campaign actively for immediate independence from Britain. In August 1942, it adopted the 'Quit India' resolution and relaunched the campaign of non-co-operation with the colonial power. Britain reacted by imprisoning Congress leaders and banning the organisation. As Britain's repressive policy took hold, almost 60,000 Indians, including Gandhi and Nehru, were detained without trial. British attempts to control the increasingly dangerous situation in India led to over 1000 people being killed.

SOURCE D

India will attain her freedom through her non-violent strength, and will retain it likewise. Therefore, the committee hopes that Japan will not have any designs on India. But if Japan attacks India, and Britain makes no response to its appeal, the committee will expect all those who look to the Congress for guidance to offer complete non-violent non-cooperation to the Japanese forces, and not to render any assistance to them. It is no part of the duty of those who are attacked to render any assistance to the attacker. It is their duty to offer complete non-cooperation.

Extract from Gandhi's 'Quit India' resolution, 1942.

Question

Is the course of action outlined in Gandhi's 'Quit India' resolution consistent with his philosophy of *satyagraha*?

Activity

Contrast the responses of Congress and the Muslim League towards Britain during the Second World War, and comment on their significance.

The Muslim League during the war

The war also created opportunities for the Muslim League. The League's leader, Jinnah, at first approached Congress with an offer of co-operation in the face of British repression. When Congress rejected this offer, the Muslim League continued to co-operate with Britain. Jinnah accepted Cripps's offer of delayed independence, but he demanded a two-state solution after independence. As the situation in India grew increasingly tense, and Congress became the target of British repression, the League moved to give full support to the colonial power's war effort. In return, Britain gave serious consideration to a two-state solution to the problem. The League was therefore in a strong negotiating position at the end of the war. Its support for Britain's actions in India would be a key factor in the emergence of the separate Muslim state of Pakistan after independence.

Fact

Subhas Chandra Bose saw the war as an opportunity to force Britain to grant independence immediately. He allied himself with the Axis powers, and tried unsuccessfully to raise an Indian Legion in Europe to fight for the Germans. When the Germans transferred him to Southeast Asia by submarine in 1943, he formed a 60,000-strong Indian National Army (INA) among Indian prisoners of war and civilians there. He also established a Free India government in the Burmese capital of Rangoon. The INA fought Allied forces in Burma, and invaded and briefly captured parts of north-eastern India, before being defeated.

The economic impact of the war on India

India made a major contribution to the Allied victory in the war. Not only did Indian soldiers fight in North Africa, Italy and Burma, but also the Indian economy was a significant factor in the final defeat of the Axis powers. An example is the Jamshedpur steel complex, which became the largest producer of steel in the British Empire for the duration of the war. The war transformed India's economic relationship with Britain. Before the war, India had been in debt to Britain. However, during the war, Britain's need to fund the war forced it to borrow heavily from India – so much so that by 1945 the economic relationship between the two states had been reversed, with Britain owing India huge sums of money.

The war also placed strains on India. Two million people died in the great Bengal Famine of 1943, which was caused partly by the loss of rice imports from Japanese-occupied Burma, and partly by a British administrative decision to divert food from the Bengal countryside to feed the military instead. However, the war also brought opportunities. The economic demands of the conflict encouraged industrialisation on a scale unknown before 1939, and Bombay became a major centre of light engineering and manufacturing of pharmaceuticals and chemicals.

Activity

Design two essay plans, one arguing that the Second World War was the critical factor in bringing independence to India, the other arguing that the war was secondary to other factors. In pairs, decide which essay plan is more convincing.

The Second World War had a negative impact on the British economy. Although Britain emerged victorious, the burden of sustaining the war effort proved costly. By 1945, Britain's economy was on the brink of collapse, and it became apparent that it would be impossible to maintain a global empire. Furthermore, the British had made serious commitments to the nationalist movement to maintain Indian support in the war against Germany and Japan. With the defeat of the Axis powers in 1945, it was time for the British to make good their promises of independence and negotiate with the nationalist leaders.

What part did Jinnah play in the struggle for independence?

Mohammad Ali Jinnah (1876–1948) was a key player in the Indian independence movement. Like many other nationalist leaders, he had a Western education. He trained as a lawyer in London in the 1890s where he was influenced by British liberal ideas. As a result his later approach to independence was firmly grounded in constitutional methods. He was a member of the Indian National Congress from 1896, but only became active in Indian politics after defending the leading nationalist Tilak at the time of the Bengal uprising in 1905.

In 1913, he joined the Muslim League and in 1916 became its president for the first time. Jinnah believed that India had a right to independence, and argued that Indians were entitled to agitate for this goal. However, he also recognised the benefits that British rule had brought to India in the form of law, culture and industry. In many ways these were the views of most Indian nationalist leaders. Jinnah initially agitated for India to be given dominion status. This was a halfway house solution to India's position within the British Empire, and would give it autonomy rather than complete independence. He had been a moderate liberal Anglophile, but Britain's failure to give independence to India after the First World War radicalised him.

Where Jinnah diverged from the mainstream nationalist movement was in his promotion of a two-state solution for India after independence. He claimed that, in a single post-colonial state, Muslims would be swamped by the Hindu majority. He was ill-at-ease with Gandhi's public image as a traditional Hindu holy man, and also with Gandhi's political tactics of non-co-operation, which he believed could destabilise the political structure.

As a result of these differences, Jinnah parted company with Congress in 1920, and the Muslim League became an alternative pressure group that the British sometimes played off against Congress. Throughout the 1920s and 1930s Jinnah campaigned for independence, but he became disillusioned at the slow progress. He fought successfully for separate Muslim representation in elections, but was bitterly disappointed about the poor performance of the League in the 1937 elections. From then on, he set out to build up support for the League as the sole representative of Indian Muslims.

During the Second World War, Jinnah astutely supported the British, and this strengthened the position of the League in later negotiations. In 1941, he started a newspaper, *Dawn*, to propagate his views, and he put considerable pressure on Cripps during the British representative's visit to the subcontinent. During this period, Gandhi made efforts to come to an agreement with Jinnah – efforts that only served to reinforce the position of the Muslim leader with his followers.

In the tense period after the war, Jinnah took advantage of the confusion to press his demand for a Muslim state. On 16 August 1946, he instructed his followers to engage in 'direct action'. This led to strikes and protests and, eventually, **communal** violence on a large scale.

Eventually the British and Congress leaders accepted the partition of India, with Pakistan as a separate Muslim state. Jinnah became its first leader, but died of a heart attack within a year. There is some debate about whether Jinnah wanted a secular or an Islamic state in Pakistan. He died before he could put policy into action. Most scholars believe that he wanted a state akin to modern Turkey. Nevertheless the new Pakistan, with its Western and Eastern zones, was a fragile political entity at best.

It is interesting to note Jinnah's comments on the nature of the state he envisaged for Pakistan in Source E (page 80), in an address he made to the first meeting of the Pakistan Constituent Assembly, on 11 August 1947.

communal Communalism is the belief in promoting the interests of one ethnic, religious or cultural group rather than those of society as a whole. Communal groups were responsible for promoting violence between Hindus, Muslims and Sikhs.

Historical debate

Some historians believe that it was Jinnah's call for direct action that caused much of the violence and bloodshed that followed. Metcalf believes that, perhaps unintentionally, Jinnah's call precipitated the 'horrors of riot and massacre that were to disfigure the coming of independence'. Ramachandra Guha states that Jinnah was deliberately trying to 'polarise the two communities further, and thus force the British to divide India when they finally quit'. However, other historians, including Bose and Jalal, believe that Jinnah's intentions have been misinterpreted and that he was merely trying to ensure 'an equitable share of power for Muslims' in a united India, and not the creation of a separate Islamic state.

SOURCE E

You are free to go to your temples, you are free to go to your mosques or to any other place of worship in this state of Pakistan. ... You may belong to any religion or caste or creed – that has nothing to do with the business of the state. ... We are starting with this fundamental principle that we are all citizens and equal citizens of one state.

Quoted in Bose, S. and Jalal, A. 1996. Modern South Asia. *London, UK. Routledge. p 194.*

Jinnah can be criticised for his adherence to a two-state solution. It may be argued that his position encouraged communal violence in the final months before independence. In his defence, however, it might be argued that such an outcome would have resulted anyway, given the tensions at the time. A more sophisticated defence of Jinnah lays the blame for the two-state solution at the feet of Congress. Some scholars, such as Seervai and Jalal, argue that Jinnah wanted a compromise federation in post-colonial India but could not get the co-operation of Congress leaders.

What was Gandhi's contribution to the independence movement?

Mohandas Gandhi (1869–1948) is one of the outstanding figures of the 20th century, so much so that it is difficult to evaluate his impact on the Indian nationalist movement and India's final transition to independence in 1947. In many ways he was similar to Jinnah. He certainly had the same liberal Western-influenced background. Where he differed from the Muslim leader, however, was in his public image as a Hindu holy man. Further, his policies of *satyagraha* were directly opposed to Jinnah's more constitutional political approach.

Gandhi was born into a middle-class Indian family; his father had been a high-ranking official in Porbander, one of the princely states. Gandhi was brought up in the Jain religious tradition, which influenced his later political belief in *satyagraha*. He trained as a lawyer at University College London. One of his first legal positions was in South Africa, where he experienced racial discrimination at first hand. He also saw Britain use extreme violence to quell opposition to its rule, in the ruthless suppression of a Zulu rebellion in 1906. These formative years led Gandhi to reject racism and injustice, not only for Indians but for all people. These experiences, together with his religious background, led him to believe that the most effective way of fighting colonial oppression was by non-violent methods. The application of any other strategy in India might lead to the same violent response by the British that he had seen in South Africa.

He returned to India in 1915, and spent over a year travelling around the country assessing local conditions. He also focused on issues of self-reliance and social mobility, encouraging the building of schools, hospitals and clean water facilities. From this early period we see a combination of Western liberal thought and a very Indian approach to non-violent agitation. By 1918, Gandhi had led the first non-violent acts of non-co-operation in the Champaran

Mohammad Ali Jinnah and Mohandas Gandhi in 1944

agitation. The success of this event established his reputation as an effective leader of mass civil disobedience. The strategy was very effective when used against a liberal democracy like Britain, where suppressing such protests was a difficult public-relations problem for the British to solve.

Gandhi became a national figure after the events of 1919, when he launched his first all-India non-co-operation campaign. Through this and later campaigns he was able to transform the nationalist struggle into a mass movement. He also proved to be adept at propaganda. The Salt March of 1930 is an excellent example of this (see page 72). By marching hundreds of kilometres in full view of the media to collect salt illegally, Gandhi made a most effective political statement. The salt tax was patently unfair and Gandhi responded with non-violent protest. The British reaction, imprisoning over 60,000 people, only served to damage their credibility as leaders of the subcontinent.

Gandhi can be seen as a social liberal. He certainly wanted reform of the Indian caste system to create greater equality, and his liberal attitude also extended to the emancipation of Indian women. He was partly successful on both counts, which is significant given the deeply rooted cultural attitudes that he was challenging.

Gandhi took advantage of Britain's involvement in the Second World War to increase the pressure for independence in the 'Quit India' campaign. He has been criticised for this because of his failure to make a stand against Nazism. He was, however, quite correct in pointing out the inconsistencies of the British position in fighting Nazism without giving self-determination to the Indian population. The events of the First World War period had also taught him that British promises could not necessarily be relied upon.

Fact

The Champaran agitation was one of Gandhi's first major successes. He supported the cause of peasant farmers in the Champaran district of Bihar, who were being forced to grow indigo for British planters, instead of food crops for their own use.

Gandhi has been criticised too for his attitude to the form of the post-colonial state in India. India was a diverse society, but 80% of the population was Hindu. Many of the ethnic and religious minorities – especially Muslims – genuinely feared Hindu domination in an independent India. Gandhi has been accused of not fully understanding the depth of Muslim fears. When Congress flirted with the idea of a federated India in 1934, in which Muslims would have some autonomy in Muslim majority provinces, Gandhi made his opinions public by resigning from the party in protest. The result of this failure to compromise arguably led to the final division of the subcontinent into India and Pakistan, an event that was accompanied by considerable bloodshed.

Historical debate

Historians often debate the impact of individuals on the historical process. One school of thought is that certain individuals can change the course of history; Gandhi is one of these individuals. Another argues that developments in social, cultural and economic structures are the key part of the historical process. In this perspective, individuals like Gandhi are nothing more than actors in a play whose lines have already been written. Re-read this unit and decide which school of thought you most favour.

Gandhi was assassinated in 1948 by a Hindu extremist, Nathuram Godse, who felt that Gandhi had weakened India by upholding secular rather than Hindu nationalist values. (You will read more about this in Unit 3.) In India Gandhi is seen as the father of the nation. Although he was not the originator of non-violence as a means of political action, he was the first to apply it successfully on a large scale. He became the pre-eminent independence politician of the day, and a great spiritual and moral leader. He became known as the 'Mahatma' – a semi-religious term meaning 'great soul'.

Activity

Read the news report published on the 50th anniversary of Gandhi's death on this website: http://news.bbc.co.uk/2/hi/51468.stm.

How valid are the criticisms of Gandhi from left- and right-wing perspectives? Does he deserve the title of 'Father of the Nation'? How appropriate is the title of this article ('The Lost Legacy of Mahatma Gandhi')?

End of unit activities

1 Working in small groups, debate the effectiveness of *satyagraha* as a political tactic. Refer to events in Gandhi's fight against British rule in India to support both sides of the argument. Report your conclusions to the rest of the class.

2 Write two letters to the press that might have appeared in *The Times of India* in 1942. The first should urge support for the 'Quit India' campaign launched by Congress. The second should argue that the special circumstances of the war require patience, restraint and loyalty to king and empire.

3 Working in pairs, hold a discussion between Gandhi and Jinnah about political tactics, attitudes towards Britain and British rule, the place of religion in society and state, and your visions for the future of India.

4 Use the information in this unit to design a spider diagram illustrating the impact of the Second World War on India. Include political, economic, social and military effects, and any others that you think are relevant.

5 'The Muslim League emerged from the Second World War in a far stronger position than it had held in 1939.' Do you agree with this view? Write a paragraph to support your answer.

6 Work in small groups of four or five. Each student should assume a role and prepare to defend the policies and actions of that role. Examples could be Gandhi, Bose or Jinnah. In turn, each character should make a short presentation, explaining his beliefs, policies and actions, and then defend them when cross-questioned by the rest of the group.

3 The formation of and challenges to post-colonial India and Pakistan

Key questions

- How was independence established in India?
- What challenges did independent India face after 1947?
- What challenges did independent Pakistan face after 1947?

Overview

- Between 1945 and 1947, British control of India collapsed, as anti-British protests mounted and demands for independence grew.
- However, there were differences of opinion between Congress and the Muslim League about the form that an independent Indian state should take.
- The Muslim League's call for 'direct action' led to an outbreak of communal violence known as the Great Calcutta Killing.
- As tensions rose, Congress accepted the concept of partition, and India and Pakistan became separate independent states in August 1947.
- After independence, violence between Hindus and Muslims led to the flight of 15 million refugees across the borders between the new states.
- India and Pakistan went to war over the state of Kashmir, which was eventually partitioned between them by the United Nations.
- Independent India faced several challenges that threatened its survival as a secular democracy, including political extremism, language divisions, communalism and Sikh separatism.
- The new government implemented policies to promote industrialisation, institute land reform, deal with rural poverty and increase food production.
- Social challenges facing the government were the position of women, inequalities resulting from the caste system, high rates of illiteracy, inadequate health services and high population growth rates.
- India adopted a policy of non-alignment internationally and, despite its attempt to maintain peaceful relations, fought wars against Pakistan and China over territory.
- Internal tensions in Pakistan resulted in the secession of East Pakistan as the independent state of Bangladesh.
- Pakistan struggled to establish a strong tradition of democratic government, with the army frequently intervening to establish military rule.
- The dispute between India and Pakistan over Kashmir resulted in three wars and ongoing tensions in the region.
- As an ally of the United States, Pakistan was significantly affected by the politics of the Cold War, which had a destabilising effect militarily, politically and economically.

Timeline

1946 Direct Action Day triggers widespread communal violence

1947 Mountbatten arrives as last viceroy of India; Pakistan and India become independent; refugee crisis in Punjab; first war between India and Pakistan over Kashmir breaks out

1948 assassination of Gandhi; death of Jinnah

1949 UN arranges ceasefire in Kashmir

1950 India's first constitution ratified

1955 Nehru attends Bandung Conference of non-aligned states

1962 war between India and China

1964 death of Nehru

1965 war between India and Pakistan over Kashmir

1971 East Pakistan becomes Bangladesh

1979 Soviet invasion of Afghanistan

1984 assassination of Indira Gandhi sparks anti-Sikh attacks

1992 Hindu extremists destroy Ayodhya mosque

1998 Hindu nationalist BJP comes to power in India; India and Pakistan become nuclear powers

1999 war between India and Pakistan over Kashmir

2001 US-led invasion of Afghanistan

How was independence established in India?

The move to independence, 1945–47

After the end of the Second World War, anti-British feelings in India intensified. In 1945, Indians who had fought in Bose's Indian National Army alongside the Japanese were put on trial for treason. The trial turned them into national heroes – they were seen as fighters for Indian freedom who were now being unfairly tried by the colonial power. Massive protests followed, and the British were forced to reduce the punishment to suspended sentences. This failed to stop the protests, which included a mutiny in the Royal Indian Navy involving 20 naval bases and 74 ships. Faced with a rapidly deteriorating situation, the British government realised the importance of reaching a settlement in India urgently. Britain had been seriously weakened by the war, and did not have the economic resources to maintain control in these uneasy circumstances.

The situation in India was further complicated by differences of opinion over the specific form of a post-colonial state. Congress wanted the creation of a single, secular state, in which religious affiliation would not be significant. The Muslim League, however, wanted India to be divided. Muslims formed only about 20% of the population at that stage, and they feared that their interests would be neglected in a Hindu-dominated state. They wanted a separate country, Pakistan, to be created in the northern parts of the subcontinent, where most Muslims lived. Congress vigorously opposed the concept of a divided India. Congress leaders, such as Gandhi and Nehru, tried to persuade Muslim leaders that they would be safe in a united India.

The leader of the Muslim League, Mohammed Ali Jinnah, put pressure on Britain to support the creation of two separate states. The League also appealed to popular fears and prejudices – Muslims of all classes flocked to join the organisation, believing that Islam was in danger. In Source A, historian Ramachandra Guha analyses the contrast between the election messages of Congress and the League in the 1946 elections for provincial assemblies.

SOURCE A

The world over, the rhetoric of modern democratic politics has been marked by two rather opposed rhetorical styles. The first appeals to hope, to popular aspirations for economic prosperity and social peace. The second appeals to fear, to sectional worries about being worsted or swamped by one's historic enemies. In the elections of 1946 the Congress relied on the rhetoric of hope. It had a strongly positive content to its programme, promising land reform, workers' rights, and the like. The Muslim League, on the other hand, relied on the rhetoric of fear. If they did not get a separate homeland, they told the voters, then they would be crushed by the more numerous Hindus in a united India.

Guha, Ramachandra. 2007. India after Gandhi: The History of the World's Largest Democracy. *London, UK. Macmillan. p. 28.*

Questions

Does Source A show a biased view? Explain how it can be argued that the language used in the source can contribute to bias. How could one establish whether it is an accurate and reliable interpretation of the situation?

Communal violence

As negotiations between the British government and Indian representatives dragged on, tensions mounted. Fearing that Britain and Congress would push forward with plans for a single state, Jinnah called for 'direct action' in support of the Muslim League's demand for partition. He wanted to show the other parties that Muslim aspirations could not be ignored.

On 16 August 1946, or 'Direct Action Day', there was rioting in Calcutta, which soon turned into widespread communal violence between Muslim and Hindu communities, with both sides committing atrocities. In this Great Calcutta Killing, as it became known, more than 4000 people were killed, and thousands more wounded or made homeless. There were violent clashes between Hindus and Muslims in other parts of India as well, and thousands more were killed. The British interpreted the violence as a sign that there were irreconcilable differences between Hindus and Muslims, an interpretation that is questioned by many historians today.

Question

How and why had the situation in India changed after the Second World War?

Partition, 1947

In an atmosphere of escalating violence, Congress came to accept that partition was the only viable solution and that British India would be divided into two separate states. The violence also exposed the weakness of Britain's position in the subcontinent, and the British decided to quit India as soon as possible.

In February 1947, Lord Louis Mountbatten was sent as the last viceroy of India, to facilitate and oversee the handover of power by June 1948. He later brought the date forward to 15 August 1947. In only six months, therefore, Mountbatten had to decide whether power would be handed over to one, two or more states, where the borders between them would be, and what was to happen to the 'princely states' – those parts of India that had remained under the control of hereditary rulers.

Mountbatten opted for the Muslim League's two-state solution and created two enclaves in north-western India and eastern Bengal, containing large numbers of Muslims, to become Pakistan. The rulers of the princely states were allowed to choose which state to join. The problems were not, however, solved by this decision. The ethnic and religious mix of the subcontinent was far more complex than implied by the simple geographic division devised by the British. For the partition plan to work, millions of people would have to relocate to one country or the other, depending on their ethnicity and religion.

In August 1947, British rule came to an end when the subcontinent became independent as two separate states: India and Pakistan. The two areas where partition was most complex were in the provinces of Punjab in the west and Bengal in the east. Both had mixed populations, so it had been decided to divide each of them between India and Pakistan.

Matters were further complicated by the fact that the new borders dividing these provinces were announced only a few days after independence. Millions of Hindus and Muslims found themselves on the wrong side of the border and tried desperately to get to safety. About 15 million people abandoned their homes and belongings in a panic-stricken scramble to get to the other side.

Theory of knowledge

Historical interpretation

Historians of the Subaltern Studies group, such as Ian Talbot, Gurharpal Singh and others, believe that it is not only the negotiations between political leaders (the 'high politics' of partition) that need to be understood. They believe the 'human dimension' is equally important – seeing ordinary people not simply as victims of partition, but also as agents of it. Some, for example, saw the economic advantages that could be derived from partition.

Theory of knowledge

Historical interpretation

Some historians think that the reality of the partition of India cannot be understood by simply examining the political events that led up to it or that followed it. They believe that this approach omits the 'human dimension', or the 'history from below' focus. Urvashi Butalia has constructed a history of partition based entirely on interviews with people who actually experienced it, called *The Other Side of Silence: Voices from the Partition of India*. What are the advantages and disadvantages of using oral evidence in history?

A convoy of refugees trying to reach East Punjab in 1947; partition led to a desperate migration of people anxious not to be caught on the wrong side of the border

The situation in Punjab was also complicated by the presence of the Sikhs, who were scattered throughout the province. Their demands for their own state had been ignored, and they feared that the partition of the province would leave their community powerless and split between two states. When the border was finally announced, they streamed eastwards out of West Punjab, along with millions of Hindus. This added to the violence. At the same time, millions of Muslims were moving westwards towards the border of Pakistan. Law and order broke down entirely, and up to a million people were killed in communal attacks. As a result of this mass migration, East Punjab ended up with a population that was 60% Hindu and 35% Sikh, while the population of West Punjab was almost totally Muslim. This process was similar to the **ethnic cleansing** that has occurred in more recent times.

ethnic cleansing The expulsion of a population from a certain area, or the forced displacement of an ethnic or religious minority. The term was widely used to refer to events in the civil wars in Yugoslavia in the 1990s.

The province of Bengal was also partitioned and Hindu refugees fled from East Pakistan into West Bengal, with Muslim refugees moving in the opposite direction. However, the migration in Bengal was a more gradual process and not accompanied by as much violence and death as in Punjab.

By the end of 1947, the new governments were able to contain the violence and restore order and control. Despite the mass migration, about 40 million Muslims remained in India, and several million Hindus in Pakistan. The resettlement of refugees was a huge financial burden for the new states, which also had to manage the economic consequences of the abrupt partition on existing patterns of communication, infrastructure, agriculture, irrigation and trade.

Map of the subcontinent after independence, showing the flow of refugees

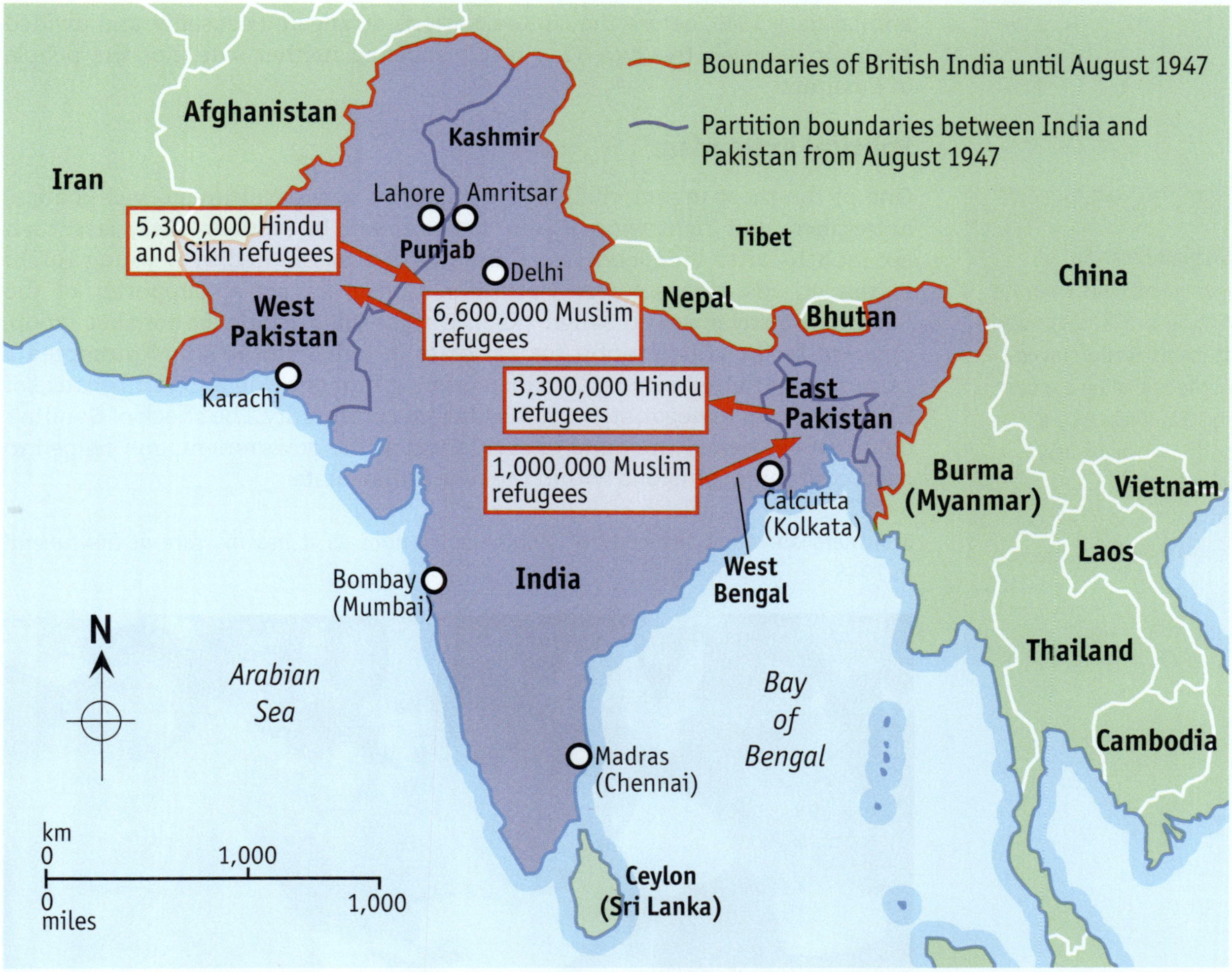

What challenges did independent India face after 1947?

After independence, India was dominated by the figure of its first prime minister, Jawaharlal Nehru, who led the country until his death in 1964. During this period India emerged as a stable democracy – a notable achievement given the large size of the country and its population, the legacies of colonial rule and the difficulties encountered during the progress towards independence.

Overcoming the colonial legacy and consolidating the new regime

The incorporation of the princely states

The 550 'princely states' occupied about 40% of British India, and their rulers had to decide which state to join. All except three of them voluntarily decided to join either India or Pakistan, in return for the right to retain some of their wealth and privileges. Two of the exceptions were Hyderabad and Junagadh, where Muslim princes ruled over large Hindu populations. Both were annexed to India by force, against the wishes of their Muslim rulers, in moves generally welcomed by their people. The third exception was Kashmir, a large state, strategically placed in the north-west and bordering both India and Pakistan. It had a Hindu prince ruling over a predominantly Muslim population. India and Pakistan fought a war for control of Kashmir between December 1947 and January 1949, before the United Nations arranged a ceasefire and divided Kashmir between the two. This result satisfied neither side, nor the people of Kashmir.

Political extremism

One of the most urgent challenges facing the new government was political extremism and right-wing Hindu nationalism. In January 1948, less than six months after independence, Gandhi was assassinated by a young Hindu extremist. His assassin was Nathuram Godse, an active supporter of the Rashtriya Swayamsevak Sangh (RSS), a right-wing Hindu nationalist group, opposed to the creation of a secular state in India. The RSS had promoted a campaign of hatred against Gandhi, accusing him of being a traitor because of his willingness to negotiate with the Muslim community. The shock of Gandhi's death strengthened the hand of secularists in the government, and helped to calm communal tensions within the new Indian state.

Fact
The Rashtriya Swayamsevak Sangh (RSS) was an openly anti-Muslim group with a vision of India as a land of – and for – Hindus. Its members portrayed Muslims as a hostile and alien element in Indian society. Claiming to be a cultural not a political organisation, the RSS formed uniformed paramilitary cells.

Mourners surround the body of Mohandas Gandhi as it lies in state at his funeral in 1948

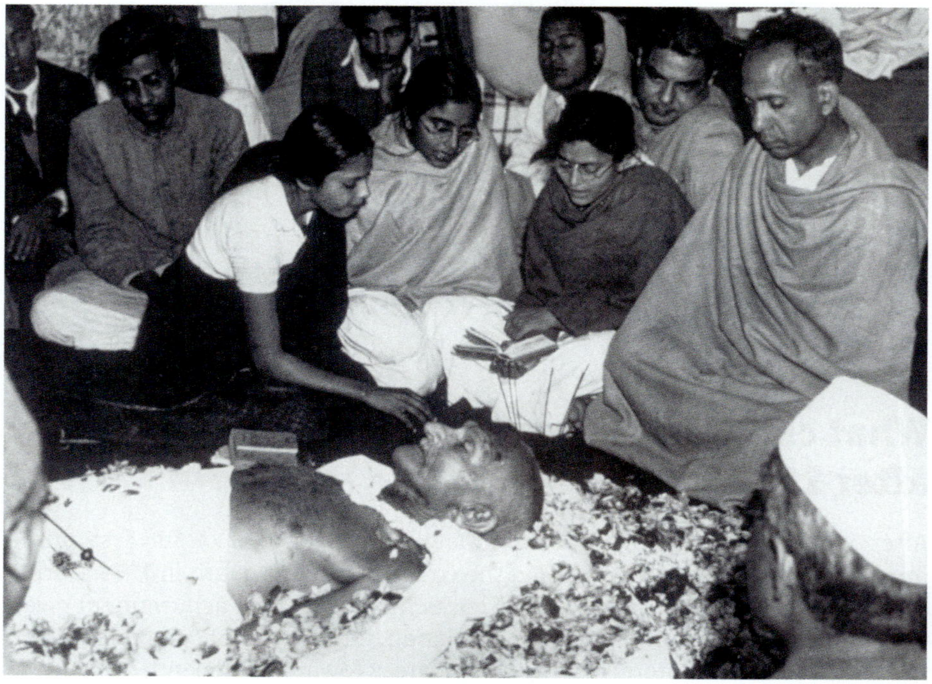

The new constitution and the first election

India's first constitution came into effect on 26 January 1950. The constitution was secular, which meant there was to be no state religion, a complete separation of religion and state, and a secular school system. The constitution recognised equality and freedom of religion for all individuals, and any citizen could hold public office.

The Congress Party won an overwhelming majority in the first election in 1952, gaining 75% of the seats in parliament. It had enormous prestige as the leader and heir of the nationalist movement as well as its links with Gandhi. Congress remained in power because the opposition was fragmented, and it managed to win successive elections during Nehru's lifetime.

Fact

Some historians and politicians incorrectly refer to India as a 'Hindu state'. In fact, India is a secular state. After partition, 40 million Muslims remained in India, compared to 60 million in Pakistan. According to the 2001 census, although the population is over 80% Hindu, there are sizeable religious minorities in India, including 160 million Muslims, 27 million Christians and 22 million Sikhs.

Language issues

There were many hundreds of languages in India, and part of the colonial legacy was English as the language of government, the law courts and of higher education, as well as that of the middle and upper classes. The most widely used language was Hindi, spoken in the north, but it was used by only half of the people in India. The constitution recognised 14 major languages, and made Hindi and English the official languages. However, it also allowed the Indian parliament to alter state boundaries, and this opened the way for different language speakers to press for their own changes. The Teluga-speaking Andhras of southern India were the first to campaign for a state of their own. Violent riots took place after an Andhra leader fasted to death, following which the state of Andhra Pradesh was created in 1953, in an area formerly part of the state of Tamil Nadu. At the same time, Tamil Nadu was recognised as a Tamil-speaking state. Protests over language also led to the division of the state of Bombay to satisfy the demands of Gujarati and Marathi speakers.

The constitution had made provision for the phasing out of English as an official language and for Hindi to take its place completely by 1965. Tamil-speakers in southern India protested violently against the use of Hindi, and several demonstrators burned themselves to death. As a result, English was retained as the language of communication between the different regions. The continued use of English perpetuated a further division in Indian society, between the educated 5% who spoke it and the rest of the population.

Sikh separatism

The Sikhs made up a distinctive religious group, numbering about 10 million, with their own history, culture and identity, as well as their own language, Punjabi. Many of them resented the fact that, while Hindus and Muslims had been accommodated in the partition plan, Sikh demands for their own state were ignored. When partition came, millions of them left their farms and villages in West Punjab and went to India as refugees. By 1951, they formed one-third of the population of Indian Punjab, and held prominent positions in politics, business and the army. The main Sikh political party was the Akali Dal, which wanted more control for the Sikhs in Punjab. Some even wanted an independent Sikh state, to be called Khalistan.

When the Akali Dal held mass demonstrations in 1955, the Indian government ordered the army to invade the Golden Temple in Amritsar, the Sikhs' most sacred holy place, which the government believed was the centre of the protests. In 1965, the Indian government finally agreed to create a smaller Punjab state with a Sikh majority, after the Sikh leader Sant Fateh Singh threatened to fast to death unless the government recognised Sikh demands. Punjab was split into a new state called Haryana, which was mainly Hindu, and a smaller Punjab, where Sikhs formed the majority. The position of the Sikhs, however, remained unresolved, and led to problems for future Indian governments. In the 1980s, a violent campaign for the creation of a separate Sikh state led to the assassination of the Indian prime minister Indira Gandhi.

Fact
Nehru's daughter, Indira Gandhi (prime minister 1966–77 and 1980–84), was assassinated by her Sikh bodyguards after she had ordered troops to storm the Golden Temple at Amritsar to arrest the leader of a militant Sikh separatist group. Thousands were killed in the process. After her death, at least 2000 Sikhs were murdered and many more made homeless in anti-Sikh riots in Delhi and elsewhere.

Communalism and Hindu nationalism

The Bharatiya Jan Sangh (BJS) was a Hindu nationalist party, which challenged the secular nature of the Indian state. Most of its leaders were also members of the militaristic Hindu nationalist group RSS (see page 88). Jan Sangh promoted Hindu culture, religion and traditions and, using the slogan 'one country, one culture, one nation', attempted to unite all Hindus. The group treated India's Muslims with suspicion, questioning their loyalty to India. In the 1952 general election, Jan Sangh won only 3% of the vote, indicating that there was little support for a communalist Hindu party at that stage. According to historian V. P. Kanitkar, Mohandas Gandhi's assassination had discredited right-wing Hindu organisations, diminishing their political influence.

Historical debate
Historians debate the reasons for the rise of Hindu nationalism. Thomas Blom Hansen sees it as a response to the economic pressures created by globalisation. Others, such as Bose, see it as a reaction against the political mobilisation of lower-caste parties.

The BJS was later succeeded by the Bharatiya Janata Party (BJP) as the main Hindu nationalist party. *Hindutwa*, or the promotion of Hindu values and the creation of a state modelled on Hindu beliefs and culture, emerged in the 1980s as a powerful force in Indian politics, as support for the BJP grew. The movement was stridently anti-Muslim, and triggered communal violence. In 1992, Hindu extremists demolished a mosque in Ayodhya, claiming that it was built on one of the holiest Hindu sites. This action started a wave of violence between Hindus and Muslims in which more than 3000 people were killed. In the 1998 general election, the Congress Party suffered its worst-ever defeat when the BJP emerged as the largest single party. The BJP ruled India as part of a coalition, until its defeat by Congress in the 2004 election.

Economic issues

The main economic challenges facing India were poverty, unemployment, landlessness and an unequal distribution of resources. The government aimed to address these problems by introducing a series of Five-Year Plans to promote economic growth. However, this was offset by high population growth rates. Efforts at land reform and rural development schemes had limited success in reducing inequality or poverty amongst the millions of landless villagers. The Five-Year Plans were more successful, however, and helped to promote industrial growth. Much of the industrialisation was financed from abroad, but Nehru was careful to limit foreign influence and avoid the dangers of **neo-colonialism**, through high tariff barriers and government control of key industries.

neo-colonialism Literally, a new form of colonialism. It refers to the economic control that industrialised countries and international companies have over developing countries. The term was first used by the Ghanaian leader Kwame Nkrumah to refer to Africa's continuing economic dependence on Europe.

The focus of economic policy from the late 1960s shifted from industry to agriculture in an attempt to make India self-sufficient in food production. This was the 'Green Revolution', which used high-yielding seed varieties, irrigation schemes and chemical fertilisers to increase agricultural output by impressive amounts. However, it intensified regional inequalities as well as social divisions. Certain regions were not suited to the new methods of agriculture, and wealthier farmers, with access to capital, larger farms and entrepreneurial skills, were the ones who benefited. Government controls over the economy were relaxed in the 1980s, as India sought to become part of the world capitalist system. Despite initial problems, the Indian economy has grown at an exponential rate since the 1990s, and India is fast becoming one of the key players in the world economy.

Villagers in India study by the light of lanterns at a night school in 1953

Fact

India is referred to as one of the BRIC countries, an acronym that covers the rapidly emerging economies of Brazil, Russia, India and China. Some economists believe that these nations have the potential to form a powerful economic bloc which could be wealthier than the current dominant economic powers by the middle of the 21st century.

Social issues

With India's low literacy rate of 16%, one of the biggest challenges was improving the state of education. Efforts to increase the number of children attending school had some success, but the aim of compulsory education for all was not achieved. However, many new universities, institutes of technology and higher research establishments were established, with an emphasis on science and technology, to support the economic goals of industrialisation and modernisation.

After independence, there were dramatic changes in the status of women. Despite strong opposition from Hindu traditionalists, new laws gave women equal rights with men in the inheritance and ownership of property, as well as greater rights in marriage. But although the legal position of women improved, it was very difficult to change traditional attitudes, especially in rural areas. There was an improvement in the number of girls attending school, although educational opportunities for girls in rural areas lagged far behind those for boys. Even decades later, the literacy rate for women in India was significantly lower than that for men.

Theory of knowledge

History and ethics

The policy of the Indian government towards the lower castes is a form of 'affirmative action'. What does this mean? How can a policy of affirmative action be justified? Does it conflict with the principle of equal opportunity?

Another social challenge was the caste system, especially the position of the Untouchables. The 1950 constitution specifically abolished this class and the practice of 'untouchability' was forbidden. Members of this caste were now free to use the same shops, schools and places of worship as any other citizen. Special government funding was set aside to give them access to land, housing, health care, education and legal aid.

However, the new laws and the special aid did not abolish social disadvantages and discrimination, and caste oppression was still common in rural areas, where acts of brutal violence sometimes occurred. In some cases these were caused by the resentment over the preferential treatment decreed by government policies.

In 1950, India had a population of 350 million, with an average life expectancy of 32 years. Millions of people died each year in epidemics of smallpox, plague, cholera and malaria. The government allocated funding to improve health services, train more doctors and nurses, and build hospitals and clinics. But this resulted in rising population growth rates, putting more pressure on land and resources. The government tried to control this by offering incentives for smaller families and promoting sterilisation programmes, to which there was considerable resistance. Between 1947 and 2010, the average life expectancy in India more than doubled to 66 years, and literacy rates improved dramatically, to 61%. However, in the same time, the population tripled to nearly 1.2 billion people.

Foreign policy

non-alignment A policy adopted by India and other developing countries unwilling to take sides during the Cold War; they declared themselves to be the 'Third World', not allied to either the First World (the West) or the Second World (the Soviet bloc). This decision was made at Bandung in Indonesia in 1955, at a meeting of newly independent Asian and African nations.

In international affairs, India opted for a policy of **non-alignment**, not allying itself with either the Western or Soviet blocs. Nehru became one of the leading proponents of the Non-Aligned Movement (NAM), which aimed to keep a balance between the two power blocs in the Cold War. India under Nehru also became a champion of anti-colonialism and anti-racism. India remained a member of the Commonwealth but, although Britain was a leading Western power in the Cold War, Nehru declared that India was not part of that conflict.

The consolidation of India was completed when small areas that had remained under colonial control were incorporated. France handed over Pondicherry and other small French enclaves in 1954, and when Portugal was reluctant to withdraw from Goa, the Indian army invaded and united it with the rest of India in 1961. The dispute with Pakistan over Kashmir remained unresolved.

India initially established a good working relationship with the People's Republic of China. The two countries shared similar problems of rural poverty and underdevelopment, and in 1957 they signed a treaty promoting trade and recognising each other's territorial rights.

Activity

In pairs, discuss the achievements and failures of independent India.

However, there was competition between them to be the leading Asian nation in the developing world, as well as disputes over territory along their border. Relations grew strained when India gave refuge to the Tibetan spiritual leader, the Dalai Lama, who fled after Chinese troops occupied Tibet. In 1962, there was a short war between them when Chinese troops occupied a disputed area in north-east India.

What challenges did independent Pakistan face after 1947?

Pakistan did not make the transition to independence as smoothly as India. The problems facing the new Muslim state included the impact of partition, military dominance in politics, the dispute over Kashmir and the impact of the Cold War.

The legacies of partition

Economic and social challenges

At the time of partition, over 90% of industries in the region were in India, as well as most of the railways and hydro-electric plants. The large cities of South Asia – Delhi, Bombay and Calcutta – were all in India. Lahore was the only city of economic and cultural significance in Pakistan. Pakistan's economy was mainly agricultural, there were few exports and most people were poor farmers.

Both countries faced the challenge of settling millions of refugees, but for Pakistan it was particularly difficult, because the refugees formed a larger percentage of the population than they did in India. In addition, many of those coming into Pakistan were unskilled rural labourers, while many who fled from Pakistan to India were professionals, skilled workers and traders. This contributed to a shortage of skills to staff the new administration.

Although the majority of the population shared a common religion, Islam, there were vast linguistic and cultural differences, not only between the people of East and West Pakistan, but also within West Pakistan, where the people of the northern frontier areas bordering on Afghanistan were accustomed to a greater degree of autonomy.

Disputes over assets

There were bitter disputes over assets and territory between India and Pakistan. As a result of its size and geographical position, India inherited most of the administrative infrastructure of British India, whereas Pakistan had to build up its government structures from scratch. There was suspicion and resentment over the division of assets, including financial reserves and government property. Pakistan believed that the Indian government intended to undermine it right from the start, by denying it a rightful share of these assets. In the end Pakistan reluctantly accepted what it regarded as an unfair division. Although Pakistan covered 23% of the land area of the subcontinent, it only received 17.5% of the financial assets. India was reluctant to hand even these over, and only did so after a fast by Gandhi put pressure on it.

The Indian Army had been the basis of British control over India, and there were disagreements too over its division. Although an agreement was reached that Pakistan would receive one-third of the troops and military equipment, most of the military stores were in Indian territory, and the transfer was plagued with difficulties. The outbreak of fighting with India over Kashmir in 1947 underlined the vulnerability of Pakistan's position, and so, according to historians Talbot and Singh, its government started to use scarce resources to build up its military forces 'at the cost of dependence on foreign aid and economic and social development'.

There was also a sense of injustice over the territorial division of India. In Pakistani eyes, some strategically important regions with Muslim majorities had been given to India. Pakistan's determination to unite Kashmir under Pakistani control must be understood in the light of these circumstances.

A divided state

Pakistan itself was divided into two parts, East and West Pakistan, separated by 1500 km (930 miles) of Indian territory. More than half of the Pakistani population lived in East Pakistan, an economically underdeveloped region with very high population densities and subject to natural disasters such as regular flooding.

The people of the two regions had little in common except their religion. The Bengali-speaking people of East Pakistan had their own culture and history, and a strong sense of national identity. They resented the political and economic dominance of the Urdu-speaking people of the western regions. Bengalis were underrepresented in the armed forces and in the administration. To them it seemed as though East Pakistan was little more than a colony, providing tax revenues and foreign exchange from the export of jute for the benefit of West Pakistan. A Bengali party, the Awami League, wanted greater autonomy, but West Pakistan maintained control by arresting its leaders and crushing protests. In 1971, West Pakistani troops crushed an uprising demanding the secession of East Pakistan. As a result, about 10 million refugees fled into India to escape the fighting. This prompted the Indian government to intervene. Indian troops crossed the border into East Pakistan, 93,000 Pakistani soldiers surrendered unconditionally, and the people of East Pakistan declared their independence as the state of Bangladesh.

Activity

Historians Talbot and Singh believe that the break-up of Pakistan, and the creation of Bangladesh as an independent country in 1971, proved that ethnicity was a more enduring bond than religion. What evidence could be used to support this argument? Work out a counter-argument to this view.

Political challenges

Pakistan did not have the same continuity of leadership experienced by India after independence. Jinnah, the founder of Pakistan and its first leader in 1947, died of a heart attack a year later. His successor, Liaqat Ali Khan, was assassinated in 1951. His death was partly motivated by a religious backlash to his secular policies, and a reaction by extremists to a perceived weakness in his negotiations with Nehru over Kashmir.

Another advantage that India had was the long experience of Congress in building up structures of leadership in the nationalist movement. Many of these leaders took positions in government after independence. The Muslim League, however, did not have this experience. The heartland of support for the League had been in the province of Uttar Pradesh, which was now part of India. Muslims from this region had moved westwards as refugees to Pakistan, and once there they had to compete with local people for access to land and employment, which put them at a disadvantage.

There were also problems surrounding the adoption of a constitution. The first drafts were rejected by Bengalis as giving too much power to the central government, and by prominent Muslim leaders who felt that the drafts did not sufficiently incorporate the principles of Islam. A constitution was finally approved in 1956, but it did not provide a stable foundation for democracy. Two years later the constitution was suspended when the head of the armed forces, General Ayub Khan, took over the government in the first of several spells of

Question

Why were some of the challenges facing Pakistan more complex than those facing India?

military rule. The circumstances of Pakistan's beginnings as an independent state – its weak economy, the dispute over Kashmir, and the belief that its borders were insecure in the face of a strong and hostile neighbour – put the military in a strong position. The army frequently justified its intervention in politics on the pretext of stamping out corruption. From the 1950s onwards there were several long periods of military rule, interspersed with interludes of weak civilian government. The position of the military was strengthened by outside circumstances, such as the Cold War and, more recently, the 'War on Terror' (see below).

Fact
Since 1987, a Muslim separatist group has been fighting a campaign in the Indian part of Kashmir to try to force the Indian government to withdraw from Kashmir altogether. Pakistan has provided support and funding to the Kashmiri militants, a source of ongoing tensions with India.

The problem of Kashmir

When the United Nations divided Kashmir in 1949, a UN peacekeeping mission remained in Kashmir to monitor the border between the two. The issue proved to be more politically divisive in Pakistan than in India. Many Pakistanis firmly believed that all of Kashmir, with its predominantly Muslim population, rightfully belonged in Pakistan. However, Pakistan did not have the military might to seize the parts of this region occupied by India by force, and this failure proved to be a source of embarrassment to a series of Pakistani governments, undermining their authority and credibility.

Since then, India and Pakistan have fought two more wars over Kashmir – in 1965 and 1999. As both states became nuclear powers in the 1990s, the ongoing conflict over Kashmir grew to be of grave concern to the international community.

Question
Why is the dispute over Kashmir so difficult to resolve?

Foreign policy

Unlike India, which followed a policy of non-alignment, Pakistan became involved in Cold War politics. The US realised the importance of Pakistan's strategic position in relation to the Soviet Union, and invited Pakistan to join the anti-communist alliances SEATO and CENTO, in 1954 and 1956 respectively, which were part of the policy of **containment**. In return, Pakistan received substantial military and financial aid, which it hoped would create an army strong enough to recover Kashmir, and also provide it with protection against perceived Indian aggression. This aid significantly strengthened the position of the military in Pakistan and contributed to the weakness of democracy.

containment This was part of the American Cold War strategy to prevent the spread of communism. The US government established a series of anti-Communist alliances around the world to stem the spread of communism. The South East Asia Treaty Organisation (SEATO) and the Central Treaty Organisation (CENTO) were two of these alliances.

When the Soviet Union invaded Afghanistan in 1979, Pakistan was once again in the frontline of the Cold War, and immediately received attention and additional aid from the US. The two countries provided support to Islamic freedom fighters, the Mujahedin, in their fight against the Soviet occupation. In this instance, American and Pakistani interests overlapped. However, this sharing of interests was not always the case, and the loss of Pakistan's independence in foreign affairs led to a general mistrust by the mass of the population of Western influence. The withdrawal of Soviet forces from Afghanistan in 1989 was hailed as a Cold War victory by the West, while the subsequent coming to power of the Taliban was welcomed by groups in Pakistan, which supported the establishment of a militant Islamic state in Afghanistan.

In the wake of the 9/11 attacks on the World Trade Center in New York, the US led an invasion of Afghanistan in 2001 in its 'War on Terror', which resulted in an ongoing war against Taliban forces there. This was to have a destabilising effect on Pakistan, militarily, politically and economically.

End of unit activities

1 Research the circumstances of Gandhi's assassination and write a newspaper report explaining the events leading up to it, and the impact of his death.

2 Read 'The Hidden Story of Partition and its Legacies', by historian Crispin Bates, on this website: http://www.bbc.co.uk/history/british/modern/partition1947_01.shtml

In what ways does this historian blame the British for the upheavals that accompanied independence in India? According to this article, what are some of the unresolved issues from the time of partition?

3 'The violence and bloodshed that accompanied independence and partition can be attributed largely to British policies and mismanagement.'

Divide the class into two groups. One group should prepare an argument to support the statement above, and the other an argument to oppose it.

4 Draw a spider diagram to illustrate the policies implemented by the Indian government after independence. Include categories on territorial consolidation, constitutional developments, and economic, social and foreign policies.

5 Draw up a table to show the problems facing Pakistan after independence.

6 Write an obituary for Mohammed Ali Jinnah, evaluating his role in the history of South Asia.

End of chapter activities

Paper 1 exam practice

Question

Compare and contrast the attitudes towards the continuation of British control in India expressed in Sources A and B (page 98).
[6 marks]

Skill

Cross-referencing

Examiner's tips

Cross-referencing questions require you to compare **and** contrast the information/content/nature of two sources relating to a particular issue. Before you write your answer, draw a rough chart or diagram to show the similarities **and** the differences between the two sources. That way, you should ensure you address **both** aspects/elements of the question.

Common mistakes

When asked to compare and contrast two sources, make sure you don't just comment on **one** of them. A few candidates make this mistake every year – and lose 4 of the 6 marks available.

Simplified markscheme

Band		Marks
1	**Both** sources **linked**, with **detailed references** to the two sources, identifying **both** similarities **and** differences.	6
2	**Both** sources **linked**, with **detailed references** to the two sources, identifying **either** similarities **or** differences.	4–5
3	Comments on both sources, **but** treating each one separately.	3
4	Discusses/comments on just **one** source.	0–2

SOURCE A

The committee is of the opinion that Britain is incapable of defending India. It is natural that whatever she does is for her own defence. There is the eternal conflict between Indian and British interests. Japan's quarrel is not with India. She is warring against the British Empire. India's participation in the war has not been with the consent of the representatives of the Indian people. It was purely a British act. If India were freed, her first step would probably be to negotiate with Japan. The Congress is of the opinion that if the British withdrew from India, India would be able to defend herself in the event of the Japanese, or any aggressor, attacking India.

Extract from Gandhi's 'Quit India' speech, 5 August 1942.

SOURCE B

It is, therefore, plain beyond doubt that Indian self-government is assured as soon as hostilities are over. A promise has been made and that promise will be carried out. Is it reasonable then for people of India, while hostilities are continuing, to demand some complete and fundamental constitutional change? Is it practical in the middle of a hard-fought war in which the United States, China and Britain are exerting all their strength to protect the Eastern world from domination by Japan? Gandhi has asked that the British Government should walk out of India and leave the Indian people to settle differences among themselves, even if it means chaos and confusion. There would be no authority to collect revenue and no money to pay for any government service. The police would cease to have any authority, courts of justice would no longer function, and there would be no laws and no order.

Extract from the response to Gandhi's speech by Stafford Cripps, the British government's special envoy to India, 6 August 1942.

Student answer

Source A states that Britain is motivated by self-interest and cannot defend India. It had involved India in the war against Japan without consultation with the Indian people. Britain should withdraw from India immediately, and leave Indian leaders either to negotiate with the Japanese or to defend India.

Source B responds by stating that Britain has committed itself to self-rule for India but only after the war is over. There cannot be fundamental constitutional changes while the war is still on. If Britain withdraws immediately, the administration would collapse and there would be chaos.

Examiner's comments

The answer simply paraphrases both sources without making any attempt to compare or contrast them. There is no attempt to link the sources, or to comment on them. The candidate has thus done enough to get into Band 3, and so be awarded only 3 marks.

Activity

Look again at the two sources, the simplified markscheme, and the student answer above. Now try to rewrite the answer, linking the two sources by pointing out similarities and differences between them, and referring to the sources without simply paraphrasing them.

Summary activity

Copy this diagram and, using the information in this chapter, make point form notes under each heading.

India: the road to independence

Independence

- British policies
- Impact of the Second World War
- Role of religion
- Role of Gandhi
- Role of Jinnah
- Partition

Rise of nationalism

- Opposition to British rule
- Impact of the First World War
- Amritsar Massacre
- Indian National Congress
- Muslim League
- Policy of non-co-operation

Independent India and Pakistan

- Challenges and problems
- Policies and achievements

Practice Paper 2 questions

1 What were the main problems that either India or Pakistan faced in the two decades after independence in 1947?

2 In what ways, and to what extent, did either left-wing or right-wing ideology play an important role in the formation of India and Pakistan?

3 For what reasons were India and Pakistan granted independence in 1947?

4 Analyse the support for, and the methods used by, Gandhi.

5 To what extent were Gandhi and his policy of *satyagraha* effective methods of achieving independence in India?

6 To what extent did British policy and actions in India contribute to the rise of the nationalist movement?

Further reading

Try reading the relevant chapters/sections of the following books:

Bates, Crispin. 2007. *Subalterns and Raj. India since 1600*. London, UK. Routledge.

Bose, Sugata and Jalal, Ayesha. 1998. *Modern South Asia*. London, UK. Routledge.

Butalia, Urvashi. 2000. *The Other Side of Silence: Voices from the Partition of India*. Durham, USA. Duke University Press.

Chandra, Bipan, Mukherjee, Mridula and Mukherjee, Aditya. 2000. *India after Independence: 1947–2000*. London, UK. Penguin.

Guha, Ramachandra. 2007. *India after Gandhi: The History of the World's Largest Democracy*. London, UK. Macmillan.

Metcalf, Barbara and Metcalf, Thomas. 2006. *A Concise History of Modern India*. Cambridge, UK. Cambridge University Press.

Pandey, Gyanendra. 2001. *Remembering Partition*. Cambridge, UK. Cambridge University Press.

Talbot, Ian. 2000. *India and Pakistan*. Arnold.

Talbot, Ian and Singh, Gurharpal. 2009. *The Partition of India*. Cambridge, UK. Cambridge University Press.

4 Vietnam

Introduction

Vietnam, Cambodia and Laos together make up the region known as Indochina. Vietnam lies to the south of China and to the east of India, and it has been influenced by both these countries. The geography of Vietnam is diverse, and at times throughout its history the varying political and cultural beliefs of inhabitants in the different regions of Vietnam have developed into ideological divisions that have split the country.

The geography and climate of Indochina as a whole have also had a significant impact on the economy of the region. Indochina has a tropical monsoon climate, with high levels of heat and humidity, and a rainy season that stretches from May to October. This climate is ideal for the production of rice if managed properly.

During the 20th century, important national independence movements developed in both Cambodia and Laos. However, the focus in this chapter will be on Vietnam – the most important of France's colonies in Indochina.

Map showing the regions of French Indochina, with the dates they were colonised by the French; Tonkin, Annam and Cochinchina eventually became Vietnam which, after 1954, was split into North and South Vietnam; the inset map shows the countries as they are today

1 The origins and rise of nationalist and independence movements in Vietnam

Timeline

1893 France sets up the French Indochinese Union, consisting of Vietnam, Cambodia and Laos

1911 nationalist revolution in China

1916 unsuccessful rebellion in Vietnam

1925 Bao Dai becomes emperor of Vietnam

1926 Cao Dai formed

1927 Nationalist Party of Vietnam (VNQDD) formed

1930 Yen Bai rising; Communist Party of Vietnam formed

1939 Second World War begins; Hoa Hao formed

1940 France occupied by Germany

1941 Japan joins the Second World War and occupies Indochina; Viet Minh formed

1945 Second World War ends; Japan defeated in Indochina; Viet Minh occupy Hanoi after the August Revolution; Ho Chi Minh declares the Democratic Republic of Vietnam; British troops arrive in Indochina and use French and Japanese troops to push Viet Minh out of southern Vietnam

Key questions

- What were the main features of French involvement in Indochina before 1941?
- What factors influenced the rise of the independence movement?

Overview

- In 1893, France – which had already established control of Vietnam, Cambodia and Laos – joined these countries together to form the French Indochinese Union.
- The nationalist revolution in China in 1911 inspired a rebellion in Vietnam in 1916; this was quickly suppressed by the French.
- In the 1920s, the first Indochinese nationalist movements were formed, despite the cultural and social divisions within the region. These included the Cao Dao in 1926 and the Nationalist Party of Vietnam in 1927. The latter group was involved in the unsuccessful Yen Bai rising in 1930.
- In the 1920s and 1930s, the French found it easy to control these independence movements; the turning point was the Second World War.
- In 1930, Ho Chi Minh and other Vietnamese exiles in China formed the Communist Party of Vietnam; the party lasted until 1945, when it was dissolved and its activities absorbed into those of the Viet Minh
- The Viet Minh formed in 1941 as a common front seeking independence from French colonial rule. It soon became the key group in the struggle for independence.
- During the Second World War, French Indochina was occupied by Imperial Japan by agreement with the Vichy French authorities. The Viet Minh became the centre of resistance against the Japanese, and received considerable aid from the Allied powers in their struggle.
- In 1945, with Japan defeated, an independent Vietnam was briefly established. In September, however, Britain used French and Japanese soldiers to push the Viet Minh out of the southern parts of Vietnam. At this point, however, the French attempted to re-establish colonial rule in Indochina. This set the scene for the First Indochina War.

What were the main features of French involvement in Indochina before 1941?

The French had first become interested in Vietnam – and the rest of Indochina – as a result of their ambitions in mainland China. In the past, Chinese emperors had controlled northern Vietnam as well as Korea. In AD 938, after nearly 1000 years of struggle, the Vietnamese had won their independence from China, but they remained subject to several invasions by the Chinese between that time and the arrival of the French in the 1850s. However, in the latter part of the 19th century China was in chaos, and the **Great Powers** sought to take advantage of this by wresting territory and trade concessions from the Chinese.

Great Powers The major states of the world. In the 19th century, these were Britain, France, the USA and Russia. After the Second World War, the world's major states were the USA and the USSR; Britain and France only fitted this description to a limited extent. Later, Communist China became increasingly powerful and important. After 1945, the Great Powers became involved in Indochina to further or protect their own economic, military or ideological interests.

In 1884–85, France defeated China in the Sino–French War, gaining control of northern Vietnam. Between 1887 and 1893, France established a federal protectorate over the three main areas of Indochina. Local rulers were usually left in place, but they were mere figureheads and real power lay with the French government. Vietnam was close to the markets of China, while Indochina in general was important for rubber production. Indochina, and especially Vietnam, was therefore one of France's most prized colonial possessions. France controlled its Indochinese territories by the policy of 'divide and rule', setting one part of the region against another, emphasising the cultural differences between them. This policy hindered the development of a coherent nationalist movement.

Although this policy mostly worked well for France, there were several limited uprisings against French rule before 1939. There was a nationalist rebellion in Vietnam from 1885 to 1895, led by Phan Dinh Phung. During and after the First World War, nationalist sentiments grew and there were further uprisings, but the French refused to make concessions. In 1930, Vietnamese soldiers in the French colonial army in Yen Bai mutinied, under the leadership of the Viet Nam Quoc Dan Dang (VNQDD), the Vietnamese Nationalist Party. This uprising was easily crushed by the French, and a wave of brutal suppression of opposition followed.

Nationalism began to increase during the Second World War, after Indochina was conquered by the Japanese in 1940. Regional rivalries, long simmering below the surface, boiled up. In the post-war period France found it impossible to control these rivalries, and this structural weakness became one of the main factors in the nationalists' victory over and ejection of the French from the region in 1954.

What factors influenced the rise of the independence movement?

Divisions within Indochina

Indochina is not a homogeneous region, and the diversity of peoples and cultures has had a fundamental impact on its history. During the period under study, these divisions led to the emergence of the three states of Indochina: Vietnam, Laos and Cambodia. In Vietnam, in the Red River Delta in the north, the people of the Tonkin region were ethnically and culturally very homogeneous. The southern part of the country, however, had a more diverse cultural and religious make-up.

The origins of Vietnamese nationalism

The opposition felt by many Vietnamese to French rule stemmed from several sources. The Vietnamese had a history of resistance to the imposition of foreign rule, and the French colonial system exploited the indigenous population. The Vietnamese people were forced to pay for the development of their country in the interests of the colonial power. In particular, taxes had to be paid in hard currency, which placed serious strain on the subsistence-farming economy that dominated the region. Peasants were forced to work on French-owned plantations and in French mines in order to meet these tax demands. The French also imposed a monopoly on the sale of salt, opium and alcohol, for which they then demanded exorbitant prices. The effect of these policies was to impoverish the region and place a significant economic burden on the indigenous population. Eventually this led to political opposition.

Question

To what extent did the history and physical geography of Vietnam hinder the emergence of a nationalist movement in the 1920s and 1930s?

SOURCE A

Part of a letter written in the early 1900s by Phan Chu Trinh, a minister at the imperial court, to the French governor.

In your eyes we are savages, dumb brutes, incapable of distinguishing between good and evil. Some of us, employed by you, still preserve a certain dignity. … and it is sadness and shame that fills our hearts when we contemplate our humiliation.

Quoted in Karnow, S. 1984. Vietnam: A History. *Harmondsworth, UK. Penguin. p. 118.*

Ho Chi Minh (1890–1969)

Ho was a Vietnamese patriot and independence leader. He led the Viet Minh from 1941 onwards, defeating both the Japanese and then the returning French colonialists in the post-war period, and establishing the Democratic Republic of Vietnam (North Vietnam). Ho had a communist background and had visited the USSR. During the Second World War, his military campaigns were assisted by intelligence from the US, but Ho became increasingly disillusioned with America after 1945. He had stepped into the background politically by 1960, but remained very much a figurehead for his country.

In the 1920s and 1930s, the French had found it easy to break up and suppress opposition groups, but anti-French feeling grew increasingly strong in the region. Eventually, in 1930, a new force appeared in Vietnamese politics that was more successful in fighting the French colonial power. This was the Communist Party of Vietnam, formed by the merger of three different communist parties. It was renamed the Dang Cong San Dong Duong (Indochinese Communist Party) later that year. The party was established by **Ho Chi Minh** and others while they were in exile in China. By 1945, the party had been dissolved and its activities absorbed into those of the nationalist–communist Viet Minh (formally the Viet Nam Doc Lap Dong Minh Hoi – the Revolutionary League for the Independence of Vietnam), which had been formed four years earlier.

The Viet Minh's immediate task was to fight the occupying Japanese forces. France, which had been defeated by Germany in 1940, offered no resistance. The Viet Minh was not the only nationalist group active around this time, however. Several others existed, often with a religious base and focused mainly in the south, but almost all of them collaborated with the Japanese and, later, with the Viet Minh. The Cao Dai, officially established in 1926, became the third largest religion in Vietnam, after Buddhism and Catholicism. It split in 1946, and most of its members supported the French, though a small section continued to work with the Viet Minh. The Hoa Hao, founded in 1939, developed its own private army, but split in 1947, with most supporting the French. The Binh Xuyen was essentially a bandit army which, like the other two groups, decided to collaborate with the French in 1948.

There are several reasons why Ho and his mainly communist movement were more successful than other nationalist groups. Parts of Ho's nationalist movement were socialist in nature, but at first it limited its objectives to creating an independent Vietnam. The organisation established itself in northern Vietnam, and its leaders were educated Vietnamese – teachers, indigenous colonial administrators and low-ranking officers in the colonial army. However, it soon became clear that the real strength of the movement was its communist roots. This created a strongly disciplined organisation characterised by a unity that previous nationalist movements had lacked. Furthermore, the Vietnamese communists were supported by both the USSR and the Chinese communists. The former supplied aid and the latter gave Ho and his people a safe haven from which to operate against the Japanese.

SOURCE B

A draft programme for Indochinese communists, written by Ho Chi Minh in 1930.

The Communist Party of Indochina is the party of the working class. It will follow these slogans:

- To overthrow French imperialism and the reactionary Vietnamese capitalist class.
- To make Indochina completely independent.
- To establish a worker-peasant and soldier government.
- To confiscate the banks and other enterprises belonging to the imperialists and put them under the control of the worker-peasant and soldier government.
- To confiscate all of the plantations and property belonging to the imperialists and the Vietnamese reactionary capitalist class and distribute them to poor peasants.
- To bring back all freedom to the masses.
- To carry out universal education.
- To implement equality between man and woman.

Quoted on http://www.fordham.edu/halsall/mod/1930hochiminh.html.

Ho was aided by French suppression of anti-colonial elements, which destroyed moderate nationalist groups whilst strengthening the hand of the more radical communists. In 1930, an abortive anti-colonial rising in Vietnam was crushed by the French, removing many of Ho's nationalist rivals. As the 1930s progressed, the communists attempted to infiltrate Vietnamese society. They followed the typical pattern of establishing cells within villages and began to organise the peasants into potential resistance groups. This had a limited impact, and once the French became aware of these activities they easily destroyed the local cells. Ho was forced to flee the country. When he returned to Vietnam in 1940 and attempted to organise another uprising, he and his organisation were once more defeated with relative ease.

Ho's chance came with the Second World War. It was at this point that the communists became the only viable indigenous resistance group, and when Ho formed the Viet Minh in 1941 he immediately received the backing of the Allied powers. Thus, factors outside Vietnam helped create the formidable independence movement that France was unable to defeat in the post-war period.

Theory of knowledge

History and language

The colonial powers often used language as a means of control, by insisting on the use of European languages in their colonies. Ho Chi Minh's father lost his job as a teacher because, as a means of protest, he refused to learn French. Ho Chi Minh, however, mastered French and lived in Paris for several years, where he was a founder member of the French Communist Party. How does this information about Ho's family history illustrate the saying that 'language is power'?

Fact

Cells were the smallest organisational units in communist parties, and were the basis for all communist work and actions – such as propaganda, recruitment of new members and organising strikes. In situations such as those existing in French-controlled Vietnam, they had to be secret, and members of one cell would often not know members of other cells. Thus, if anyone was captured – and probably tortured – they would be unable to reveal many names. Eventually, these cells built up into a national network.

Jiang Jieshi (1887–1975) Also known as Chiang Kai-Shek, Jieshi was the leader of the Guomindang, the Chinese nationalist party, which engaged in a lengthy civil war with the Chinese communists. The nationalists were defeated by the communists in 1949, and Jieshi was forced to retreat to the island of Formosa (Taiwan).

guerrilla warfare A method of waging warfare that places emphasis on small raids, assassination and sabotage. Guerrilla soldiers do not wear uniforms and blend into the local population.

Question

Why did many Vietnamese tend to support the Viet Minh rather than other nationalist leaders before 1945?

The impact of the Second World War

The internal politics of Vietnam, and Indochina generally, were radically changed by the outbreak of the Second World War in 1939. In the spring of 1940, France was attacked by Germany and rapidly defeated. This created a new political situation. In Europe, Germany occupied the north of France, while the south was governed by the pro-German Vichy regime. Vichy also controlled France's overseas empire. To Indochinese nationalists, France's prestige had been fatally compromised. Japan's rapid victories over European colonial powers in the region also destroyed the myth of Western and white superiority. Though the British, French and Dutch tried to re-establish their former colonies after 1945, by 1961 the entire region had been decolonised.

Vietnamese nationalists were drawn together into the Viet Minh by Ho Chi Minh. The group began to step up resistance activities against the Vichy administration in Vietnam. In September 1940, the situation changed again when Japanese troops entered Indochina – initially with Vichy co-operation – and established control over the region. Just over a year later, on 7 December 1941, Japan attacked the US Pacific naval base at Pearl Harbor, triggering the USA's entry into the Second World War.

The Viet Minh's position was now transformed. It was the only organisation able to effectively resist the Japanese in Indochina, and, despite its communist leanings, it soon began to receive aid and encouragement from the Allied powers. Viet Minh fighters were trained in China by one of **Jiang Jieshi**'s warlords, and the USA supplied Ho's guerrillas with equipment. The Viet Minh's anti-Japanese **guerrilla warfare** during the war was mainly limited to the Tonkin region, in the far north of the country, but these operations legitimised the Viet Minh's claim to be the leaders of the Vietnamese people and a potential post-colonial government. The Viet Minh also provided a model for other countries in Indochina – especially as many other nationalist leaders tended to collaborate with the French and Japanese, seriously damaging their credibility in the eyes of the general population.

The Viet Minh's real chance came in the last year of the Second World War, when Japan's position became increasingly precarious. Allied strategy to defeat Japan involved two thrusts across the Pacific towards the Japanese home islands. As Japan attempted to resist the main Allied attacks, areas such as Indochina became secondary to Japan's main military effort. In Vietnam, the Japanese sought to reduce their military presence by replacing the Vichy French regime with a nominally independent Vietnam under a French-controlled 'puppet' leader, the Vietnamese emperor Bao Dai. Thus, as the war came to an end, the Japanese had created a difficult problem for the post-war French re-imposition of colonial rule.

In August 1945, the USA dropped atomic bombs on the Japanese cities of Hiroshima and Nagasaki. Japan collapsed quickly in the wake of the disaster, leaving most of its former empire without central direction. The Allies were not numerous enough to quickly occupy this empire by force, and for a period of time Ho Chi Minh and his Viet Minh guerrillas had a free hand. By August 1945, they controlled most of Vietnam and, in the middle of that month, they marched unopposed into Hanoi, the capital of French Indochina. This became known as the August Revolution. On 2 September Ho declared the whole country as the new Democratic Republic of Vietnam. However, the French did not recognise the Viet Minh as legitimate rulers. US president Franklin D. Roosevelt had supported the idea of an independent Vietnam, and Ho had hoped for continued US support after the war. However, the USA's attitude changed in the wake of Harry Truman's succession to the presidency and the onset of the Cold War.

SOURCE C

An extract from Ho Chi Minh's speech declaring Vietnamese independence, 2 September 1945.

For more than eighty years, the French imperialists ... have violated our fatherland and oppressed our fellow citizens. ... They have enforced inhuman laws: to ruin our unity and national consciousness. They have carried out three different policies in the north, the centre and the south of Viet-nam. ... In the autumn of the year 1940 ... the French imperialists ... surrendered, handing over our country to the Japanese. ... From that day on, the Vietnamese people suffered hardships. ... The result of this double oppression was terrific ... two million people were starved to death in the early months of 1945. ... We declare to the world that Vietnam ... has in fact become a free and independent country.

Quoted in Buss, C. A. 1958. Southeast Asia and the World Today. *Princeton, USA. D. Van Nostrand. pp. 154–55.*

The emperor Bao Dai had predicted this turn of events and quickly abdicated. This, together with the Viet Minh's military record in the war years, left Ho without significant Vietnamese opponents to his seizure of power. He began to implement communist reforms, redistributing land and promising elections. He also embedded his control in the countryside, establishing military cells in peasant villages. The Viet Minh suppressed other nationalist opposition groups, such as the Constitution Party and the Party of Independence.

While Ho Chi Minh was busy establishing the Democratic Republic of Vietnam, the major powers had very different ideas about what should happen to Vietnam in the aftermath of the Second World War. The Western Allies had agreed that northern Vietnam should be given to the Chinese, while Britain had been allocated responsibility for implementing post-war arrangements in southern Vietnam. However, Vietnam was not high on Britain's list of strategic objectives. On 12 September 1945, a small British military force arrived in southern Vietnam, but was not nearly strong enough to secure control over the whole of the country. Despite this, and with the help of French and Japanese soldiers, the British managed to push the Viet Minh out of the south and secure Saigon. They then sat back and awaited the arrival of French reinforcements.

Although northern Vietnam had been allocated to the Chinese, Jiang Jieshi was facing civil war against the communists in his own country, and was unable to maintain significant forces in Vietnam for long. Once again Ho and his guerrillas were given time to consolidate their control over the north. The French began to arrive in force in early 1946, and it was clear they meant to re-establish control of Vietnam. However, it was equally clear that very few Vietnamese wanted the French back.

Fact

The French Union was set up by the government of France in October 1946. It was intended as a replacement for the old colonial system and included France itself, along with its overseas territories. Former colonies such as Vietnam became protectorates and were ostensibly granted a degree of self-government. The Indochinese states left the French Union in 1954.

The French continued the British policy of clearing the Viet Minh from the south, and re-established a substantial military presence in both Laos and Cambodia. In March 1946, Ho reached an agreement with the French. He was to be allowed an army, and the territorial integrity and independence of the Democratic Republic of Vietnam was to be maintained, although it would remain a French protectorate as part of the French Union. At first it seemed that Ho had achieved an independence of sorts, but later France refused to honour these promises to grant local autonomy. Instead, the French created the Indochinese Federation, over which they retained substantial control. The Viet Minh, however, demanded full independence, and Ho Chi Minh went to France to negotiate a more permanent settlement.

The French government, under premier Charles de Gaulle, was determined to recover as much of its pre-war colonial empire as possible, partly for economic reasons but also to restore some of France's international prestige – which had taken a severe battering by the country's defeat and occupation by Germany. Furthermore, French settlers in Cochinchina in southern Vietnam were pushing for the re-establishment of French colonial power in the region. As a result, French troops were ordered north to reoccupy Tonkin in the first steps towards re-establishing colonial rule. In November 1946, the French took Hanoi and bombarded the port city of Haiphong. In December they overthrew Ho's government, the Viet Minh withdrew to their village strongholds and a full-scale war broke out.

In conclusion, the Second World War gave the Viet Minh a huge boost. It allowed the group to gain legitimacy and for a period of time it had established an independent state in the Tonkin region. The power of the French had been eroded by the war – and not only in Indochina. The French domestic economy and the prestige of their armed forces had been severely damaged. Ho and his guerrillas had taken full advantage of this opportunity, and they would prove more than a match for the French army in Vietnam.

Activity

'Historical development is evolutionary rather than revolutionary.'

Carry out some further research on the history of Vietnamese nationalism from 1900 to 1946. Then explain and discuss your answer with other members of your class.

End of unit activities

1 http://www.rationalrevolution.net/war/collection_of_letters_by_ho_chi_.htm

Read the extract on this website entitled 'In France, December 26, 1920'. Using the information, draw a spider diagram to illustrate the impact of French colonisation on the people of Indochina.

2 Working in pairs, work out a dialogue between two American State Department officials, discussing the wisdom of supplying weapons to the Viet Minh during the Second World War.

3 Find out what you can about the Japanese occupation of Southeast Asia during the Second World War.

4 'The attitude and actions of the French after the Second World War were the main cause of the outbreak of war in Vietnam in 1946.'

Divide into two groups. One group should prepare an argument in support of this statement, and the other group an argument to oppose it.

5 Read up on the early life of Ho Chi Minh, noting information about his education, his travels and any other factors that you think contributed to the development of his ideas. You can start by looking at this website: http://www.historylearningsite.co.uk/ho_chi_minh.htm.

6 'To what extent was the Second World War a turning point in the fortunes of the Vietnamese nationalists?'

This type of question demands that you place a historical development in context. It also challenges the nature of the historical process. Is historical change caused by long-term developments or by rapid spurts of development usually caused by a single cataclysmic event – in this case a war?

Divide into groups and brainstorm two responses to the question, one affirmative and one negative, creating a spider diagram for each. Then create a balanced response with a third spider diagram by rating each of the ideas in the original exercise on a scale of 1 to 5, from unconvincing (1) to very convincing (5). From this, create an essay plan and then write the essay.

2 Methods of achieving independence in Vietnam

Timeline

1946 French troops reoccupy Indochina; First Indochina War breaks out

1954 Battle of Dien Bien Phu; defeat of France; Geneva Conference

1955 US recognises the Republic of South Vietnam

1957 formation of the Viet Cong (VC)

1959 start of Second Indochina War; VC begins guerrilla war in South Vietnam

1960 National Liberation Front in South Vietnam formed; Cambodian Communist Party formed

1963 demonstrations begin in Vietnam against Diem regime; Diem ousted by a military coup; John F. Kennedy assassinated; Lyndon Johnson becomes president of the USA

1964 Gulf of Tonkin incident; USA begins bombing North Vietnam; Gulf of Tonkin Resolution

1965 US ground troops fight first large battle of the Second Indochina War; battle of Ia Drang

1967 Operations Cedar Falls and Junction City clear the Iron Triangle

1968 Battle of Khe Sanh; Tet Offensive; massive domestic opposition to the war in the USA; Richard Nixon elected president

1972 ARVN, backed by massive US air power, stops major NVA (North Vietnamese Army) invasion of the South

1975 NVA forces enter Saigon, ending the Second Indochina War with communist victory

Key questions

- What were the main events of the First Indochina War, 1946–54?
- How did the Cold War affect the Vietnamese struggle for independence?
- What political steps were taken to resolve the situation?
- Why did the Second Indochina War, or Vietnam War, begin?
- What were the main stages of the Second Indochina War, 1959–75?
- Why did North Vietnam win the Second Indochina War?
- What part did Ho Chi Minh play in the struggle for independence?

Overview

- During the period 1946–75, two wars were fought in Indochina – the First and Second Indochina wars.
- The first war took place between the Viet Minh and the French. By the end of 1954, after the battle of Dien Bien Phu, the French had been defeated and their colony in Indochina had been destroyed.
- Developments in Vietnam started to cause concern in the West, where the 'domino theory' of states falling one after the other to communism began to take hold.
- At the end of the First Indochina War, the Geneva Conference outlined the structure of Vietnam. A two-state solution was agreed, with a communist North and a pro-Western South Vietnam.
- The agreements at Geneva disappointed both sides, and soon war broke out again, with the North attempting to reunite the country.
- In the first phase of fighting, Ho Chi Minh's leadership was critical to northern victories.
- In the early 1960s, pressure from the North increased and the flimsy political structure of the South appeared to be on the brink of collapse.
- This caused the USA to intervene in the conflict to prop up the southern regime and to prevent the communist domination not only of Vietnam but of the whole of Southeast Asia.
- In 1965, the first major battle involving American troops took place. As the decade went on, US commitment to the conflict increased.
- In 1968, the Tet Offensive ended in military defeat for the communists, but US television coverage of the event caused a major backlash at home and forced the US to begin the process of disengagement.
- In the early 1970s, this disengagement was facilitated by the 'Vietnamisation' of the conflict. However, this failed, and, in a major offensive in 1975, the North overran the South and created a united Communist Republic of Vietnam.
- The USA, a superpower, had been defeated by a country in the developing world.

What were the main events of the First Indochina War, 1946–54?

In 1946, the struggle for Vietnamese independence entered the first of two phases. The First Indochina War (1946–54) was the conflict that eventually eliminated French colonial control. This was followed by the Second Indochina War (1959–75), which aimed to eliminate Western – and especially US – influence in the area and establish an independent and unified Vietnam. These two conflicts are known as the Indochina Wars because nationalist movements appeared in all three Indochinese states. However, most of the early fighting took place in Vietnam. Although the Vietnamese succeeded in driving out the Japanese and then the French, it took almost another 30 years of painful and costly armed struggle to banish US influence and involvement.

In November 1946, the French attacked the port of Haiphong, killing many civilians and sparking the First Indochina War. By December 1946, the situation across the region had deteriorated. The Viet Minh were massing for a full-scale uprising and the French were pouring troops into the region. For the next eight years, the French increasingly struggled to maintain their strongholds in urban areas, while the Viet Minh quickly established widespread popular support in the rural agricultural areas. By the time the conflict ended, the French had suffered 92,000 killed, 114,000 wounded and more than 20,000 missing.

Initially the French were confident that the size of their army and their superior weapons technology would enable them to defeat the Viet Minh easily. Strategically, too, the French had the upper hand because they controlled the major towns and the communications infrastructure of Vietnam. This was even true in the northern Tonkin region, a Viet Minh stronghold. The French controlled all the economically valuable parts of the country, whilst the Viet Minh were forced to shelter in the highland regions, which were little more than wilderness.

The military leader of the Viet Minh was **Vo Nguyen Giap**, who proved to be a gifted general. When the Viet Minh made their bid to take over Vietnam in 1945, Giap was made minister of war. For the first four years, he concentrated on building up the Viet Minh army and gathering peasant support. Initially, he followed a guerrilla strategy in the First Indochina War, but in the later phase of the conflict he switched to more **conventional warfare**. By 1954, Giap commanded 117,000 troops, against 100,000 French plus 300,000 Vietnamese in France's colonial army.

Vo Nguyen Giap (b. 1911) Giap was highly educated and a graduate of Hanoi University. He had originally been a teacher, but rose to be the Viet Minh's military leader after joining the Indochinese Communist Party in 1931. He was a student of military history, with a special interest in Napoleon and Sun Tzu. He had practical military experience fighting the Japanese in the Second World War. He was a gifted military commander and leader of the communist armies throughout the two Indochina wars. His most notable victory was that at Dien Bien Phu.

conventional warfare Warfare between well-defined, uniformed forces fighting set-piece battles. On several occasions, wars in Indochina began as guerrilla wars before entering a conventional phase.

A Viet Cong supply convoy, using reinforced bicycles

From guerrilla tactics to conventional warfare

At first, France's optimism seemed well-founded. In late 1946 and early 1947, the Viet Minh suffered a series of serious military defeats. The French, however, did not have the military might to hold the entire country, and the highlands became safe havens for the Viet Minh. The French tried to change the strategic situation in October and November 1947 by launching a series of major raids into the area to the north of Hanoi, with the objective of capturing Viet Minh leaders. These raids failed due to the dense terrain, which favoured Giap's guerrilla army. The French simply policed the region as best they could with garrisons and outposts. Thus, after some initial French success, the situation soon reached a stalemate.

In the following months, the Viet Minh began building up their strength. In 1949, Mao Zedong and his communists emerged as victors in the Chinese Civil War, and declared the People's Republic of China – creating a sympathetic communist state on Vietnam's northern border. This gave Giap's soldiers bases from which to operate, as well as access to Chinese-supplied weapons of increasing sophistication, including heavy artillery. In 1950, Giap switched his strategy to a more conventional form of warfare.

Fact

The Red River Basin was strategically important to the French. Its high agricultural output would provide a vital food supply to the Viet Minh, and the French also feared the region's 10 million inhabitants falling under the control of the Viet Minh should it be captured. Some historians have suggested that the need to maintain French troops in the Red River Basin rather than sending them as reinforcements to Dien Bien Phu may have contributed to the French defeat there.

This was successful at first, with victories along the China–Vietnam border at Lang Son and Cao Bang. Having secured his supply lines, Giap then sought to liberate the entire Red River Basin (see map on page 117). However, the Viet Minh suffered a series of serious defeats in conventional battle against the French line of defence around Hanoi. A reversion to guerrilla tactics allowed the Viet Minh to rebuild their strength and slowly extend their influence over the next three years. The events of 1950 showed that, although the Viet Minh could be defeated on the battlefield – especially if they engaged in conventional stand-up fights – they always had the option to go to ground and recover. The French, and later the Americans, would learn that military strategy had to be accompanied by political initiatives if they were to capitalise on their victories.

From the start of the First Indochina War, the French had been at a political disadvantage in Vietnam. The Second World War, and the power vacuum created by the withdrawal of Japanese forces in 1945, had allowed the Viet Minh to become firmly established in the northern Tonkin region. Furthermore, the Viet Minh had acquired substantial military strength as part of a more general Allied war effort against the Japanese. France's political strategy was ineffective and the regime under the emperor, Bao Dai (see pages 106–107), was so obviously under French influence that it did not draw many non-communist Vietnamese nationalists away from the Viet Minh. As the cost of the conflict escalated – in both men and resources, the French attempted to negotiate with the Viet Minh. This came to nothing, as Ho Chi Minh sought to wear down his enemy's resolve through guerrilla warfare.

Dien Bien Phu, 1954

In 1952, Giap pushed into Laos. Late the following year, French colonial troops were parachuted into the hill country around Dien Bien Phu, on the Vietnam–Laos border, to establish a fortified position in an attempt to disrupt Viet Minh supply routes from Laos. The French reasoned that if the base posed a serious threat, it might draw the Viet Minh into a set-piece battle where superior French firepower – especially from air attacks – could inflict a serious defeat and return the strategic and political initiative to France.

Aware of the French presence in the area, Giap surrounded the base and, in January 1954, launched his first attack at Dien Bien Phu. On 7 May, he captured the base. The fall of Dien Bien Phu was attributed to several factors (see Source A). However, one of the main reasons for the Viet Minh's victory was that Giap went to immense efforts to drag Chinese-made field and anti-aircraft artillery to the area. In particular, he organised 80,000 peasants to deliver food, weapons and ammunition through the jungle on bicycles.

SOURCE A

Dien Bien Phu highlighted the shortcomings of French strategy. Located near the Laotian border in a rugged valley of remote north western Vietnam, Dien Bien Phu was not a good place to fight. The base depended almost entirely on air support for supply. The French occupied the place to force a battle, but they had little to gain from such an engagement. Victory at Dien Bien Phu would not have ended the war; the Viet Minh would have retired to their mountain strongholds. On the other hand, the French had much to lose, in manpower, equipment, and prestige.

Demma, V. H. 1989. American Military History. *Washington, DC, USA. Center of Military History, US Army. p. 340.*

French troops being led to a prison camp after their capture during the Battle of Dien Bien Phu

Question

Why did the Viet Minh win the First Indochina War?

Fact

In some ways, Vietnam became entangled in the Cold War by accident. Many Vietnamese nationalists were communists, and a communist state – China – abutted the region. However, without the actions of the French and, later, the Americans, it is highly unlikely that Indochina would have become one of the major battlegrounds of the Cold War.

Korean War A war fought in 1950–53 between communist North Korea backed by the People's Republic of China, and the pro-Western South Korea backed by the USA. The North came close to victory before the conflict ended in a stalemate.

Lyndon B. Johnson (1908–73)
As a Democrat member of the House of Representatives (1937–48) and then the Senate (1948–60), Johnson became known as a liberal. However, this reputation, and his 'Great Society' programme, were overshadowed by his escalation of the USA's involvement in the Second Indochina War, which he began after assuming the presidency in 1963. Under him, the war became increasingly costly and unpopular and, in March 1968, he announced that he would not stand for re-election.

France's colonial army in Indochina was shattered by the defeat at Dien Bien Phu, and its reputation lay in tatters. Once again, it looked as if Ho Chi Minh's dream of an independent Vietnam was about to be realised.

How did the Cold War affect the Vietnamese struggle for independence?

The history of Vietnam – and of Indochina – cannot be fully understood without a general survey of the Cold War. In the immediate post-Second World War era, the world had quickly polarised into a Western bloc led by the USA, and a communist-dominated Eastern bloc. In 1939, the only communist state in the world had been the USSR; by 1945 this state had emerged as a regional superpower that dominated half of Europe.

By 1954, the situation in Indochina seemed to the West to have further developed in favour of communism. By 1949, Mao Zedong's Chinese Communist Party had emerged victorious from its struggle with Jiang Jieshi's nationalist regime to establish the People's Republic of China. In 1950, the **Korean War** began, as communist-dominated North Korea attacked the pro-Western South. The United States and its allies had been able to contain this attack only with considerable military effort.

From an American perspective, communism appeared to be a growing threat across the globe but particularly in Asia. Indochina was seen by the government in Washington as part of this anti-Western development, and the victories of the Viet Minh were viewed with some alarm by the US administration. As a result, following its policy of containment, the US increasingly placed the events unfolding in Indochina within a broader global perspective, seeing the region as the front line in a larger conflict between the opposing ideologies of capitalism and communism. This perspective began to condition American reactions to developments within Indochina in general and specifically in Vietnam.

In the US, the fear of the spread of communism took the form of the 'domino theory'. This envisaged one state after another falling in sequence to communism, like a line of dominoes. It appeared especially relevant in Southeast Asia when president Dwight D. Eisenhower advanced a scenario in which first Vietnam 'fell', and then in turn Laos, Cambodia and Thailand, with the process culminating in a communist takeover in Australia. The domino theory underpinned policies throughout the administrations of both John F. Kennedy and his successor **Lyndon B. Johnson**. Thus, Vietnamese communism, which was essentially a nationalist movement with very limited objectives – the independence of Vietnam from its former colonial masters – was perceived by the US as a direct threat to its own interests in the region.

What political steps were taken to resolve the situation?

The Geneva Conference, 1954

France began to negotiate a settlement at an international conference convened in Geneva in 1954 to discuss the general situation in the Far East. The USSR had managed to add Indochina to the agenda and in fact, prior to the talks, Britain and France supported this, hoping that an agreement could be reached to bring about a ceasefire. Initially the Americans believed it would be bad for US interests for France to pull out of Indochina; the US hoped that a military solution was still possible.

However, the Viet Minh victory at Dien Bien Phu occurred just as the Geneva delegates were preparing to meet, leaving American policy in tatters. The US had propped up French colonial rule in Indochina, but now it seemed that the Viet Minh had been completely successful. The first domino was about to fall. It is important to understand just how concerned the US was about a possible French defeat at Dien Bien Phu. The joint chiefs of staff – the main military planning body in the USA – seriously considered giving US air support to the French, and the deployment of American ground troops was also discussed.

Activity

In pairs, discuss and write down the reasons why Vietnam, and Indochina in general, was an important region in the Cold War.

On 21 July 1954, the Geneva Accords ruled that Indochina should be divided into its constituent parts: Vietnam, Laos and Cambodia. Furthermore, Vietnam should be temporarily divided in two along the **17th parallel**. The Viet Minh would hold the north of Vietnam, and withdraw from the south, as well as from Cambodia and Laos. French troops would withdraw to the south. There would be a demilitarised zone (DMZ) in between the two parts. This would create the conditions for a ceasefire and, once accomplished, elections would be held in Vietnam by July 1956, as the first step to creating a united country again.

17th parallel A line of latitude dividing North and South Vietnam. The demilitarised zone to the south was intended to act as a buffer and prevent communist incursion to the south. In fact, the communists simply went round it, through Cambodia.

Delegates arrive for the Geneva Conference in 1954, including (left to right on the steps in the foreground) Viet Minh leader Pham Van Dong, French prime minister Pierre Mendès France and British minister of foreign affairs Anthony Eden

Both the US and the Viet Minh accepted the Geneva Accords. Although by this time the Viet Minh controlled nearly 75% of Vietnam, they had come under pressure from their Soviet and Chinese backers to make peace. Both these powers feared full-scale US intervention in the region, and China in particular felt vulnerable to such a development. The Viet Minh also needed time to reconstruct their army and economy. The main reason for Ho's acceptance of the accords, however, was that he was genuinely convinced he could win the planned elections in view of the strong nationalist feeling in the country. Fear of this outcome was why, in the event, the US and South Vietnam refused to hold the elections. Eisenhower later conceded that Ho would have won 80% of the vote had the elections been allowed to take place.

Theory of knowledge

History, language and perspective

The choice of words to describe a historical event can affect your perspective on it. To the Viet Minh, the Battle of Dien Bien Phu was seen as a 'victory'. To the French and the Americans, it was a 'disaster'. Language and historical bias are thus closely linked. How might you describe the result of the battle in neutral language?

SOURCE B

Comments made on 16 July 1954 by Ngo Dinh Diem, prime minister of South Vietnam.

We did not sign the Geneva Agreements … we will struggle for the reunification of our homeland. We do not reject the principle of free elections as peaceful and democratic means to achieve that unity. Although elections constitute one of the bases of true democracy, they will be meaningful only on the condition that they are absolutely free. Faced now with a regime of oppression as practised by the Viet Minh, we remain sceptical concerning the possibility of fulfilling the conditions of free elections in the North.

Quoted in Cole, A. B. (ed.). 1956. Conflict in Indo-China and International Repercussions. *New York, USA. Cornell University Press. pp. 226–27.*

Instead of the promised elections, a permanent partition of Vietnam was created and the situation was formalised in June 1955, when the USA gave its support and recognition to Ngo Dinh Diem as leader of the new Republic of South Vietnam. This was one of the main causes of further conflict in the region, as the North Vietnamese attempted to unite the entire country through force. It would lead to the Second Indochina War, in which America would play such a key and costly role.

With Ho Chi Minh and the Viet Minh in control of North Vietnam, the USA rushed to give South Vietnam support – military, political and financial – and set up a pro-Western regime. Once committed to supporting this state, which should have been reunited with the North according to the Geneva agreement, the US found it difficult to disengage. It would be drawn deeper and deeper into the politics of the region until, by the 1960s, it was forced to deploy US ground forces in support of South Vietnam.

North Vietnam after the Geneva conference

North Vietnam – the Democratic Republic of Vietnam – was recognised by all the communist states, but faced considerable problems in the immediate post-Geneva period. The division of the country along the 17th parallel cut the northern population off from the main rice-growing areas in the Mekong Delta, and the threat of famine was very real. In addition, much of the fighting in the recent war had taken place in the North, and all the damage inflicted would have to be repaired before the country could function properly. Finally, although the North was backed by the USSR and Communist China, neither saw the region as a priority. The North Vietnamese also viewed China with considerable suspicion given its historical interest in the region (see page 103). Compared to the significant economic aid offered to the South by the USA, North Vietnam's communist allies were of limited use.

North and South Vietnam during the Second Indochina (Vietnam) War

At first, Ho concentrated on establishing control in the North, rather than spreading revolution southwards. He moved to eliminate the influence of French sympathisers – sometimes via executions. The Catholic Church was also brought under control. Ho initiated a programme of land reform, and the redistribution of land from rich landlords was popular, as was the abolition of rents. However, this policy was accompanied by the execution of thousands of the wealthier landlords, in an action decided on by groups known as People's Agricultural Tribunals. In some places, local leaders widened the net to include those who had not been significant landowners, and these actions disrupted agricultural production. In August 1956, Ho and Giap publicly admitted these 'errors', and production was increased. Later, though, when Ho began to implement the **collectivisation** of agriculture along Chinese lines, the move was less popular, and met with considerable resistance from those peasants who simply wanted land redistribution, not to be herded into huge collective farms under state control. In all, about 1 million refugees fled from North to South Vietnam.

Ho also sought to take advantage of the North's limited mineral wealth and encourage the development of industry. To do this he needed the support of the Soviets. Following the collapse of Sino–Soviet relations in the 1950s, this was a difficult objective to achieve without alienating the Chinese, who were a much more important and immediate military ally than the USSR. Given the mainly agricultural economy of the Tonkin region, this attempt at industrialisation had a negligible effect and in no way prepared North Vietnam for the conflict ahead. At the same time, Ho attempted to rebuild the army, placing an almost unbearable burden on the economy of the North.

So the new state of North Vietnam was not well placed to wage a war against a new enemy, the Republic of South Vietnam, now backed by the powerful USA. The task facing Ho was far more difficult than forcing the French out of the region. However, Ho helped the Viet Cong (see page 119) in the South form the National Liberation Front – a coalition of nationalists and communists. He also helped the construction of what became known as the Ho Chi Minh Trail through Laos and Cambodia, along which supplies could reach the Viet Cong.

collectivisation A method of organising agriculture by grouping farms into large, state-owned collectives. The method was first used in the USSR in the late 1920s.

South Vietnam after the Geneva Conference

The regimes in the South – before and after 1954 – had one thing in common: they were corrupt, undemocratic and brutal. In 1949, the French had installed Bao Dai, the Vietnamese emperor, to be the puppet leader. However, he had been weak (and was blamed for his collaboration with the Japanese), and the French had been forced to withdraw, despite receiving $3 billion from the US in their fight against the Viet Minh. It was difficult to select a leader for South Vietnam, as there was simply no one with Ho Chi Minh's stature in the pro-Western camp. In 1954, the US convinced Bao Dai to recall **Ngo Dinh Diem** as his prime minister, but the following year Diem ousted Bao Dai and, after a clearly rigged referendum, declared the independent republic of South Vietnam with himself as president.

Ngo Dinh Diem (1901–63)
Diem came from a Catholic background and had worked at the emperor's court. He established himself as a champion of Vietnamese independence and resigned his cabinet post in the 1930s in protest at French failures to increase the region's autonomy. In the Second World War he had, unlike Ho, stood aside from guerrilla activity and in 1950 he emigrated to America. Whilst there he was introduced to the Kennedy family – who were also Catholics – and cultivated an image of the 'acceptable' face of Vietnamese nationalism.

On the face of it, Diem was a good choice. He was pro-Western, conservative and had connections in America. In reality his Catholic background – a northern trait – made him unacceptable to the bulk of the Buddhist South Vietnamese. He was also highly élitist; he has been described as a mandarin (a bureaucrat of Chinese or Vietnamese origin), and lacked the common touch so important in the world of modern politics. He was inclined to talk over others and was a poor listener. He was, however, a survivor, and with American aid he thwarted a series of attempted coups between 1960 and 1963.

Activity
In pairs, establish a case that in the mid 1950s North Vietnam was essentially too weak to wage a war of liberation in the south.

Another problem faced by the new republic was the displacement of large numbers of Catholic Vietnamese from the north. During the French occupation the colonial power had sought to convert the indigenous population to Catholicism, with some localised success in the Tonkin area. The virtual mass migration of these people – 850,000 moved south – added a new dimension to the already volatile ethnic mix in the South. Measures taken by Diem's government to grant the Catholic refugees land in the Mekong Delta only increased the tension.

Vietnam was also divided internally. The French had encouraged the growth of a series of religious 'sects' that possessed huge private armies and considerable political influence. The most powerful of these were the Cao Dai and Hoa Hao (see page 104). The former had 2 million followers and could command an army of 20,000 men; it controlled much of the Mekong Delta. On top of this, a mafia-style organisation called the Binh Xuyen had an army of 25,000 men and considerable assets in the form of gambling and prostitution rackets in Saigon. Each of these organisations demanded recognition by the government and virtual independence within their local areas of influence. Diem crushed these groups with his army, but at considerable cost in lives and money.

Diem also had problems with the **Army of the Republic of South Vietnam (ARVN)**. It was large – numbering over 250,000 men – but morale was low and corruption was common at all levels. What is more, the French had taken all the ARVN's equipment with them when they left. However, by 1960, the US mission in Vietnam, with the help of $85 million per year, had created a fairly effective and modern army. The ARVN still had weaknesses – its officer corps was ineffective and the training given was more suited to a conventional battlefield than to the counter-insurgency warfare needed to stop the Viet Minh.

Army of the Republic of South Vietnam (ARVN) South Vietnam's standing army was equipped to high standards by the USA. Some ARVN units were very effective, but most suffered from poor motivation and leadership. The army was heavily infiltrated by the Viet Cong.

The southern economy had also been badly damaged in the fighting. Once again, the USA stepped in with aid, rebuilding the infrastructure and subsidising the economy.

Troops of the Army of the Republic of South Vietnam (ARVN) man a machine gun in Danang

It was in the area of politics that the most serious problems lay. Diem and his brother, Ngo Dinh Nhu, rejected any notion of democracy and established a dictatorship. Diem's family dominated the government and, although Diem himself was an honest man, this gave the impression of corruption. Furthermore, his government ignored the needs of the people.

In particular, Diem had a very different approach to the land question than that followed by the Viet Minh in North Vietnam, and this lost him popularity among the peasant classes. Up until 1954, the Viet Minh had redistributed 600,000 hectares of land in the south to the landless peasants and had abolished high rents. Diem, however, sided with the large landowners and thwarted attempts by the peasants to acquire their own land. In 1955, Diem reversed the Viet Minh's earlier redistribution policy and ordered the peasants to resume paying rents. In 1958, he forced them to buy the land they farmed in six annual instalments. This was very costly, and alienated most of the peasant population. Against this backdrop the Viet Minh agenda, which emphasised the redistribution of land and wealth, had real influence on the affiliation of the southern peasantry.

The final reason for Diem's unpopularity was that he gave the best positions in the government to Catholics rather than to Buddhists – even though Buddhists made up about 90% of the population. Diem held on to power by ruthless suppression of all political opposition, but this created even more widespread resistance to his regime. His refusal to hold the elections agreed to in the Geneva Accords also played into the hands of the growing opposition. Although the Viet Minh had withdrawn from the South, the group's southern Vietnamese members – as many as 15,000 of them – had remained. In 1957, these nationalists and communists formed the **Viet Cong (VC)**. The VC was the core of the new resistance to Diem's government in South Vietnam.

Viet Cong (VC) The name given by Diem and the US to the guerrilla movement based in the South. The term Viet Cong (short for 'Vietnamese communists') was an attempt to label all resistance as communist. In fact, the locally born VC drew recruits from a broad section of the South Vietnamese population. It consisted of three groups: main-force units of regular soldiers, provincial forces and part-time guerrillas. The part-time guerrillas – men and women – farmed by day and fought by night. The VC generally avoided large-scale military operations, favouring guerrilla tactics.

The VC began to assassinate government officials and, in the villages, the group often formed alternative political bodies to undermine the central government and to get local peasants involved. They used terror against government officials, but their operations usually left ordinary villagers untouched, unlike those carried out by the ARVN and US troops.

At first the VC comprised largely autonomous cells working independently of each other – and of North Vietnam. This structure meant that if any VC members were caught by the ARVN or US troops, they could not yield much information, even under torture. The VC were therefore very difficult to identify. Though they soon received military supplies from the North, most of their operations were decided and designed by local commanders, who had good knowledge of their areas. In 1960, the **National Liberation Front (NLF)** was formed as the political arm of the VC.

National Liberation Front (NLF) A political coalition of communists and other nationalists, intended to unite the southern resistance. It also had growing links with the North Vietnamese Army (NVA) and North Vietnamese government.

SOURCE C

Comments made by Truong Nhu Tang, a founding member of the NLF.

I saw that the Diem government made many fundamental errors: First, it was a government of one family. Second, Diem suppressed many patriots who participated in the war against the French. Third, he put the Christian religion above the interest of the nation. I am personally not a Buddhist, but eighty percent of the Vietnamese population are Confucian or Buddhist.

From 1958 some resistance was formed, which led to the formation of the National Liberation Front in December 1960. … I had been the comptroller of a large bank, and later became Director General of the Sugar Company of Vietnam and secretary-general of the Self-Determination Movement.

The mobilisation committee for the [NLF] was formed by intellectuals: the architect Huynh Tan Phat; the doctor Phung Van Cung; the lawyer Trinh Dinh Thao; myself; and others. … Our idea of independence came from what we saw in free countries in the West. … I was not a Communist.

Quoted in Santoli, A. 1985. To Bear Any Burden. *New York, USA. E. P. Dutton. pp. 76–77.*

The US decided to support the Diem government, much as it had done the French. From 1955 to 1961 the US poured $1 billion dollars into South Vietnam, and over 1500 Americans were present in the country, offering support in various ways. From 1956, the US took over responsibility from the French for training the ARVN. Without this US support, the Diem regime would have collapsed.

Question

Why couldn't South Vietnam maintain a democratic form of government?

Thus, by the early 1960s the Republic of South Vietnam had made progress in many areas, but there were inherent weaknesses in the state. These would encourage the growth of opposition and severely hinder the Republic's ability to resist it. This situation did not change over time, and is one of the reasons why the US was drawn ever deeper into the war in Indochina.

Viet Cong guerrillas advance through the jungle

Why did the Second Indochina War, or Vietnam War, begin?

The Americanisation of the conflict

After Geneva, the USA became more directly involved in Indochina, as the main supporter of South Vietnam. The VC began operations in the South as early as 1957, with the assassination of local officials and attacks on government buildings. North Vietnam pledged support and began to construct the routes needed to supply and support the VC in South Vietnam. These routes became known as the **Ho Chi Minh Trail**.

Ho Chi Minh Trail A series of communication and supply routes through Laos and Cambodia, which connected the VC in the South to their allies in the North.

In 1960, the political wing of the VC – the NLF – was formed with the objective of achieving an independent and reunited Vietnam. Despite this, the North grew afraid that the situation would lead to conflict before it had recovered enough to fully support the armed struggle in the South. The impact of the VC was obvious – in 1958, 700 government officials were assassinated, rising to 4000 in 1961.

The success of the VC was due mainly to the alienation of the peasant class. They did not benefit at all under Diem's regime, and these peasants were described at the time as 'a mound of straw ready to be ignited'. The VC were careful to target recognisable supporters of the government, whereas Diem's army was indiscriminate in its reaction – shelling and strafing villages with little regard for the civilian population. Soon the VC had thousands of supporters in the countryside. To deprive the VC of its bases, the US and the South Vietnamese government attempted to isolate the peasant population from the VC by relocating whole villages to areas that could be more easily policed by the ARVN. In theory these new settlements – known as 'strategic hamlets' – were supposed to have new schools, medical facilities and electricity, but this was rarely achieved. Furthermore, the peasants resented being removed from their homes, which had strong religious connections with their ancestors. The strategic hamlets were also regularly patrolled by the ARVN, whose behaviour alienated the peasants even more, increasing support for the VC.

CIA The Central Intelligence Agency – the USA's spy and covert operations organisation.

coup A seizure of political power by an army, usually by force.

Alongside this, Diem faced rising opposition from other quarters. In 1960, he clamped down on journalists, students and other groups opposed to his regime, imprisoning many. The Washington administration was warned by the **CIA** of the impending collapse of Diem's regime. In November 1960, there was an abortive army **coup**.

Religious tensions

The existing Civil Guard – a sort of badly armed local militia – had been expanded and re-equipped. New ARVN Ranger Battalions were created and trained by US specialists. By 1961, the number of US military advisors in Vietnam had risen to 800, in total disregard of the agreements made at Geneva. The situation began to spiral out of control in 1963, when it became obvious that the inherent religious tensions had reached crisis point, with outright opposition to the Diem regime by thousands of Buddhists.

Buddhists had been historically suppressed by Vietnam's rulers, who preferred the Chinese philosophy of Confucianism. Diem was a Catholic, and hundreds of thousands of his co-religionists had migrated south after Geneva. The tension was partly caused by ideological differences, but the biggest factor in Buddhist opposition was the monopoly of power held by Catholics in government.

The first major demonstrations came in May 1963 in the Hué region. The government reacted with vicious counter-measures, sending armoured vehicles against the demonstrators, killing many and arresting hundreds. This simply encouraged greater opposition and the demonstrations spread to Saigon. Again the South Vietnamese security forces, under the control of Diem's brother Nhu, attempted to crush the anti-government campaign by force. As well as marching in the streets, the Buddhists also lobbied the administration and allies within the army. The most striking example of their opposition to Diem was the self-immolation (suicide by burning to death) of a Buddhist monk, Thich Quang Duc, on 11 June 1963. This act was broadcast around the world, along with the Buddhists' message of protest against Diem's authoritarian rule. It seemed that Diem was losing control, jeopardising US influence in Vietnam.

Aged 73, the Buddhist monk Thich Quang Duc burned himself to death in protest at the persecution of Buddhists by Diem's government

Theory of knowledge

History and religion

Religion and religious persecution have sometimes been a powerful force in history. What role did they play in the downfall and death of Ngo Dinh Diem?

On 21 August 1963, Diem ordered the ARVN to attack Buddhist temples in Hué. Many Buddhists were killed or arrested, and more monks set themselves on fire. It was a public-relations disaster, and the US ambassador to Vietnam, Henry Cabot Lodge, decided that Diem must be removed from power. The nature of Diem's fall is of great importance. At first the US simply pressured Diem to resign, but when this failed, President Kennedy gave tacit support to an army coup. On 1 November 1963, the generals made their move – backed by the CIA – and Diem was deposed. He and his brother, Ngo, were shot. General Duong Van Minh became the new leader of the junta (military-led government), but he failed to unite the regime or gain popular support. In 1964, five more coups took place. Eventually, in 1965, General Nguyen Van Thieu became president of South Vietnam, but he still led a corrupt and brutal regime.

The North Vietnamese leadership in Hanoi was not blind to these developments, and ordered regular **North Vietnamese Army (NVA)** units to the South to reinforce the VC. This order began to affect events in the South within a year and, by 1964, the government in South Vietnam (and the US) was faced with a situation that was spiralling out of control.

North Vietnamese Army (NVA) The NVA was the regular army of North Vietnam. It was well equipped, with high morale and good leadership. From 1964 onwards, the NVA was found in ever-increasing numbers fighting alongside the Viet Cong in South Vietnam.

Peasant support

After Diem was killed, there were some attempts at land reform in the South. In 1954, 60% of peasants had been landless and 20% had less than a hectare. Tenant farmers had been forced to pay almost 75% of their annual crop to landlords. This was why the Viet Minh's redistribution of land in the 1940s and 1950s had been so popular among the peasant class. After 1954, the VC continued to support these redistribution policies, and so maintained popularity with many peasants. To reduce this support, in 1968, Thieu gave land to 50,000 families; in 1970, the Land-To-The-Tiller Act ended rent payments, and gave ownership to those who worked the land, with a maximum holding of 15 hectares. In all, by 1972, 0.6 million hectares had been distributed to 400,000 landless peasants. By 1973, all but 7% of peasants in the South owned land.

Discussion point

In groups, prepare a class presentation outlining why the USA became increasingly drawn into the conflict in Indochina.

What were the main stages of the Second Indochina War, 1959–75?

As early as 1957, the VC had begun assassinating public officials. In the spring of 1959, the VC began to engage the ARVN in direct combat using guerrilla tactics. The ARVN was not trained to cope with this method of warfare. In addition, many of the South's army officers had gained their posts through family influence or corruption, rather than as a result of competence. The ARVN was also often infiltrated by the VC.

The government in North Vietnam decided to renew the conflict in 1959. While this decision was clearly tied to Cold War politics, it was also very much a continuation of the struggle for an independent Vietnam. In July 1959, the Central Committee of the Workers' Party in the North met to formalise the reopening of hostilities in this second phase of Vietnam's fight for independence. The group believed that reunification was necessary in order to achieve socialism.

Despite attempts at land reform, the corruption and brutality of the government and the ARVN continued, alienating many in the South. In addition, the VC and the NVA were determined to continue the struggle for an independent and united Vietnam. The events of the Cold War, combined with the incompetence of the ARVN, caused the US to step up its aid and eventually to commit troops to the conflict in Indochina. This growing US involvement turned a war of independence into an anti-imperialist war, in which it would be necessary to expel the US if the nationalist aim of an independent Vietnam were ever to be achieved. Consequently, the North began to send men and supplies to the VC in the South via the Ho Chi Minh Trail.

From 1964 onwards, the USA became increasingly involved in the struggle in Vietnam. With South Vietnam unable to cope, and in fear of Vietnam becoming the first communist 'domino' (see page 114), the US appealed to the Southeast Asia Treaty Organisation (SEATO), established in 1954 to stop the spread of communism in the region, to send troops. Soon, Australia and New Zealand – which feared a communist Vietnam backed by the USSR and China – had also sent troops to fight alongside American forces.

Historical debate

Historians have conflicting opinions about the USA's motive for involvement in Vietnam:

- William Duiker supports the geo-strategic motive of global resistance to communism. This is modified by Melvyn Leffler, who argues that the US grossly overestimated the threat of both China and the USSR to its own position in the world.
- Gabriel Kolko argues that the US was only interested in Indochina's natural resources and markets. Patrick Hearden modifies this view further to argue that the US had – and has – a huge neo-colonial empire and that intervention in Vietnam was intended to preserve this empire.
- David Shaplan argues that US involvement was simply driven by a desire to support France.
- David Halberstam argues that whatever the initial motive, US involvement began as a small-scale affair and escalated out of control. In many ways, the US leadership were to blame for allowing their country to slip into war.
- David Anderson argues that no single factor prompted the USA's involvement in Vietnam, but rather a combination of factors were at play.

Escalation and Operation Rolling Thunder, 1964–65

In March 1964, NVA regulars began to infiltrate South Vietnam via the Ho Chi Minh Trail. By this time, an estimated 170,000 VC were operating in the South. The trail was located for the most part in Laos, and US president Lyndon Johnson made it clear that he was prepared to support ARVN raids into Laos to disrupt this activity. On 2 August 1964, the Gulf of Tonkin Incident took place – the American destroyer USS *Maddox* was fired upon by North Vietnamese patrol boats in the Gulf of Tonkin. The *Maddox* had been in, or very near, North Vietnamese territorial waters and had been supporting South Vietnamese naval operations in the area. On 4 August, Johnson ordered US war planes to attack targets in the North, dramatically escalating the war. On 7 August 1964, the US Senate passed the Gulf of Tonkin Resolution, giving the president a free hand to prosecute the war in Vietnam as he saw fit.

As 1964 went on, tension continued in the South. An attempt to introduce a new constitution in August prompted more student and Buddhist demonstrations and sparked off another coup, out of which Air Marshal Nguyen Cao Ky emerged as leader. VC activity increased, and US troops were actively targeted. In December, the Brink Hotel in Saigon, which was used as US officers' quarters, was bombed. In February 1965, a major VC attack on a US base at Pleiku killed eight American servicemen. On 2 March, the US launched Operation Rolling Thunder, a major air offensive against the North. Next, the USSR began to supply increasingly sophisticated military equipment to the North Vietnamese. By July 1965, the NVA was deploying Soviet-made surface-to-air missiles to defend their airspace.

SOURCE D

Comments made by North Vietnamese politician Pham Van Dong, 1964.

The US can go on increasing aid to South Vietnam. It can increase its own army. But it will do no good. I hate to see the war go on and intensify. Yet our people are determined to struggle. It is impossible for westerners to understand the force of the people's will to resist and to continue.

Quoted in Chandler, M. and Wright, J. 1999. Modern World History. *Oxford, UK. Heinemann. p. 110.*

On 8 March 1965, the first large-scale deployment of US troops took place. This development soon led to the commitment of US army and marine forces to full-scale battle. At first, skirmishes between marine patrols and VC guerrillas took place around Da Nang in the south-central region of Vietnam, but on 18 August 1965, a full-scale marine attack took place on a VC regiment located 20 km (12 miles) south of the American base at Chu Lai. Within three and a half years, half a million US ground troops would be committed to fighting the VC and the NVA.

Search and destroy

The early part of 1966 was fairly static. The NVA had been severely damaged by the events of 1965, and was rebuilding its forces. However, guerrilla activity did not cease. From mid 1966, the first large-scale US **search and destroy** operations were put into effect. These operations aimed to seal off areas of South Vietnam and to saturate them with US troops. The first of these operations, El Paso, took place in May and June in the area around Loc Ninh.

search and destroy An anti-guerrilla strategy used by the USA, search and destroy involved sealing off large areas of territory and then searching for and defeating the enemy in battle. In practice, it often resulted in the destruction of Vietnamese villages and the deaths of civilians.

Search and destroy had a limited effect. The strategy did result in the capture or death of many VC guerrillas and severely disrupted the VC's military infrastructure. However, its political effects were less convincing, sometimes even counter-productive. The US could clear large areas of South Vietnam of VC and NVA soldiers, but it could only hold on to these areas by permanently garrisoning them. Once the US forces had left an area, the VC slowly crept back in and recommenced guerrilla operations. Furthermore, both phases of these operations could be very damaging to the civilian population, often driving them into supporting the VC. It was not uncommon for entire villages to be destroyed, while the fighting killed many civilians and damaged their property.

In other areas of the country, Australian troops used the different strategy of **counter-insurgency** (COIN). This also involved military operations – for example, the Australians won a major battle against the VC on 18 August 1966 at Long Tan. However, their tactics were co-ordinated with extensive civic-aid programmes designed to improve the living conditions of the peasants through provision of better medical care, education and living standards. The local populations thus equated progress with co-operation with the Australians, making it far more difficult for the VC to re-establish control. The problem was that this strategy only worked effectively in very small, self-contained areas.

counter-insurgency A method of combating guerrilla warfare that uses a mixture of military action and socio-economic improvement for peasant communities.

An Australian soldier helps a young Vietnamese girl; Australian medical teams worked in South Vietnam as part of counter-insurgency operations to improve the lives of local people

The US carried out a series of major air attacks on North Vietnam throughout 1967. Similar operations had been ongoing since 1965, but the strategic impact on the North had been minimal. North Vietnam simply did not have the industrial base to provide easy targets, and it was almost impossible to disrupt agriculture by air attacks. The best that US air power could achieve was to disrupt communications and supply routes from China, and wage a fairly ineffective campaign to bring down the morale of the northern population. In 1967, the North began to develop improved air defences based on surface-to-air missiles. It also established its own air force. NVA airmen were now using sophisticated Soviet-supplied MiG-21 interceptor aircraft, and by the end of 1967, 455 US planes had been lost. Once again, the limits of a purely military solution to the situation in Vietnam had been demonstrated. On the ground in South Vietnam more search and destroy operations were launched in 1967. VC/NVA units were badly damaged but not destroyed, and, despite strenuous US efforts, survivors were able to retreat to the safety of Cambodia.

SOURCE E

Comments made by Ho Chi Minh in 1967.

Vietnam is thousands of miles from the USA. ... Contrary to the 1954 Geneva conference, the USA has ceaselessly intervened in Vietnam. The US government has committed war crimes. ... Half a million US troops have resorted to inhuman weapons. ... Napalm, toxic chemicals and gases have been used to massacre our people, destroy our crops and raze our villages to the ground. ... US aircraft have dropped thousands of bombs, destroying towns, villages, hospitals, schools. We will never submit to force; never accept talks under threat of bombs.

Quoted in Walsh, B. 2001. Modern World History. *London, UK. John Murray. p. 360.*

Historical debate

Historians have debated the relative successes and failures of each side during the military engagements of the war, and most agreed that it was a serious defeat for the US. Recently, historians such as William Duiker and Robert Buzzanco have argued that Tet was a massive setback for the Viet Cong. The most serious challenger to the received wisdom is C. Dale Walton, who argues that it was possible for the US to have won the war on the battlefield as it was actually successful in most of its military operations. If you believe these authors then you must look beyond the battlefield to find reasons for nationalist victory.

Khe Sanh and the Tet Offensive

From January to April 1968, the Battle of Khe Sanh took place. Khe Sanh was a US base in the central highlands near the demilitarised zone, and was intended to block the infiltration of the NVA from the Ho Chi Minh Trail into the central coastal plain. The NVA high command reasoned that the strategic situation of Khe Sanh was so similar to Dien Bien Phu – isolated in the dense terrain of the central highlands – that they could impose a second conventional defeat on their enemies. In April, the NVA sent two full divisions to Khe Sanh. The battle raged for months, but the US managed to destroy the NVA's heavy artillery. In April, after very hard fighting, the NVA retreated – leaving an estimated 20,000 dead. The battle was a major defeat for the North.

At the same time as the Battle of Khe Sanh was being fought, the Viet Cong launched the Tet Offensive, which proved to be the turning point of the war. It was a massive and widespread offensive, intended to attack military and political targets across South Vietnam. The offensive was timed to coincide with Tet, the Vietnamese New Year, which was normally a time of truce. The Viet Cong thus hoped to catch ARVN forces off guard and to encourage a general rising of the South Vietnamese population through a display of massive military power. The VC attacked on 31 January, deploying 84,000 troops. However, the ARVN managed to hold out until US reinforcements arrived, and the offensive failed.

Viet Cong guerrillas lie dead after the failure of the Tet Offensive

Tet was a serious strategic defeat for the Viet Cong, who suffered high casualties (over 40,000 dead), and were never able to regain their previous strength. By abandoning their guerrilla tactics and coming out into the open, the VC were badly mauled by superior US firepower and mobility. In particular, the VC's overall structure was shattered by the defeat. A good example of this is the subsequent recapture of the northern capital, Hué, by US marines after a month-long battle that left over 5000 Viet Cong dead. The US suffered 147 dead and 857 wounded. However, while the Tet Offensive was a disaster for the VC, it was an important development for the independence movement. NVA troops moved in to take the place of the defeated Viet Cong, and they were much better matched to the conventional methods of warfare used by the ARVN and US troops.

SOURCE F

Comments by Nguyen Tuong Lai, a Viet Cong guerrilla leader.

Tet was a great loss for the NLF forces. Our forces had to be restructured afterward. There were three phases of fighting during the offensive: During the first phase in my area the NLF forces did the fighting. We lost too many men and in the second phase had to be reinforced by North Vietnamese units. And in the third phase, the fighting was done exclusively by North Vietnamese units. … The southern forces were decimated … and from that time on mostly served as intelligence, logistics, and saboteurs for the northerners.

Quoted in Pollock, A.1995. Vietnam: Conflict and Change in Indochina. Melbourne, Australia. Oxford University Press. p. 77.

However, the main effect of Tet was not military but political, as it helped turn US public opinion – appalled by the images of the offensive that were broadcast into American homes – against the war.

fragging US slang for killing an unpopular officer with a grenade.

Increasing opposition in the US was just one factor that adversely affected the morale of US troops. Among others were the impact of VC booby traps, and the growing numbers of casualties, both of US troops and of civilians. The '**fragging**' of officers became more common, as did drug-taking. There was a rise in racial tension within the army. Desertion and outright insubordination increased.

The My Lai Massacre

In March 1968, the impact of the Tet Offensive was deepened by the notorious massacre at My Lai, in which US troops killed 400–500 civilians. This further encouraged the rural Vietnamese in the South to side with the VC, as well as reinforcing opposition to the war in the US. Furthermore, the American commander in Vietnam, William Westmoreland, demanded more troops – 206,000 – and permission to attack into Cambodia and Laos to capitalise on the success of Tet. The American public was outraged at the massacre and strongly objected to the drafting of yet more American troops to this foreign battlefield.

Historical debate

The impact of the media on the eventual outcome of the war has been the focus of historical debate. Peter Braestrup argues that media coverage of the Tet Offensive and My Lai moulded opinion and helped tip the US public against the war. William Hammond, however, argues that the media supported the war until the politicians in Washington changed their position, claiming that the media *reacted* to public opinion rather than moulding it. The same debate has surrounded the widespread anti-war protests. Melvin Small argues that the protests greatly influenced the US administration, whereas Adam Garfinkle claims that the protesters were so radical that they outraged public opinion and actually prolonged the war.

Politically, the US now began to look for a way out of Vietnam. On 31 March 1968, President Johnson announced that all bombing of the North would be suspended. In May, the first peace talks opened in Paris; they lasted until 1973. After Richard Nixon became president, the US representative at the talks was the secretary of state, Henry Kissinger. The North was represented by Le Duc Tho.

Vietnamisation and the end of the war

The Nixon administration took office in January 1969, and soon announced plans for a phased withdrawal of US troops in Vietnam – 25,000 to leave in 1969, with 150,000 more in 1970. At the same time, the US was entering a period of the Cold War known as détente (see page 34). During this time, the USA attempted to improve relations with the two great communist powers, the USSR and China, to create greater global stability and open up markets for American trade. However, 'Vietnamisation' – the attempt to make the ARVN capable of fighting the NVA without US troops – proved ineffective due to the inherent problems within the ARVN, and the political and social structure of Vietnam. It soon became apparent that the US would be forced to withdraw from South Vietnam, leaving the region without the strength and unity to resist a concerted VC/NVA attack.

Victims of the My Lai Massacre

North Vietnam wanted the withdrawal of all US troops and the replacement of the government in the South with a coalition. As the ARVN and US suffered more defeats, the pressure on the US to withdraw increased. By 1971, this was being openly discussed and the North withdrew its demand for a coalition government, improving the atmosphere of the talks. However, when the US permitted South Vietnam to make some changes to preliminary agreements, the North withdrew from the talks. The US followed up with an intensive bombing campaign, which succeeded in driving the North back to the negotiating table.

By 1972, the VC/NVA had rebuilt their forces after the defeat in the Tet Offensive. NVA regulars moved into South Vietnam, fighting a guerrilla campaign to begin with but soon waging more conventional warfare. The renewed US bombing of the North eventually drove all sides into a negotiated settlement at the talks in Paris. The USSR and China both forced the government of North Vietnam to make an agreement. They wanted better relations with the USA, and the events of 1972 had shown that total military victory would be difficult to achieve. On 27 January 1973, formal agreements were made that would allow the US to disengage from the conflict. The Agreement on Ending the War and Restoring Peace in Vietnam was signed by South and North Vietnam, the NLF and the USA. The US agreed to withdraw all troops within 60 days, and a ceasefire was set to begin on 28 January. By March 1973, all US and SEATO troops had left Vietnam.

By 1975, Giap had accumulated enough NVA reserves to begin a protracted conventional campaign, and the war for reunification resumed. The North already had troops south of the border, and the Paris agreements had resulted in the withdrawal of vital US air support.

The government in the South was corrupt and unpopular. Food shortages and inflation further eroded support. At the same time, increasing numbers of ARVN troops deserted. In March 1975, the NVA launched its final campaign. Despite some isolated victories, the ARVN proved unable to stop the advance of the NVA; many ARVN units simply disintegrated, and the South collapsed after only two months. Thieu resigned on 21 April and fled to Taiwan. NVA and VC troops entered Saigon on 30 April 1975 – completely unopposed. The war was finally over, and the early nationalist aims of an independent and reunified Vietnam were finally achieved.

Activity

In groups, prepare a chart. On one side list the military events of the Second Indochina War. On the other side, decide who came out best from each event – the NVA/VC or the US/ARVN.

Why did North Vietnam win the Second Indochina War?

At first the reasons for the North's victory may seem obvious. Despite overwhelming military and financial might from the USA, the South was unable to sustain a war against the forces of the VC and NVA. In addition, many in the US – and the rest of the world – had come to see American interference in Vietnamese affairs as damaging and unnecessary. In particular, the war in Vietnam was viewed as essentially a war of national liberation begun by Ho Chi Minh rather than the attempted communist conquest of another country from outside, as portrayed by the US government.

After Tet and the My Lai Massacre, the war became politically untenable for the US and it began to withdraw from the conflict. The South – wracked by internal divisions – was unable to resist on its own, even with a massive injection of US military aid in the final stages of the war. But this analysis, although convincing, needs to be developed and placed in a more rounded historical context.

Historical debate

There is discussion about Richard Nixon's contribution to the outcome of the war. Jeffrey Kimball argues that Nixon made up policy as he went along, and withdrew from Vietnam in a messy and badly planned way. Larry Berman and Melvin Small argue that Nixon was motivated by the need to achieve 'peace with honor' as a solution to the crisis. Ted Morgan argues that Nixon had no other choice but to expand the war into Cambodia in order to cover the US retreat from the main theatre of war in Vietnam.

Military factors

It is clear that in the First Indochina War the communists won the upper hand militarily. They were fighting against a weakened European power emerging from the Second World War – France had been under German occupation for almost four years, and simply did not have the military will or economic reserves to sustain a war in Indochina. Thus, the guerrilla tactics wore down the French willingness to fight, and the catastrophic defeat at Dien Bien Phu made the war politically unsustainable for France.

SOURCE G

Draft of a memo from US secretary of state Henry Kissinger to President Gerald Ford, titled 'Lessons of Vietnam', 12 May 1975.

We cannot help draw the conclusion that our armed forces are not suited to this kind of war. … This was partly because of the nature of the conflict. It was both a revolutionary war fought at knife-point during the night within the villages. It was also a main force war in which technology could make a genuine difference. Both sides had trouble devising tactics that would be suitable for each type of warfare. But we and the South Vietnamese had more difficulty with this than the other side.

Presidential Country Files for East Asia and the Pacific, Gerald R. Ford Library.

However, during the Second Indochina War this analysis does not apply. The problem was not wholly a military one, and the US armed forces could not defeat the VC/NVA outright. The VC/NVA could always retreat to a network of safe havens in the wake of defeat, where they could re-evaluate and regroup. It was only later in the war that Nixon ordered ground forces into Cambodia to deny the VC/NVA such refuges. Even so, North Vietnam remained out of bounds for US ground forces (see page 126) and the US was never able to totally cut off the Ho Chi Minh Trail, which connected the NVA's bases in the North to their VC allies fighting in the South. Furthermore, the methods used to fight the large battles of the war tended to alienate the rural peasantry of the South, who made up the bulk of the population. Thus, although severely damaged, the VC could always recruit new fighters and rely on the local population to support their guerrilla operations.

The structures and ideologies of the North and South Vietnamese states

North Vietnam was better suited to fighting a war of attrition. This state had a quite definite strategic goal – the reunification of Vietnam under communist rule. Ho Chi Minh provided strong leadership in pursuit of this goal. The nature of the state also helped towards victory – the Tonkin region was very culturally homogeneous compared with the southern part of the country. North Vietnam's communist ideology and the fact that its government had emerged from a revolutionary struggle also created unity. Both these factors created great social discipline, and the sharp focus of the struggle for unification kept internal disunity to a minimum. North Vietnam did, however, face problems. The country, a developing-world state with almost no industry, was fighting the most powerful economy in the world. The support of China and the USSR was also, therefore, a significant factor in the North's success.

Fact

China and the USSR had their own interests, which sometimes conflicted with those of North Vietnam. There are points in the history of the conflict when the USSR limited its backing due to international considerations. The limit on support applies even more to China, which had historical interests in Vietnam that Ho and his regime actually perceived as imperialistic.

On the other hand, the North's largely agricultural economy was very difficult for the US to damage, and its massed air raids on the North – which dropped three times the tonnage of bombs that had been used on Germany in the Second World War – were not a decisive factor in the outcome of the war. On balance, therefore, the unity of purpose of the North Vietnamese equipped them better for the long-drawn-out war of attrition that their fighters had created by their tenacious struggle in the South.

Because decisive victory could not be achieved on the battlefield alone, the political weaknesses of the Republic of South Vietnam became key to the outcome of the conflict. In theory, the war of attrition this created should have been won by the USA, with its vastly superior resources. This proved impossible, however. The ethnic, political and cultural differences within the South created so many divisions that South Vietnam could not survive without direct US military support. This can be seen by comparing the events of 1972 to those of 1975. In 1972, a large communist attack was halted by the use of massed US air power. In 1975, despite massive US aid to the ARVN, the NVA swept all resistance aside. Thus, one of the major reasons for the North's victory in the war was the failure of the emergence of a coherent state in the South – the reasons for which were deeply rooted in Vietnamese history.

Historical debate

The historian George Herring argues the case that some US politicians believed foolishly that military success could offset the inherent weakness of the South Vietnamese regime. Robert Thompson modifies this, arguing that military action, especially aerial bombing, only served to force the rural population into the arms of the Viet Cong. Larry Cable believes that the Americans should have concentrated more on counter-insurgency and abandoned their damaging search and destroy strategy.

The influence of the Cold War

The conflict in Indochina cannot be analysed in isolation from the Cold War. The Cold War conditioned US reaction to events in Vietnam and Indochina. In particular, the USA's policy of containment and belief in the domino theory resulted in support for pro-Western factions whatever the cost.

When an independent Vietnam emerged from the Second World War, Ho Chi Minh genuinely believed that the US would maintain its support, as it claimed to be an anti-colonial force. The Cold War also brought the large communist powers China and the USSR into the conflict as supporters of the North. The ideological nature of the war thus gave the North access to large amounts of money and modern weaponry. This is especially interesting given China's rather ambiguous role in the region and general Vietnamese fears that, by relying on China, they were encouraging a re-imposition of its historical dominance over their country. Thus, despite the battering that VC/NVA forces received at the hands of America's armed forces, they were always able to survive.

SOURCE H

During the 1950s and 1960s, the Vietnamese Communists confronted formidable enemies, the French and the Americans, in their quest for national unification. Ho Chi Minh avidly sought advice and weapons from China. But sentiments of distrust were never far below the surface. The Chinese, for instance, were suspicious of Hanoi's intentions to incorporate Laos and Cambodia in an 'Indochinese Federation', while the North Vietnamese guarded closely their 'special relationship' with Laos when China increased its aid to the Pathet Lao.

Zhai, Q. 2000. China and the Vietnam Wars, 1950–1975. Chapel Hill, USA. University of North Carolina Press. p. 119.

North Vietnamese tanks move through the streets of Saigon in May 1975

Conclusion

The outcome of the war was the result of a combination of factors, but at its heart lay the North's extreme resilience. US and ARVN forces could inflict debilitating defeats on the VC/NVA, but due to the existence of safe havens and the willingness of the North Vietnamese to continue the struggle, they always re-entered the conflict once they had rebuilt their strength. The North Vietnamese could tolerate the war of attrition, whereas the US could not. The failure of the US to create a South Vietnamese state with a similar resilience meant that, once domestic opinion about the conflict turned against Washington, the war was effectively lost.

Question

Why was North Vietnam finally able to win what it saw as its war of independence?

What part did Ho Chi Minh play in the struggle for independence?

An important factor in the success of the communist resistance, first to the French and then to the Republic of South Vietnam and its US backers, was the leadership of Ho Chi Minh. He was charismatic, intelligent and ruthless. He had been educated in France and had joined the French Communist Party in 1920. He had spent the early 1920s in Moscow, where he had made strong contacts with the Russian Bolshevik Party. During his time in Russia, Ho had formulated a model of communist revolution based not on a rising of industrial workers but on an organisation based around agricultural peasants. Thus, like Mao in China, he modified classic Marxism to fit into a developing-world context. In 1924, he travelled to Canton – a Chinese communist stronghold – and there began to form his Vietnamese communist organisation.

In 1941, Ho returned to Vietnam and led the guerrilla war against the Vichy French and the Japanese. His movement was supported in these operations by the USA. With the defeat of Japan in 1945, he emerged as leader of an independent Vietnam after ruthless purges of his opponents. Ho was initially friendly towards the US, which he saw as an opponent of European colonial empires, but his communist credentials ruled out any possibility of US support for the newly created Vietnam. Thus, in 1950, he successfully negotiated with the USSR and the People's Republic of China for support against French attempts to reinstate colonial rule in Indochina. He attempted to strike a deal with the French, but talks broke down due to the unwillingness of the former colonial power to negotiate. Ho devised the general direction of the war against the French but wisely left the details of military planning to his minister of war, Vo Nguyen Giap.

With the defeat of the French in 1954 and their replacement by the Republic of South Vietnam, the war for independence took a new direction. Ho remained staunchly opposed to any negotiated settlement whilst foreign troops remained in South Vietnam. This was even the case when wider strategic considerations caused his Soviet and Chinese backers to pressure him to compromise with the South. Even in the dark days of 1967, Ho realised that US public opinion would not support the war forever and that South Vietnam and its army were fundamentally weak. He put in place the long-term strategy of attrition that would eventually lead to victory. He authorised the Tet Offensive and began the Paris talks that were the outcome of this public-relations disaster for the US government.

Ho Chi Minh did not live to see the fruits of his efforts, dying in September 1969. His death was greeted with shock by his people and his successes as leader created a cult around him.

End of unit activities

1 Draw a spider diagram to compare the two sides in the First Indochina War, showing the disadvantages facing the French and the advantages of the Viet Minh. Include information on military strength, tactics, allies and foreign aid, support from the Vietnamese people, political factors, and any other consoderations that you think are relevant.

2 Draw up a table to contrast the two Vietnamese states in the period after the Geneva Conference of 1954. Use the table below as an example, and add any other categories that you think are necessary.

	South Vietnam	North Vietnam
Problems facing the country		
Economic situation		
Political structure		
Quality of leadership		
Foreign Aid		

3 In 1960, opponents of Diem formed the National Liberation Front (NLF), the armed wing of which was the Viet Cong. Read about the NLF on at least two of the websites listed below, and make notes to answer these questions:

- How did the NLF try to win over the peasants?
- How did the Viet Cong operate?
- Why were they able to resist US forces?

http://www.spartacus.schoolnet.co.uk/VNnlf.htm
http://www.historylearningsite.co.uk/national_liberation_front.htm
http://www.pbs.org/battlefieldvietnam/guerrilla/index.html

4 'North Vietnam won the war because the government in the South was seen as an unpopular regime propped up by the US.'

Divide into two groups. One group should work out an argument in support of this statement; the other group should work out an argument to oppose it.

5 Use the information in this chapter, from books and from the internet to find out about the impact of the war on the people and environment of Vietnam.

6 It is 1969. The Paris peace talks have started and there are signs that the new Nixon administration will soon begin to scale down American involvement in Vietnam. Imagine that you are a journalist working in North Vietnam. Prepare a list of questions that you would have liked to ask Ho Chi Minh about his political career and achievements, and compose the answers that you think he may have given.

Activity

Read this unit again. Why do you think historians have come up with such radically different interpretations of the impact of the media on the war in Vietnam?

3 The formation of and challenges to post-colonial Vietnam

Timeline

1976 establishment of a united Socialist Republic of Vietnam

1978 Vietnamese forces invade Kampuchea/Cambodia and topple Pol Pot's Khmer Rouge regime

1979 clashes between communist Vietnam and China

1986 start of the economic policy of *Doi Moi* (or 'reconstruction')

1993 US grants diplomatic recognition to Vietnam

1994 US ends trade embargo against Vietnam

1995 Washington reopens diplomatic relations with Vietnam

Key question

- What form did Vietnam take after independence, and what challenges did it face?

Overview

- After 1975, Vietnam attempted to reconstruct its economy, which had been badly damaged by the war, using the USSR as a model. This was at best only partly successful.
- The social impact of the North's victory took its toll on the South and further restricted economic activity. As a reaction, thousands of Vietnamese fled the country in small boats, many of them dying in the attempt.
- Vietnam emerged as a genuinely independent state; it was not a satellite of the USSR and was prepared in 1979 to defend its frontiers successfully against a much more powerful China.
- The situation in post-war Indochina was desperate, partly because of the social and economic dislocation caused by the war and partly due to ill-conceived policies by the communist successor regimes in the region.
- By 1990, Vietnam had begun to introduce economic reforms and to intervene in the politics of its neighbours.
- By the later 20th century, the region was beginning to recover.

What form did Vietnam take after independence, and what challenges did it face?

After 1975, Vietnam proved to be independent of its backers, especially China. In fact, in 1978, Vietnam invaded Kampuchea (Cambodia) and overthrew the tyrannical government of the Khmer Rouge leader Pol Pot, who had aligned himself with the Chinese communist regime. This increased the traditional historical tensions between Vietnam and China, and in 1979 there was a series of major clashes along the Sino–Vietnamese border, as the newly created united Vietnam successfully repelled Chinese incursions into its territory. Thus, Vietnam did not become a puppet of the larger communist states as American strategists had feared throughout the 1950s. A US trade embargo on the new communist state, however, made recovery from the war slow and difficult. It is only now that Vietnam is beginning to prosper.

The cost of the war for all sides was enormous. Fifty-eight thousand US soldiers were killed or missing and 300,000 sustained wounds. In South Vietnam, 220,000 soldiers were killed, and over 5000 of America's allies, from Thailand, South Korea, Australia and New Zealand, were also dead. The North Vietnamese suffered appallingly, with up to a million military dead (NVA and VC). The combined total of Vietnamese civilian deaths has been estimated at 400,000, and it is believed that over a million South Vietnamese civilians were injured between 1964 and 1975. In Cambodia, between 500,000 and a million died. Economically, the US spent $150 billion and this commitment of resources was one of the main contributing factors in the worldwide recession of the 1970s.

Question

Were earlier US fears about Vietnam becoming a puppet of the USSR or China borne out after 1975?

Post-war Vietnam

Post-war Vietnam was in ruins. The war had taken its toll on the population and had shattered the economy of the entire country. Furthermore, there were extreme political and social divisions, as the population of the South had to be incorporated into a united communist state. This was not too difficult in the countryside, but in the urban areas of the South, where the population had led a more Western lifestyle, it caused extreme social instability.

The Northern government also had problems switching to functioning as a peacetime administration. The communists had effectively been at war since 1941 and they found rebuilding the country a huge challenge. This situation was exacerbated by the USA's blockade of Vietnam and its diplomatic efforts to ensure that most of the West placed an embargo on trade with the new country.

Politically and socially, the impact of the North's victory was immediate and far-reaching. After 1975, the North imposed a single-party state and communist policies in the South, such as forced collectivisation and the expansion of heavy industry. In 1976, the whole country was renamed the Socialist Republic of Vietnam. About 80% of the population of this new state were poor peasants living in rural areas. The government was based on elected legislative and executive bodies, but the Communist Party decided who could be candidates. However, unlike many other recently unified and independent states, the North Vietnamese leadership was experienced in administration.

Many South Vietnamese who were closely associated with the previous regime had fled with the Americans. There were, however, about 300,000 individuals who were considered by the communists to be members of the bourgeoisie, and thus class enemies. These people, including civil servants, army officers and the professional classes of the South, were quickly identified and arrested. Large numbers were forcibly re-educated in camps where conditions were atrocious and beatings commonplace. By 1990, international pressure forced the regime to allow these people to emigrate. Most of them did, depriving Vietnam of the skilled people required to run a modern economy.

The secret police – known as the Cong An – helped maintain order, and kept a close watch on any potential anti-government activity. To remove colonial, imperialist and Western capitalist influences, pre-1975 art and literature were banned. All new works had to be sanctioned by the government, which insisted on pro-nationalist and pro-communist messages. The new government also controlled or supervised the new agencies, and owned the newspapers as well as the radio and television services.

As 90% of Vietnamese were from the same ethnic group, there were no significant problems with ethnic or racial minorities. However, religious groups were brought under government control, with only state-controlled churches allowed to function. The Protestant Montagnard of the central highlands (many of whom had worked with US forces) and the Hoa Hao Buddhists in the South protested about persecution and the seizure of their lands.

The most visible expression of the social backlash against the North's victory was the 'boat people'. Social and economic conditions in Vietnam became so bad that between 1975 and 1990 over a million people attempted to leave the country in small boats. The number of boats used for this mass exodus was so large that it had an impact on the country's fishing economy. Many of the 'boat people' died in their attempt to leave their homeland. Others ended up in Australia, New Zealand or the USA. In 1990, Vietnam agreed to allow voluntary migration, and the phenomenon of the boat people stopped.

Question

What do you understand by the term 'boat people'?

Vietnam's economic problems

The country's economic problems were rooted in the damage done by the long-drawn-out war of independence, the essentially agrarian nature of the united Vietnam and the political alienation of the southern middle classes. Even the most advanced states would have found it difficult to rebuild an economy that had been so badly damaged. To overcome these problems – and to implement communist policies – the new government moved to a centralised economy. From 1975 to 1985, heavy industry was developed, and state-owned agricultural collectives were established in the countryside. The latter policy brought about

Civilians survey the wreckage of their bomb-damaged homes in Hué, South Vietnam, in 1968

the biggest changes for the peasants. Private businesses were nationalised, and the government attempted to oversee the entire war-shattered economy. As a way of recovering as quickly as possible, Vietnam joined **Comecon** and, until Mikhail Gorbachev took over as leader of the USSR in 1985, Vietnam received $3 billion a year in aid from the Soviet Union, and 4000 Soviet advisors and technicians were sent to help reconstruction.

Comecon The Council for Mutual Economic Assistance, set up in 1949 between the USSR and the Eastern European countries, as a Soviet response to the Marshall Plan. At first the terms of trade were advantageous to the USSR, but were later equalised under Nikita Khrushchev.

However, communist attempts to follow the Soviet model and create an industrialised economy had mixed results – a common experience for countries in the developing world in their immediate post-colonial phase. In particular, the economy lacked several of the raw materials and the capital and skills required to complete such an ambitious task. While the USSR provided aid to its ally, the Soviet model still proved difficult to establish in Vietnam.

In the countryside the communists attempted to repeat the collectivisation of agriculture that they had accomplished in the North, but the peasantry resisted collectivisation. The Mekong Delta was the rice basket of Indochina, and these unpopular policies prompted passive resistance by the peasants. They preferred to leave land uncultivated rather than hand over their produce to the government, and they were prepared to slaughter their own livestock for the same reason. The peasants resorted to a **black market** for their goods. The net effect of this was to cause food shortages on a massive scale.

black market Secret trading without the knowledge of the government.

These economic problems had not been so widespread when the North turned to communism, because it was essentially an agrarian society. In the South, with a more developed commercial and manufacturing base, the problems were much greater. The economy slowly ground to a halt, and shortages and hyper-inflation led to austerity measures in the early 1980s.

The leadership was divided. Reformers wanted a shift towards **market socialism** to overcome the stagnating economy, while hardliners feared that any moves towards economic liberalism would lead to the erosion of socialism. The reformers won the debate and, in 1986, a 'renovation' of the economy began. This was known as *Doi Moi*. Several of the policies were similar to those being introduced in both China and the USSR. The regime allowed small-scale private businesses to produce consumer goods, while the peasants were given a free hand in the production of food. From 1990, Vietnam's economy began to improve.

market socialism An economic system in which enterprises are owned by the state or by public co-operatives, but production and exchange of goods are determined mainly by market forces rather than by state planning.

Vietnam experienced an increase in gross domestic product (GDP) of 8% a year during the period 1990–97, while foreign investment rose by 300%. A relaxation of state control also encouraged tourism, and Vietnam now gains a substantial proportion of its income from this source. In 1993, the US granted diplomatic recognition to Vietnam, and in 1995 normalised its relations, lifting all sanctions.

Vietnam and China

For centuries, Vietnam had been under the influence of Imperial China. Although the Viet Minh had received help from China after the communist victory in 1949, Vietnamese nationalists were keen to limit Chinese influence. Conflicts with China over Cambodia, and Vietnam's alliance with the USSR, led to a three-week border war with its powerful northern neighbour in 1979. China attempted to enforce its influence in the region but its invading army was badly beaten in the jungles of northern Vietnam against a determined and experienced Vietnamese army. Although there has been no more fighting, relations remain strained.

The border war highlights several important factors relating to Vietnam's position after it achieved independence. Firstly, Vietnam was a Soviet, not a Chinese, ally. Secondly, Vietnam was so distant from the USSR that it was essentially a sovereign state, with none of the problems of satellite status experienced by the countries of Eastern Europe. Thirdly, Vietnam's historical antipathy towards China surfaced almost as soon as the war was over. The border war of 1979 shows how foolish US strategy in Vietnam had been from the start. The US had propped up the South in order to prevent the expansion of Chinese power into the region. Ironically, as soon as the US had withdrawn and Vietnam was united, China attempted to reassert its influence in the region.

Fact

Soviet aid to Vietnam after 1979 was significant. As well as military aid and technical training, the Soviet Union provided Vietnam with more economic aid than any other country and became its biggest trading partner, a role it maintained until the late 1980s.

Immediately after the 1979 war, the Soviet Union gave more training and aid to build up the Vietnamese army, but this came to an end in 1989–91 when the USSR and the Eastern European regimes collapsed. The loss of aid and trading partners caused problems for the Vietnamese economy.

Despite these issues, and after nearly 60 years of turmoil, conflict and suffering, Vietnam has developed a stable and independent government. Although it has moved towards a form of capitalist economy, it has followed China's example in attempting to keep communist political control, and the Communist Party remains the only political party in Vietnam.

End of unit activities

1 Draw up a table to summarise the challenges involved in reuniting the two Vietnams after 1975. Include sections on political, social and economic challenges.

2 Find out what you can about the 'boat people', and make notes on the following: who they were; why they were leaving Vietnam; how many people were involved; what problems they encountered; and how successful their mission was.

3 Use the information in this chapter to write notes on Vietnam's relationship with China, the United States and Cambodia since 1975.

4 Use the information on the websites below, together with information from books and other websites, to prepare an oral presentation on Pol Pot, the Khmer Rouge and the Cambodian genocide, and to discuss its connection to the situation in Vietnam.

   http://www.edwebproject.org/sideshow/khmeryears/index.html
   http://www.time.com/time/asia/asia/magazine/1999/990823/pol_pot1.html

5 'Although American policy in Southeast Asia was designed to prevent the domino effect, American actions instead caused such an effect.'

   Prepare an argument to oppose or support this statement.

End of chapter activities

Paper 1 exam practice

Question

With reference to their origin and purpose, assess the value and limitations of Sources A and B below for historians studying the Vietnam War.
[6 marks]

Skill

Utility/reliability of sources

SOURCE A

The war in Vietnam is a new kind of war, a fact as yet poorly understood in most parts of the world. Vietnam is not another Greece, where indigenous guerrilla forces used friendly neighbouring territory as a sanctuary. Vietnam is not another Malaya, where Communist guerrillas were, for the most part, physically distinguishable from the peaceful majority they sought to control. Vietnam is not another Philippines, where Communist guerrillas were physically separated from the source of their moral and physical support. Above all, the war in Vietnam is not a spontaneous and local rebellion against the established government. ... In Vietnam a Communist government has set out deliberately to conquer a sovereign people in a neighbouring state.

A US government document describing the war in Vietnam in 1965.

SOURCE B

'I had a terrible dream of ghosts floating through the village and into our house and into my mouth and nose and I couldn't breathe. I woke up to find my father's hand over my face and his voice whispering to me to lie still.' In many ways the Vietnam War was a fight to control the countryside of South Vietnam and the loyalty of its people. Before the war most of the people in South Vietnam lived in small, rural villages and supported their families by farming. They tended to be quite poor, and few of them could read or write. They lived simple lives that emphasized the importance of family ties and cultural traditions. They did not know or care much about politics. But when the war began, the South Vietnamese peasants were caught in the middle.

A Vietnamese peasant, Le Ly Hayslip, writes about the war, 1993.

Utility/reliability questions require you to assess **two** sources over a range of possible issues/aspects – and to comment on their value to historians studying a particular event or period of history. The main areas you need to consider in relation to the sources and the information/view they provide, are:

- origin and purpose
- value and limitations.

Before you write your answer, draw a rough chart or spider diagram to show, where relevant, these various aspects. Make sure you do this for **both** sources.

Common mistakes

When asked to assess **two** sources for their value, make sure you don't just comment on **one** of the sources! Every year a few students make mistakes like this, and lose as many as 4 of the 6 marks available.

Simplified markscheme

Band		Marks
1	**Both** sources assessed, with **explicit consideration** of **BOTH** origins and purpose **AND** value and limitations.	5–6
2	**Both** sources assessed, but without consideration of **BOTH** origins and purpose **AND** value and limitations. **OR explicit consideration** of **BOTH** origins and purpose **AND** value and limitations, **BUT** only for **one** source.	3–4
3	**Limited** consideration/comments on origins and purpose **OR** value and limitations. Possibly only one/ the wrong source(s) addressed.	0–2

Student answer

One problem or limitation of Source A is that it is a US government document, so it might be biased – though this would depend on whether it was intended for publication (in which case it might be propaganda); or whether it was an internal document, which would be likely to be more reliable. Although the fact that it says the war in South Vietnam is not a local rebellion makes it more doubtful. However, even if it is propaganda, it is useful as an example of how the US tried to 'sell' its involvement. If it were an internal document, it would be useful for historians to know how the policymakers were thinking – even if they were wrong.

Examiner's comments

This is good assessment of Source A, referring explicitly to both origin and possible purpose and to value and limitations. The comments are valid and are clearly linked to the question. The candidate has thus done enough to get into Band 2, and so be awarded 3 or possibly 4 marks. However, as there are no comments about Source B, this answer fails to get into Band 1.

Activity

Look again at the two sources, the simplified markscheme, and the student answer. Now try to write a paragraph or two to push the answer up into Band 1, and so obtain the full 6 marks. As well as assessing Source B, try to make a linking comment to show value – e.g., do the two sources provide similar information?

Summary activity

Copy the spider diagram opposite and, using the information in this chapter, make brief point form notes under each heading.

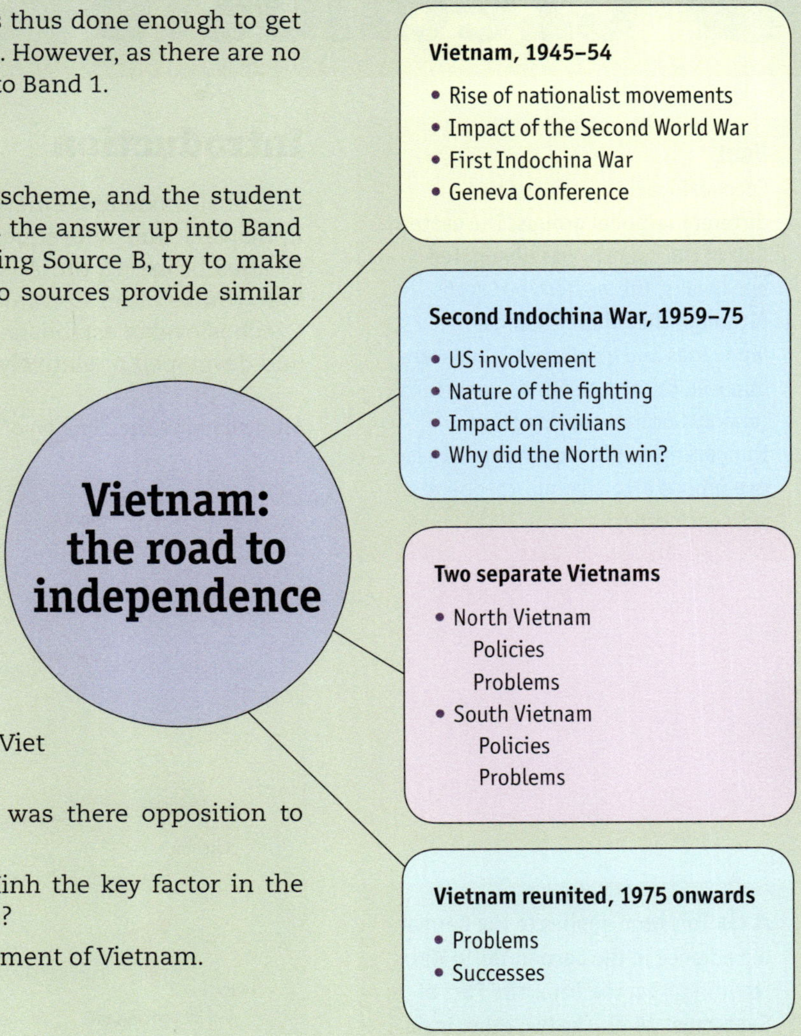

Practice Paper 2 questions

1. Assess the successes and failures of either/or North or South Vietnam.
2. Analyse the emergence and development of the Viet Minh and NLF.
3. For what reasons, and with what justification, was there opposition to colonial rule in Indochina?
4. To what extent was the leadership of Ho Chi Minh the key factor in the defeat of French colonialism in Indochina by 1955?
5. Assess the impact of the Cold War on the development of Vietnam.
6. Why did the North win the war in Vietnam?

Further reading

Try reading the relevant chapters/sections of the following books:

Anderson, David L. 2005. *The Vietnam War*. Basingstoke, UK. Palgrave Macmillan.

Duiker, William J. 2000. *Ho Chi Minh: A Life*. New York, USA. Hyperion.

Herring, George C. 2001. *America's Longest War: The United States and Vietnam, 1950–1975*. Maidenhead, UK. McGraw-Hill Higher Education.

Karnow, Stanley. 1994. *Vietnam: A History*. London, UK. Pimlico.

Kolko, Gabriel. 1985. *Anatomy of a War*. New York, USA. Pantheon.

McAlister, John T. 1970. *Viet Nam: The Origins of Revolution*. London, UK. Allen Lane.

Pike, Douglas. 1991. *Viet Cong: The Organization and Techniques of the National Liberation Front of South Vietnam*. Cambridge, USA. De Capo Press.

5 Czechoslovakia

> **Fact**
> Czechoslovakia comprised two different national groups. The eastern half of the country was dominated by Slovaks, the western by Czechs. Although they shared similar languages and ethnic ties – and were opposed to the non-Slavic minorities (mainly German-speaking and Hungarian) in Czechoslovakia – these two groups often did not co-operate with each other.

Introduction

Czechoslovakia first emerged as an independent state as a result of the political upheavals and subsequent treaties that occurred in 1919 and 1920. These treaties broke up the Austro-Hungarian Empire at the end of the First World War. Unlike other Central and Eastern European states in the 1920s and 1930s, Czechoslovakia established a democratic system along Western European lines and developed a relatively prosperous industrial economy.

Map showing the division of Europe after the treaties of 1919 and 1920

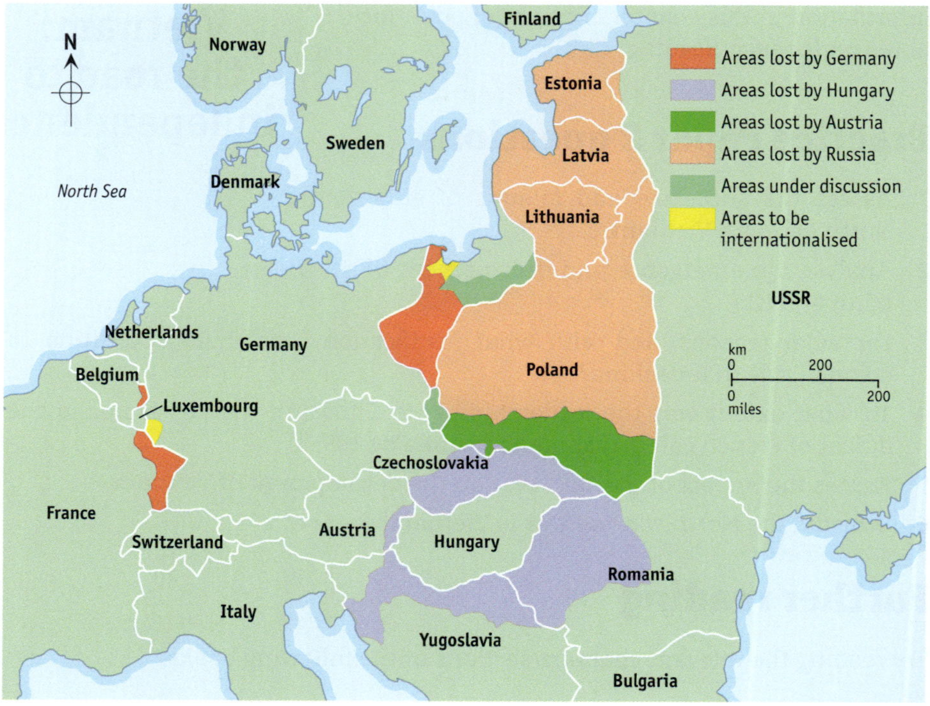

The rise of Nazi Germany in the 1930s posed a significant threat to Czechoslovakia, as a substantial minority German population lived in the Sudetenland, an area along the Czech border. In October 1938, Hitler pressured Britain and France to support German occupation of this region and, in an infamous move, the Western powers abandoned Czechoslovakia, despite the USSR's offer of military assistance to turn back the Nazi tide. In March 1939, Hitler's army occupied the rest of Czechoslovakia without any resistance from the West. The Czechs never forgot this 'betrayal'. Hitler proceeded to incorporate Bohemia, the western half of the region, into Germany and set up a pro-Nazi **Axis** satellite power in Slovakia in the east. This was a dictatorship, ruled by president Josef Tiso, an ex-Catholic priest who declared the Slovak Republic's independence from Czechoslovakia in March 1939. Tiso quickly allied Slovakia to Nazi Germany, and supported the German invasions of Poland and the USSR in the same year. In 1944, Tiso's troops helped crush the Slovak National Rising.

> **Axis** This term applies to the German-led alliance in the Second World War, resulting from the Tripartite Pact of September 1940. The two other main members of the alliance were Italy and Japan, thus it is often known as the Rome–Berlin–Tokyo Axis. Romania, Bulgaria, Hungary, Finland and Slovakia were also members of this alliance. Slovakia joined in November 1940, and declared war on Britain and the US in 1942. These actions caused tensions between the Czechs and the Slovaks.

> **Activity**
> Find out what happened at the Munich Conference in 1938. Why did many Czechs believe that they had been betrayed or even sacrificed by Britain and France?

Eastern Europe in the Second World War; Slovakia was a state set up by the Nazis after their invasion of Czechoslovakia

Czechoslovakia's former president, Edvard Beneš, established a government in exile in London, which was formally recognised by the Soviet leader Joseph Stalin in 1943. Czechoslovakia was liberated at the end of the Second World War, largely by Soviet Red Army troops. Following the Yalta agreements in 1945, the US withdrew from the small area in the west that it had occupied – and Czechoslovakia soon fell firmly into the communist bloc.

Once within that sphere of influence, Czech independence movements and political organisations at odds with the Soviet view of communism found it very difficult to survive, let alone make progress. With the strength of the **Warsaw Pact** behind it, the USSR could impose its political will on states within the communist bloc by the use of armed force if necessary. The events of the Cold War also meant that Czechoslovakia was isolated from any Western aid. Thus, without radical changes in the USSR, Czechoslovakia had little hope of following an independent course in its own affairs.

Warsaw Pact The Soviet-led military alliance established to counter the West's NATO. It was founded in 1955 and dominated Eastern Europe until the collapse of the USSR in 1991.

As the Cold War developed, Stalin established pro-Soviet communist regimes throughout Eastern Europe. Although there were common patterns of economic and social development within each of the communist states under Soviet influence, aspects of Czechoslovakia's political and economic background eventually brought it into conflict with the USSR. In 1968, attempts to liberalise the communist regime in Czechoslovakia resulted in an armed invasion by Warsaw Pact forces.

Throughout the 1970s and 1980s, Czechoslovakia's internal economic development continued but, fearing Soviet intervention, the government firmly maintained the communists' political position. In the later 1980s, the country was caught up in the general crisis engulfing the entire communist bloc, and in 1990 it emerged from the communist era as an independent state.

1 The origins and growth of movements challenging Soviet and centralised control of Czechoslovakia

Timeline

1919 Treaty of Versailles establishes an independent Czechoslovakia

1935 Edvard Beneš becomes prime minister

1938 Hitler occupies the Sudetenland after Munich agreement is signed

1945 Beneš becomes president of post-war Czechoslovakia

1948 Berlin Blockade

1949 Comecon established

1953 death of Stalin; currency reform in Czechoslovakia causes a rise in food prices resulting in strikes; rising in East Germany suppressed by the Red Army

1956 uprisings in Hungary and Poland suppressed by the Red Army

1957 Antonín Novotný becomes president of Czechoslovakia

Historical debate

Some historians see the motive for the extension of Soviet control into Eastern Europe as deeply rooted in Bolshevik ideology as a way of spreading communism. Others accept the genuine security concerns of the USSR, based on the belief that the capitalist imperialist states of the West would seek to overthrow the communist state in Russia.

Key questions

- How did the USSR begin to establish control over Czechoslovakia?
- What factors influenced the growth of movements that challenged Soviet control?

Overview

- After 1945, a pro-Soviet communist state was established in Czechoslovakia.
- The initial communist state was built very much along Stalinist lines and mirrored the structure of the USSR. As a result, the early communist state of Czechoslovakia was extremely repressive.
- The society and economy of this state was highly centralised, once again along Soviet lines.
- Stalin's death in 1953 resulted in changes to Czechoslovakia's economy and society, as it did elsewhere in the communist bloc.
- In 1957, a new form of communism was established, based on the principles of market socialism, and Czechoslovakia experienced a period of growth and prosperity.
- Under Antonín Novotný, a balance was reached between economic development and the supremacy of the Communist Party in everyday life.

How did the USSR begin to establish control over Czechoslovakia?

All of Eastern Europe fell into the Soviet sphere of influence at the end of the Second World War. The continent was divided in two roughly along the line of the River Elbe (which runs through Czechoslovakia and Germany to the North Sea), with the Red Army occupying the eastern half. For reasons of ideology and security, Stalin was determined that Eastern Europe should be placed firmly under Soviet influence.

Russia had been invaded many times by Western states. Between 1918 and 1922, a series of military interventions were staged by the USA, Britain, France and Japan to support forces fighting against the Red Army during and immediately after the Russian Civil War. Poland invaded in 1920–21. Added to these were the German invasions of 1914 and 1941. All this suggested to Stalin that the USSR's security was under long-term threat. In 1945, therefore, he decided to create a series of satellite states (countries that, although technically independent, are heavily reliant on a more powerful state), which would effectively push Russia's sphere of influence so far to the west that the country would be protected from future invasions. Stalin did not actually absorb these states into the USSR – he wanted Eastern

SOURCE A

Comments by the Czech historian Z. A. B. Zeman on the events of 1968.

Twice in this century the Russians have had to face an onslaught from the centre of Europe. Only they know the extent of their losses in the last war [the Second World War] ... and the country is still governed by the men who fought in it. The Russians have no intention of dismantling their defences to the west.

Quoted in Fisher, P. 1985. The Great Power Conflict After 1945. *London, UK. Basil Blackwell. p. 40.*

Europe to act as a buffer zone. Simply extending the Soviet border westwards would increase, not decrease, the vulnerability of the USSR. In addition, the states of Eastern Europe had far higher living standards than the USSR and their full incorporation into the Soviet state might cause internal political instability.

That these satellite states should have communist regimes that mimicked the USSR's was entirely logical given the political context of the emerging Cold War. The problem was that the Soviet-style regimes were highly authoritarian, and many people living within the new sphere of influence opposed their imposition. The power of the USSR in 1945, however, made resistance to Stalin's policy futile, as the populations of Eastern Europe had been weakened by the social and economic impact of the Second World War.

The post-war years, 1945–53

The first president of post-war Czechoslovakia was **Edvard Beneš** of the Czech National Social Party. In October 1945, the National Assembly unanimously confirmed him as president, even though no elections had been held. Stalin ordered the leader of the Czechoslovakian Communist Party, Klement Gottwald, to co-operate in a National Front coalition, and the communists secured control of important ministries, including the police and the military. In May 1946, the first post-war elections saw the communists emerge as the largest party, winning 38% of the vote in a free election. Gottwald became prime minister of a new coalition. By then, however, emerging Cold War tensions led Stalin to order him to increase communist control. Because Czechoslovakia was relatively developed and prosperous compared to the rest of Eastern Europe, a 'class war' against the rich resulted in a redistribution of wealth, which was supported by most of the population. However, Czechoslovakia's limited independence – and Stalin's determination to control the USSR's satellites – was demonstrated when the USSR stopped Gottwald applying for **Marshall Aid.**

Until 1948, Beneš led a government that was left-leaning and friendly towards the USSR, but which also displayed many Western values. However, non-communists were increasingly victimised. Václav Nosek, the communist minister of the interior, dismissed eight police inspectors in the capital, Prague, in an attempt to remove non-communists from the police force. The cabinet voted to reverse his decision. However, these events prompted anti-government riots by students in Prague and, in February 1948, a Soviet-supported coup was carried out. Beneš resigned in June of that year. New elections were held – with no opposition parties – and Gottwald became the new president.

Edvard Beneš (1884–1948)
Beneš was a key player in the Czechoslovakian independence movement, and became the country's first foreign minister in 1919. He represented his country in most of the key international conferences in the 1920s and early 1930s. He became president in 1935, but spent the Second World War in London, leading the Czechoslovakian government in exile. Beneš was a socialist and on friendly terms with Stalin. For example, he signed a co-operation agreement between his country and the USSR in 1943.

Marshall Aid A post-war initiative by the USA to refinance and economically reconstruct Europe. Historians debate the USA's motives in giving Marshall Aid. On the face of it, the Marshall Plan was an altruistic act by the USA to rebuild the economies of the West. However, the government in Moscow – and many historians since then – interpreted the move as an attempt to establish US economic control in the region.

Question

Why was the USSR keen to establish satellite states in countries such as Czechoslovakia after 1945?

Josip Tito (1892–1980) Tito (real name Josip Broz) emerged as a communist resistance fighter in German-occupied Yugoslavia. His partisans had liberated the country by themselves as the Nazi empire collapsed at the end of the Second World War. Tito was therefore not beholden to the USSR, and sought to maintain an independent stance for Yugoslavia in international affairs.

The reasons for the coup in February 1948 were fourfold:

1 Stalin was paranoid about the possibility of the collapse of Soviet control of Eastern Europe.
2 Domestic national tensions within Czechoslovakia seemed to be pushing the country towards civil war.
3 A situation was developing in Yugoslavia, where the socialist leader **Josip Tito** was distancing himself from the USSR.
4 In the elections held in January 1948, the communists' share of the vote dropped to 25%.

Had it not been for these developments, the Soviet communists may well have found Beneš's regime acceptable.

Under Gottwald, Czechoslovakia became subservient to the USSR, and many of the characteristics of Soviet communism were introduced, including one-party rule and the replacement of private ownership by a nationalised and centrally controlled command economy (see page 150). Civil society (churches, unions and clubs) came under communist control or were closed down. The secret police and other security forces were used to intimidate and imprison opponents.

Afraid of further defections like that of Yugoslavia, in the period 1950–52 Stalin ordered a series of **purges** and **show trials**, which resulted in the execution of the leading Communist Party members Rudolf Slánský, Vladimír Clementis and Otto Šling for the crimes of 'Trotskyism' and 'Titoism'. Labour camps similar to the Soviet **gulags** were also created and, between 1948 and 1954, there were 150,000 political prisoners in Czechoslovakia.

Question

Why was Stalin's attitude towards Eastern Europe more complex than many Western politicians believed at the time?

Rudolf Slánský, secretary-general of the Czech Communist Party, at his show trial during Stalin's purges in 1952

purges A Stalinist method of social control, where large numbers of people – often innocent – were arrested, imprisoned or executed to maintain an atmosphere of terror and, hence, social control.

show trials Politically motivated public trials of opponents of a totalitarian regime. Commonly used by Stalin to remove opposition in the USSR.

gulag A prison camp, usually for political prisoners. Gulags were used to supply forced labour.

Stalin ensured control of Eastern Europe by establishing a Red Army presence and by banning any political associations between the different states. For example, Czechoslovakia considered resurrecting a pre-war mutual defence pact called the Little Entente with Yugoslavia and Romania, but this was blocked by the USSR. Each state of Eastern Europe had unilateral relations with the USSR and every other state in the region.

During the late 1940s, this arrangement came under pressure because of the increasingly independent stance taken by Tito's socialist Yugoslavia as well as events in the Cold War, especially the Berlin Blockade of 1948. In 1949, Stalin established Comecon, an economic organisation designed to balance the USA's Marshall Plan, which had been set up to aid the reconstruction of Western Europe. Czechoslovakia was one of Comecon's founding members, and the organisation bound the whole of communist Eastern Europe politically and economically to the USSR. In 1955, Czechoslovakia entered into the full military alliance of the Warsaw Pact with the USSR and the other states of Eastern Europe.

Fact

In response to the West's formation of Trizonia (the division of post-war Germany into American, British and French zones) and the introduction of a new currency for their regions of Germany, which he saw as the first moves in reviving an anti-Soviet Germany, Stalin imposed a blockade. Lasting from 1948 to 1949, this cut off West Berlin from the outside world. The Western powers supplied the city successfully by air, causing the Soviet leader to back down.

Reasons for communist takeover

Although Czechoslovakia had a democratic tradition, this only lasted 20 years (1919–39). Beneš and his government had attempted to maintain strong links with the West, but they also recognised the need for a strong Soviet influence in Central Europe. These politicians had experienced the dangers of a powerful Germany in 1938, and were always conscious of the fact that they had been abandoned by the Western powers at that time. They saw the USSR as a protector against a potentially resurgent Germany. In addition to this, Beneš was not prepared to act unconstitutionally against the communists.

By 1949, the political, social and economic structures of Czechoslovakia were all copies of the Soviet model. Communist rule was based on the concept of 'democratic centralism' – once decisions had been made by the central authorities, they were not to be questioned by local officials. The Communist Party was at the centre of political life; it had a rigid hierarchy with locally elected officials in places of work or districts. Large elements of the population were party members – 45% in Czechoslovakia by 1978 – and the party played a central role in all aspects of life, from education to the availability of luxury consumer goods such as cars. This gave ordinary people a stake in the system. The Communist Party also maintained internal security organisations to ensure social discipline. In Czechoslovakia this took the form of the secret police organisation known as the StB. By 1968, 100,000 key posts in Czechoslovakia were reserved for those deemed trustworthy by the state.

Question

How appropriate is the term 'democratic centralism' to describe the political system in Czechoslovakia?

What factors influenced the growth of movements that challenged Soviet control?

De-Stalinisation and its impact on Czechoslovakia

Stalin died on 5 March 1953. His method of maintaining dominance had been based on the use of terror, and his death heralded a radical change in the USSR's political and social policy. The Soviet Union's **Politburo** was now controlled by a group that favoured a 'New Course', which relied less on fear and more on liberalisation and the production of consumer goods for Soviet citizens. Following the 'secret speech' in 1956, in which the new Soviet leader, Nikita Khrushchev, attacked Stalin, there were also attempts at de-Stalinisation in the rest of the Eastern bloc. However, whilst these developments were taking place, new problems were emerging in several of those Eastern European states.

Politburo Short for 'Political Bureau', this was the top political decision-making organisation in the USSR and the Eastern European states.

Question

Does the fact that the writer of Source B was living in West Germany make it more or less valuable to a historian studying this period?

SOURCE B

An account in a German newspaper of events in 1953 by a Czech writer living in West Germany.

Communist economic policy had resulted in an unprecedented economic decline and an increasing impoverishment of the population. The workers became increasingly dissatisfied. Faced with a pressing food shortage caused by the collectivisation of agriculture, there was an increasing refusal to work. Gottwald's successor knew no other remedy than a drastic currency reform, which destroyed people's savings. This fuelled the explosive atmosphere among the workers.

Quoted on http://www.zeit.de/2003/22/S_86_Vorspann_Pilsen?page=1

Antonín Novotný (1904–75)
Novotný was general secretary of the Communist Party of Czechoslovakia from 1953 to 1968, and president of Czechoslovakia from 1957 to 1969. By nature a conservative, he sought to maintain party control over all aspects of society, even in the face of mounting pressure for reform resulting from economic developments. (See also pages 150–51.)

Gottwald died just a few days after Stalin. He was succeeded as first party secretary by **Antonín Novotný**. In May 1953, the Czechoslovakian government announced a currency reform, and almost immediately food prices rose by 12%. Widespread demonstrations followed, the most serious of which took place at the Skoda plant at Pilsen, where 20,000 workers went on strike. The strikers attacked communist officials, as well as lynching several secret-service informers. In June 1953, a serious uprising took place in East Germany, which had to be suppressed by the Red Army.

Question

Why did de-Stalinisation have a limited impact in Czechoslovakia?

Activity

Research the causes and results of the uprisings in Poland and Hungary in 1956.

Khrushchev encouraged the satellite states of Eastern Europe to follow the USSR's lead in diversifying and decentralising economic activity, and relaxing social control. The motive for this change was twofold – to provide a more stable political atmosphere and to reform economic structures in the hope of achieving genuine growth. To encourage these reforms, Comecon assumed a much more active role. Czechoslovakia was well placed to take advantage of these changes. The country was one of the most industrially advanced regions of the Soviet bloc and reacted positively to the relaxation of social control. Furthermore, the population was not as anti-Russian as some other parts of Eastern Europe, partly because of the Western abandonment of the country at Munich (see page 143), and partly because it believed that alliance with the USSR offered protection against any new threat from Germany. Thus, whilst de-Stalinisation caused instability and uprisings in Poland and Hungary in 1956, Czechoslovakia remained relatively stable.

Gustáv Husák (1913–91)
Husák was president and secretary of the Communist Party of Czechoslovakia from 1969 to 1987. He was a victim of the purges of 1950–52, and spent a long period in prison before being rehabilitated in 1963. He became deputy secretary during Alexander Dubček's brief reign as Czech leader (1968–69), but then supported the ending of Dubček's reforms. After 1968, he initiated a process known as 'normalisation', by which communist authority was restored after the events of the Prague Spring (see page 155).

Czechoslovakia's economy in the 1950s

In 1951, wages stood at 86.6% of their 1937 level, and poverty and food shortages were a common experience for the Czechoslovakian population. At first, the communists attempted to control these problems by repression, instigating show trials such as that of **Gustáv Husák**.

However, during the 1950s, Czechoslovakia experienced a period of economic growth, as the state instigated a series of five-year plans. These were assisted by limited aid from Czechoslovakia's communist partners, co-ordinated by Comecon. The plans included changes to working conditions. Although it was still illegal to leave a job, and stringent measures were put in place to counter absenteeism, the new initiative did at least outline more realistic production targets. The five-year plans were initially successful and their introduction created a burst of economic activity that sustained Czechoslovakia until the late 1950s. The rural economy was reorganised into groups of farms known as collectives, and the different areas of agricultural production were brought together into large enterprises called combines, which were owned and run by the state. By 1956, 80% of Czechoslovakia's rural population were either members of collective farms or employed by state-controlled combines. There was also a certain amount of private industry, and from 1954 onwards the production of consumer goods slowly rose in Czechoslovakia.

Historical debate

Geoffrey Swain has argued that the agricultural changes in Czechoslovakia were not as radical as those imposed on the Soviet Union, and were a mixture of collectivisation and recognition of traditional farming practices. This was an effective combination, mixing large-scale agricultural production with a small-scale area of economic activity which in many ways presaged market socialism.

Although Antonín Novotný continued using Stalinist methods of political control, the relative prosperity of Czechoslovakia after 1953 meant there was no widespread discontent with general living standards. As a result, Novotný's government faced little pressure for political concessions or liberalisation. In the late 1950s, when economic problems began to emerge, there was a purge of economists instead of reform – violence in Hungary against leading communists in 1956 meant that the Czech leaders were keen to prevent reforms.

Market socialism

In 1957, the president of Czechoslovakia, Antonín Zápotocký, died and was replaced by Antonín Novotný. Novotný reluctantly introduced limited social and political reform to Czechoslovakia. In the economic sphere, a radical reform called 'market socialism' (see page 150) was introduced. However, Novotný was unable to reform the economy without the introduction of equal social and political changes.

A worker in a steelworks near Prague in the 1960s

command economies Economic systems that are entirely controlled by a central govenment. In a command economy, the state makes all the decisions about the production and distribution of goods and materials in every economic sector.

market socialism An economic system in which enterprises are owned by the state or by public co-operatives, but production and exchange of goods are determined mainly by market forces rather than by state planning.

Until the 1960s, communist economies had been **command economies** – with industry and agriculture controlled and directed from the centre. Central planning agencies determined the economic needs of the state, and organised labour and resources to meet these needs. This system had transformed the USSR from a backward agrarian state into a major industrial power. There were, however, weaknesses in the centralised system. In peacetime and in economies with established industrial bases – such as in Czechoslovakia – centralised economic decision-making was often inefficient and did not accurately assess the needs of the population.

The shift towards **market socialism** was designed to address the weaknesses of the centralised system. The key sectors of the economy – energy production, heavy industry, and so on – would remain under the central planning system. However, there would be more diversification in other parts of the structure, especially light industry and those parts of the economy concerned with the production of consumer goods. Market socialism was intended to provide economic development without fundamentally undermining Marxist ideology, which would be protected by the power of the Communist Party. Czechoslovakia was well placed to take advantage of these changes.

However, there were some disadvantages to the introduction of market socialism. Firstly, the system greatly empowered local managers, who were allowed to set wage levels and hire and fire at will. Secondly, the economic changes were not accompanied by political and social reforms, yet market socialism created a middle class that wanted access to political as well as economic power. In 1965, therefore, a programme of further reforms was initiated. The command economy was modified by limited market reorganisation so that consumers could have more influence on economic activity. Enterprises were grouped together into trusts, which were given greater independence from central control. Factory owners were allowed to assess their own needs and acquire their own natural resources. They were also allowed to keep profits, and these could be shared amongst the workforce or reinvested. Private enterprise was permitted in some parts of the service sector, but other areas of the economy remained centrally controlled.

Antonín Novotný

Comintern An international organisation founded in Moscow in 1919 and controlled by the USSR. Its function was to encourage and support communist revolution anywhere in the world.

When Novotný became president in 1957 his reputation as a hardline Stalinist caused the reformers within the Czechoslovakian Communist Party to view him with some suspicion. Novotný had been a member of the Communist Party since 1921 and had worked for **Comintern**.

Novotný served as first secretary of the Czechoslovakian Communist Party from 1951 (with a short break in 1953), and clashed with Gottwald's successor, Antonín Zápotocký, who wanted to take advantage of Khrushchev's accession to power and introduce reform to Czechoslovakia. From late 1953, Novotný was effectively the leader of the state. Despite Khrushchev's lead, Novotný continued with Stalinist-style state control. He even developed a cult of personality, although his uncharismatic and unimaginative character did not fit him for such a role.

One of the key areas in which Novotný resisted change was in rehabilitating those who had been 'purged' during the period of the establishment of communism in Czechoslovakia. Novotný had been deeply implicated in these purges – which had fallen heavily on the Slovakian part of the population – and could not distance himself from these events without causing serious political damage. Furthermore, he felt that relaxing the party's grip on society would cause a serious nationalist backlash amongst the Slovakian part of the population, and that this might even lead to civil war. There were certainly changes – pressure from Khrushchev was difficult to resist – but Novotný did the minimum to keep on the right side of the Soviet leader.

Questions

What is a 'personality cult'? Apart from Stalin, which other historical figures developed such a cult? Which modern leaders have tried to do a similar thing?

End of unit activities

1 Go to this website: http://www.history.com/this-day-in-history/communists-take-power-in-czechoslovakia. Read this account of the communist takeover in Czechoslovakia in 1948. Use this information, together with information from other sources, to explain the Western reaction to these events.

2 To what extent is it fair or accurate to blame Beneš for the collapse of democracy in Czechoslovakia in 1948?

3 Draw a spider diagram to illustrate how the system of market socialism operated in Czechoslovakia.

4 Find out what you can about the purges in Czechoslovakia in the 1950s.

5 Draw a table to summarise the achievement and failures of each of the Czech leaders between 1945 and 1968. You could use the table below as a template.

Leader	Dates in office	Achievements	Failures/shortcomings
Beneš			
Gottwald			
Zápotocký			
Novotný			

Theory of knowledge

History and perspective

Why is it important to take into account different perspectives when studying historical events? How would Soviet and Western views differ in their assessment of the situation in post-war Czechoslovakia?

2 Methods of achieving independence from Soviet and centralised control

Timeline

1961 Khrushchev denounces Stalin for a second time

1962 Czechoslovakian economy enters a period of crisis

1963 Alexander Dubček made first secretary

1967 Czechoslovakian intellectuals openly criticise Communist Party; student protests break out in Prague

1968 Dubček replaces Novotný as party secretary; series of reforms published; attempts to liberalise communist regime in Czechoslovakia result in armed intervention by the USSR and Warsaw Pact; Dubček replaced by Husák

1969 Novotný resigns as president and is replaced by Svoboda

1975 Gustáv Husák becomes president

1979 Soviets invade Afghanistan

1985 Mikhail Gorbachev becomes leader of USSR

1987 Milouš Jakeš replaces Husák as first secretary of the Czechoslovakian Communist Party

1989 demonstrations in Prague; Václav Havel elected president of Czechoslovakia

Fact

The problems in Czechoslovakian industry are demonstrated by the fact that in 1963, Thursday was designated 'meatless' because of problems co-ordinating agricultural production.

Key questions

- What were the main challenges to Soviet/centralised control?
- What role was played by Alexander Dubček and the events of 1968?
- What brought about the end of Soviet control after 1968?
- Why did Eastern European states last so long?

Overview

- From 1960 onwards, opposition to the Communist Party developed as a result of the introduction of market socialism to Czechoslovakia.
- In 1962, Czechoslovakia entered a period of crisis, demonstrating that whilst there was economic expansion there tended to be social instability.
- Throughout the 1960s, Czechoslovakian intellectuals and others began to openly question the socialist model in their country.
- In 1967, students began to agitate for reform. This led to the election of the reformist Alexander Dubček.
- Dubček's policies allowed a brief liberalisation of politics in Czechoslovakia. However, this alarmed his allies within the Warsaw Pact and the USSR.
- In 1968, Soviet and Warsaw Pact troops invaded Czechoslovakia and the power of the Communist Party was restored.
- Despite 'normalisation' and a 'social contract' under Gustáv Husák, by the 1980s the Czech economy had begun to stagnate.
- Opposition reappeared – often influenced by the comments and policies of Mikhail Gorbachev in the USSR after 1985.

What were the main challenges to Soviet/centralised control?

Czechoslovakian social and economic changes from 1962

Before 1962, efforts were made to push up wages in Czechoslovakia, especially those of male skilled workers. This created an élite within the working population – for example, miners earned 150% more than the average industrial worker. This élite resisted change, and there was little incentive to meet the upper targets set by the five-year plans. As a result, by the early 1960s production began to tail off radically. This seriously hindered the country's capacity to trade, and prevented the development of export markets. Production and supply within the Czechoslovakian economy was also seriously out of balance by the early 1960s. This created a situation in which parts of the industrial complex were standing idle due to a lack of raw materials.

In 1962, economic growth was 6.7%, compared to the 9.4% that had been predicted as part of the existing five-year plan. By August of the same year, the situation was so serious that the plan was abandoned and replaced with a new seven-year plan. This measure proved totally ineffective, and in 1963 there was virtually no growth at all in the Czechoslovakian economy.

In addition to this, the communists recognised that Czechoslovakia was economically worse off than Poland and Hungary, which were both poorer than Czechoslovakia in the inter-war period. The winter of 1962–63 was particularly bad, as resources were being diverted to support the crisis in Cuba.

Problems elsewhere in the communist bloc were affecting the Czechoslovakian economy: the breakdown in Sino–Soviet relations had severely disrupted trade with China. The USSR was facing problems of its own, and was unable to provide support in the form of industrial plant (especially railway equipment), food or finances. By 1963, these problems were so apparent that a reformist political rival to Novotný, the Slovak **Alexander Dubček**, was made first secretary of the Slovakian branch of the Czechoslovakian Communist Party. Dubček urged economic and political reform. Although Novotný resisted, he was unable to gather much support, in part because he was a Czech who had been antagonistic towards the Slovaks. Support for Dubček, particularly in the Slovakian parts of the country, forced Novotný to make some limited reforms.

Under the system of market socialism factories no longer received subsidies, and, in 1966 alone, 1300 factories closed. The reforms also shifted the balance of power within the workplace, as managers were able to benefit disproportionately from profits made from the reforms. This challenged some of the basic tenets of communism – often referred to as 'workerism' – that had developed during the 1950s.

Limited changes were also taking place in social policies. Education was reformed, and gymnasia (upper secondary schools) were reintroduced for those wishing to study at university. The humanities were also given more prominence in the curriculum. Censorship was relaxed, news reporting became more balanced and American television programmes were aired. It was now possible to challenge censorship in the courts. Restrictions on religious practice were also relaxed and Czechoslovakians could travel outside the communist bloc with greater ease.

Despite these changes, reformers grew increasingly frustrated with what they considered to be Novotný's conservative policies towards social and economic reform. As agitation for greater reform heightened, social and political tensions grew in Czechoslovakia.

Political reform

Political reform also slowly took place. Stalin's **Marxism–Leninism** had been exported to the USSR's satellite states in the period after 1945. In Czechoslovakia, however, this model of Marxism was less convincing.

The biggest problem was the existence of different interest groups within Czechoslovakian society. Due to the 'workerism' developed during the Novotný period (see above), a working-class élite had been created. With the development of market socialism, a managerial group had been added to the social structure. Czechoslovakia also had a large body of intellectuals and students – both important interest groups. The state, therefore, had to introduce measures and reforms that would meet the aspirations of all these groups.

Fact

Cuba had become a Soviet ally soon after the revolution of 1959, and later became a communist state. The Cuban Missile Crisis of 1962 drew it even closer to the USSR. The Soviets gave disproportionate amounts of aid to Cuba because it was the only communist state in the Americas, and an obvious propaganda victory for the Eastern bloc.

Alexander Dubček (b. 1921)

Dubček was briefly leader of Czechoslovakia, between 1967 and 1968. He was a reformist who may have lost control of events in his country when many Czechs, responding to his policies during the Prague Spring (see page 155), pushed for even more far-reaching reforms, and thus perhaps triggered the subsequent Warsaw Pact invasion of 1968.

Question

What were the advantages and disadvantages of the economic reforms that were introduced in Czechoslovakia in the 1960s?

Marxism–Leninism Under classic Marxism, human societies move through a series of phases until they enter a final, classless communist phase, in which the means of production are socially – not privately – owned. However, tsarist Russia had clearly not entered its advanced capitalist phase by 1917. Lenin thus modified classic Marxism and argued that the party, led by a revolutionary élite – in Russia's case the Bolsheviks – would act as custodians of the state until Russia could make the transition to capitalism and then socialism. The concept was used by Stalin to legitimise both repression and a permanent one-party state.

Initially, the pressure for political reform was resisted by the conservative Novotný, who alarmed intellectuals by seeming to move towards more repressive methods of controlling reforms. At a writer's congress in 1967, the noted intellectual Ludvík Vaculík electrified delegates by denouncing the Czechoslovakian constitution as obsolete. In August 1967, another intellectual, Ladislav Mňačko, argued that Czechoslovakia should follow a foreign policy more independent of the USSR.

Fact
One of Novotný's supporters, General Jan Šejna, began plotting a military coup against the reformists in December 1967, but it went seriously wrong. He found little support and the plot was exposed in February the following year. That a high-ranking communist had plotted against the reforms raised a public outcry. Over 4500 letters were written demanding that Novotný be sacked from his remaining office as president. The collapse of Novotný's faction within both parliament and the party promptly followed.

Novotný also faced problems with the Slovakian part of the country. This region was not as industrialised as the western, Czech, half of Czechoslovakia. The purges of the 1950s (see page 146) had hit the Slovaks hard, and Novotný was closely associated with these actions. The Slovaks felt that the Czechs held all the power and that the balance should be redressed. Alexander Dubček openly argued with Novotný in a central committee meeting in October 1967. Thus, the Slovakian question added national tensions to the situation and created infighting within the Czechoslovakian Communist Party.

On 31 October 1967, students invited journalists to inspect the conditions in which they were forced to live in the Strahov hostel in Prague and then proceeded to march in protest at these conditions. The students were opposed by the police, who attacked with batons, water cannon and tear gas. This only encouraged more frequent and larger student demonstrations. Novotný was isolated at the top of the party, and rumours began to circulate of a planned coup by the security forces to stop Dubček's reforms.

Question
Why was there an increase in social, economic and political tensions in Czechoslovakia by the end of 1967?

On 8 December 1967, Novotný invited Leonid Brezhnev, general secretary of the Soviet Communist Party, to a central committee meeting in the hope that his presence would underpin Novotný's authority. Significantly, however, Brezhnev gave no obvious indications of support. He stated that the Czechs and Slovaks should choose their own leader – an announcement that ended Novotný's political career.

Fact
Novotný retained his role as president until March 1968, when he resigned and was replaced by Ludvík Svoboda, one of Dubček's supporters.

Eventually, on 8 January 1968, the central committee of the Czechoslovakian Communist Party removed Novotný from his position as first party secretary and replaced him with Dubček. Dubček almost immediately began to put forward his plans for reform and the establishment of what he called 'socialism with a human face'.

What role was played by Alexander Dubček and the events of 1968?

Dubček argued for wholesale reform of the country. He had been a party member since 1938, when he had joined the Slovak Communist Party. He was a pragmatic man rather than an intellectual, and he was the first Slovakian to rise to high office. He had been educated in Moscow between 1955 and 1958, and had been a classmate of Mikhail Gorbachev (see page 164).

Dubček was impressed with Khrushchev's policies and was dismayed at the failure of his fellow countrymen to follow the USSR's lead. Despite disagreements over reform policies, Dubček maintained cordial relations with Novotný, and distanced himself from Slovakian nationalists. His first act as party secretary was to travel to Moscow to show that he was still committed to socialism and the Warsaw Pact. However, his actions soon demonstrated that his reforms went far beyond anything that the powers in Moscow would tolerate.

Dubček's proposals for reform

From the start, Dubček seemed intent on introducing widespread and radical reforms. In April 1968, reformers in the Czechoslovakian Communist Party set out their proposals in the Action Programme – a plan for a fully democratic socialist state. The programme called for increased democracy, including more open debate and opinion polls, greater autonomy for Slovakia and the freedom to travel abroad. This was the beginning of what became known as the 'Prague Spring' – a short period of political liberalisation in Czechoslovakia.

It seems that Dubček initially intended to maintain the basic socialist structure of his country rather than establishing a political system along Western lines. Although economic reforms in line with market socialism were to continue, companies remained state-owned. Despite this, they were encouraged to compete and to follow the forces of supply and demand. Dubček also made it clear that alliance with the USSR would remain at the centre of Czechoslovakia's foreign policy. As he began to relax the party's hold on society, however, all the political tensions inherent in Czechoslovakian society rose to the surface. Writers and artists tested the limits of the new freedoms by openly criticising the Communist Party's past mistakes. Soon, events went beyond the party-led democracy outlined by Dubček in the Action Programme. By the summer of 1968, it appeared that Dubček was losing control of the situation in Czechoslovakia. This caused concern amongst the leaders of neighbouring Eastern European states, and both East Germany and Poland asked the USSR to intervene.

SOURCE A

The Action Program declared an end to dictatorial, sectarian, and bureaucratic ways. It said that such practices had created artificial tension in society, antagonizing different social groups, nations, and nationalities. Our new policy had to be built on democratic cooperation and confidence among social groups. Narrow professional or other interests could no longer take priority. Freedom of assembly and association, guaranteed in the constitution but not respected in the past, had to be put into practice. However, the Soviets were not happy that the program had been composed without their advice and consent.

Dubček, A. 1992. Hope Dies Last. *Tokyo, Japan. Kodansha International. p. 102.*

The Prague Spring

The impact of Dubček's proposed reforms on Czechoslovakian society was immediately apparent. Between January and April 1968, the party published its proposals, sparking an intense debate about the future political and social path that the country should follow. This included Slovakian aspirations to improve their position within the state and the national media. All aspects of Czechoslovakian society came under intense scrutiny. Groups demanded that the secret police be abolished, that all party and state officials should be accountable to the law, and that the Communist Party should disengage itself from society and allow civil groups to organise themselves as they saw fit. Dubček's reforms facilitated this debate as he lifted censorship on news organisations within Czechoslovakia.

In economic terms, the reforms took market socialism a step further. The state would now only be responsible for general economic planning and policy, although it would have a role in protecting the interests of consumers. However, the ruling party failed to deal with the difficult problems of wage regulation and price setting. These two areas were critical to differentiating between market socialism and a full market, or capitalist, economy. Thus, in some ways the economic aspects of the reforms were not as radical as they might seem. The Action Programme also called for an equalising of Czechoslovakia's economic relationship with the Soviet Union. The establishment of Soviet control in Eastern Europe after the Second World War had created a series of disadvantageous relations between the satellite states and the USSR. Now, Czechoslovakia would trade on equal terms with its ally.

Question

How appropriate is the term 'Prague Spring' for the reforms initiated by the Dubček government in 1968?

The Action Programme was also very conservative in its treatment of foreign policy – Czechoslovakia would remain a member of the Warsaw Pact and an ally of the Soviet Union. The reason for Dubček's lack of reform in this area lay with Czechoslovakia's history. In the 1930s, the country was left isolated by the West and was overrun by the Nazis. Dubček saw the Warsaw Pact as a guarantee of independence against a possible German resurgence.

Question

Why was the term 'socialism with a human face' used to describe the Prague Spring reforms under Dubček?

The most radical part of the Action Programme was the reform of civil liberties. The programme promised complete freedom of speech, debate, travel and association. Arbitrary arrest was made illegal, and the courts and security services were made accountable to parliament. Censorship effectively ceased to exist in Czechoslovakia. The role of the Communist Party in civil life was the most difficult for the reformers to address. The party did not lose its leading role in Czechoslovakian society, but its power and influence were reduced. However, this was a radical step – and a threat to Moscow's political vision for the Eastern bloc.

Historical debate

When assessing the Prague Spring reforms, historians are divided over the question of Dubček's aims and intentions. Some – such as Marie Dowling and William Shawcross – consider his hope for 'socialism with a human face' as a genuine attempt to make communism in Czechoslovakia both democratic and popular. Others have seen him as consciously attempting to undermine both Soviet control and Czechoslovakia's socialised economy.

SOURCE B

An extract from the Action Programme of the Czechoslovakian Communist Party.

Social advancement in the Czech lands and Slovakia has been carried in the twentieth century by the two strongest currents: the national movement of liberation, and socialism. ... We shall experiment, give socialist development new forms, use creative Marxist thinking and the experience of the international workers' movement, rely on the correct understanding of social development in Czechoslovakia. It is a country which bears the responsibility, before the international communist movement, for the evaluation and utilization of its relatively advanced material base, uncommonly high level of education, and undeniable democratic traditions. If we did not use such an opportunity, nobody could ever forgive us.

Quoted in Zeman, Z. A. B. 1969. Prague Spring. *Harmondsworth, UK. Penguin. p. 121.*

The reforms also addressed the Slovakian issue. A federal relationship between the Czech and Slovakian parts of the state was promised, and Slovakia was granted its own assembly in Bratislava. Furthermore, the government would be reorganised along federal lines. This met all the demands of the Slovaks and the only condition was that the reforms would not be fully instigated until Slovakia caught up economically with the Czech part of the state.

The emergence of non-communist organisations

The development of alternative political organisations to the communists swiftly followed the announcement of reforms. By mid June 1968, over a quarter of a million people had joined farmers' unions, which sprang up all over the country. They were followed by associations of former soldiers, political prisoners, artisans and even a small landowners' union. The Sokol, a youth sports movement disbanded during the First World War, was revived. The Catholic Church was also revitalised, and organisations such as the Catholic boy scouts came into being. National minorities such as the Slovaks, Hungarians, Poles and Ukrainians formed youth movements. However, the churches were never as important in Czechoslovakia as, for example, in Poland.

The students who had been instrumental in the party's change in policy left traditional communist youth organisations in droves and formed their own, more decentralised, associations. At first these groups were civic organisations, but soon potential opposition parties emerged, such as K-231, which represented the demands of ex-political prisoners to be fully 'rehabilitated'. In May 1968, KAN – Club for Committed Non-Party Members – was formed from members of the Czechoslovakian Academy of Sciences. This group put forward the views of non-communists, and agitated for greater political freedom and the right to form fully fledged political parties. One of its leading members was **Václav Havel**.

An opinion poll in 1968 showed that 90% of the population supported the demand for political parties to be allowed. The government gave in and an opposition party of sorts, the National Front, was formed. Despite this concession, the government refused to reinstate the Social Democratic Party, which had been one of the leading parties before its abolition by the communists in 1948. Its re-emergence would cause serious political opposition and Dubček decided that such a development was a step too far. The communists were also concerned that the revival of the SDP in Czechoslovakia might encourage similar developments in other Eastern bloc states, posing a threat to the internal political stability of Czechoslovakia's allies.

Economic developments

Economic developments continued. The Czechoslovakian government began to make tentative contact with capitalist organisations in the West, including the International Monetary Fund (IMF). On 17 August 1968, Dubček announced that serious consideration was being given to raising loans from Western institutions. Given earlier Soviet rejection of the Marshall Plan, it is easy to see how the USSR would view this development with considerable suspicion and fear of the extension of Western economic influence east of the **Iron Curtain**.

Certain groups of workers had benefited greatly from the development of the command economy (see page 150), and in general terms the communist system provided great security of income and jobs. The introduction of a more extreme form of market socialism changed this arrangement. Many industrial concerns went bankrupt as a result of the demands for greater efficiency. Some workers went on strike and formed workers' councils to oppose the reforms.

Discussion point

How can the reforms initiated by Dubček's government be considered a mixture of both radical and conservative elements?

Václav Havel (b. 1936) Havel was a Czech playwright and dissident. His involvement in the Prague Spring resulted in his plays being banned and his own confinement within Czechoslovakia, but he spent the 1970s and 1980s agitating for reform once more. He became the first post-communist president of Czechoslovakia. (See also pages 172–73.)

Fact

The IMF was established in 1944 with the purpose of regulating the world's money market. Its key role is to create stability and prevent economic problems like the Wall Street Crash and the Great Depression of the 1930s. Member states contribute to a pool of money that can be lent to solve economic problems in times of crisis.

Iron Curtain A term referring to the invisible border between Western and Eastern Europe after 1945. The term was used in a speech given by Winston Churchill in March 1946, at the start of the Cold War, but was first mentioned by the leading Nazi Joseph Goebbels in February 1945.

Further political developments

In June 1968, Dubček promised the establishment of a trade union congress, and hinted that the Communist Party would lose control of the appointment and promotion of military officers. In August – in preparation for a meeting of the general assembly of the Communist Party scheduled for the following month – discussions were held about how the party should be reformed. It was decided that elections would be by secret ballot, and no state or party office could be held for more than two terms. To some it seemed that the intelligentsia were taking over the party and that the welfare of the working classes would no longer be the organisation's main concern. It appeared that a democratic system was emerging, in which the party's role in civic life might be challenged. For the conservatives, all these factors were proof that the Action Programme was threatening the existence of socialism in Czechoslovakia, and of the Communist Party itself.

The figures on the left, standing next to the bust of Karl Marx, are Kosygin, the prime minister of the USSR and Brezhnev, the general secretary of the Communist Party in the Soviet Union in 1968

" Talking of censorship, Comrade Kosygin, we can't have our friends reading this inflammatory stuff."

Questions

How does the cartoonist portray Dubček as a hero? Why is Brezhnev's comment so ironic?

Soviet concerns

Although Dubček's reforms were very popular in Czechoslovakia, many had demanded even more radical change, and this seriously threatened the Communist Party's leading role. Soviet concerns about developments in Czechoslovakia had emerged as early as February 1968, when Brezhnev visited Prague and warned Dubček about moving too far too fast. In March, Dubček was summoned to Dresden in East Germany to receive the same warnings from an assembly of all of the Warsaw Pact leaders, including East German leader Walter Ulbricht, who was particularly concerned by what he considered to be the 'counter-revolutionary' events unfolding in Czechoslovakia. Dubček was offered the aid of Soviet troops should he be forced to defend the party's control of the country in the face of greater demands for reform; thus the threat of military action against the reforms came into play very early on. To lessen the tension, Dubček offered to hold the next round of Warsaw Pact military exercises on Czechoslovakian territory. Once he had made concessions to his domestic audience, however, Dubček could not be seen to cave in to Soviet threats. He was therefore forced to make further political concessions in the form of a reduction in communist influence within Czechoslovakia – a development that was not well received by the Warsaw Pact. The subsequent threat of invasion was hinted at in a document called 'Two Thousand Words', produced for a group of scientists by the radical Ludvík Vaculík.

SOURCE C

First of all we shall oppose the views, which have been expressed, that it is possible to carry out some democratic revival without the communists, or possibly against them. It would be neither just nor sensible. The communists have their organizations and it is necessary to support the progressive wing in them. They have experienced functionaries and, after all, the various buttons and levers are still under their control. But their action programme stands before the public ... and no one else has another, equally concrete programme.

Extract from Vaculík's 'Two Thousand Words'. Quoted in Zeman, Z. A. B. 1969. Prague Spring. *Harmondsworth, UK. Penguin. p. 153.*

The 'Two Thousand Words' pressed for further democratic reform, calling for all hardline and pro-Soviet communists to be forced from office. It was so radical that the leadership of the party swiftly condemned it. Once again, this act only served to increase popular pressure for reform. The Soviet reaction was to delay the withdrawal of Red Army units on manoeuvres in Czechoslovakia, further provoking the radicals. An ex-political prisoner called Eugen Loebl openly declared that the USSR had ruined Czechoslovakia's economy.

On 14 July 1968, the leaders of the USSR, Poland, Hungary, East Germany and Bulgaria met in Warsaw to discuss the situation in Czechoslovakia. This meeting resulted in the 16 July Warsaw Letter, which demanded a complete reversal of the Czechoslovakian reforms. Dubček flatly refused to comply, and appeared on television informing the Czechoslovakian people of his decision.

The situation then worsened when the Czechoslovakian chief of military affairs, General Prchlik, publicly stated that, by refusing to withdraw its troops, the Soviet Union was in contravention of the Warsaw Pact; he even went so far as to criticise the fact that the Warsaw Pact senior command was entirely in the hands of Soviet officers. It seemed that the reforms in Czechoslovakia were beginning to have an impact on the people and institutions of the Eastern bloc as a whole.

The Soviets demanded that Dubček fly to Moscow to discuss developments. When he refused, they met him at the Czechoslovakian frontier town of Čierna-nad-Tisou. During a tense meeting, the Soviets accused the Czechoslovakian leaders of throwing away all the progress that had been made since 1948. Despite this, Brezhnev eventually backed down and agreed to a further meeting in Bratislava in August, but once again the intervention of the Soviets caused a backlash amongst the Czechoslovakian radicals. They distrusted Dubček and wondered what concessions he had made to Brezhnev. Such fears resulted in even more anti-Soviet rhetoric in Czechoslovakia.

Eventually, having warned Dubček of the consequences if he persisted with his reforms, Brezhnev authorised an invasion of Czechoslovakia by Warsaw Pact troops in August 1968. He later justified this action in a statement that became known as the Brezhnev Doctrine.

A young Czech man stands in front of a Soviet tank in Bratislava, as Warsaw Pact forces invade Czechoslovakia in August 1968

The Warsaw Pact invasion

On the night of 20–21 August 1968, Warsaw Pact troops crossed the Czechoslovakian border in strength and overwhelmed a totally unprepared Czechoslovakian army and air force. It was the largest military operation since the Second World War.

SOURCE D

Yesterday, August 20, 1968, around 11:00 p.m., the armies of the Warsaw Pact crossed the borders of Czechoslovakia. This happened without the knowledge of the Czechoslovakian president or government. The government appeals to all citizens of our Republic to keep calm and not to resist the armed forces moving in. Therefore neither our army or security forces have been ordered to defend the country. The government believes that this act contradicts not only all principles of relations between socialist countries but also the basic norms of international law.

Extract from a statement issued by Dubček's government, 21 August 1968.

Activity

Compare and contrast Sources D and E about the invasion of Czechoslovakia by Warsaw Pact troops.

SOURCE E

The party and government leaders of the Czechoslovak Socialist Republic have asked the Soviet Union and other allies to give the Czechoslovak people urgent assistance, including assistance with armed forces. This request was brought about … by the threat from counter revolutionary forces … working with foreign forces hostile to socialism.

A Soviet news agency report, 21 August 1968. Quoted in Walsh, B. 2001. Modern World History. *London, UK. John Murray. p. 405.*

The Czechoslovak Communist Party immediately reaffirmed its support for the ideals of the Prague Spring, but Dubček ordered the Czech army not to resist the invasion. Doing so seemed futile against a force that deployed tanks on the streets of Prague and other cities. Despite this, many citizens decided to fight back. Unofficial radio stations made broadcasts stating that the invasion was *not* the 'fraternal assistance' for which the Czechs had asked to help them deal with 'counter-revolutionaries'.

Despite many brave acts of Czechoslovakian resistance, the invasion succeeded. About 500 people were wounded and 108 died, most of them civilians. However, opposition to the crushing of Dubček's reforms continued after August 1968. On 16 January 1969, for example, a student called Jan Palach committed suicide by burning himself to death in Prague's main square.

Activity

Study the two pictures on this page. What evidence is there to suggest that the protesters were more anti-Soviet than anti-communist?

Young Czech protesters in 1969; the posters in the background are supporting Dubček, and say: 'Socialism yes, Occupation no!'

Questions

What is the meaning of this cartoon? What sort of emotion does it hope to evoke? How can artists draw on emotion to make a political comment or to inspire people to take action?

A street cartoon showing Lenin weeping, from the time of the Warsaw Pact invasion of Czechoslovakia; cartoons like these appeared on walls and were distributed in the streets of Prague as a form of protest and resistance

The entire Czechoslovakian leadership was arrested and flown to Moscow. However, the Soviets found themselves facing a political dilemma. They had expected conservative Czechoslovakians to form a replacement government – but none was forthcoming. The Czechoslovakian Communist Party even managed to hold its 14th Congress in Prague during the invasion. It denounced the actions of the Warsaw Pact, and a poll in September 1968 showed that 94.6% of the public remained firmly behind the reforms. Eventually Brezhnev bullied Dubček and the Czechoslovakian leadership into acquiescence. They signed a document accepting the official Soviet version of the reasons for the invasion, and agreed to return home and 'normalise' relations. This meant the restoration of full communist domination of civil life.

Dubček was forced to resign in April 1969, and was expelled from the party the following year. He went on to work for the Forestry Service in Slovakia, and later played a part in the Velvet Revolution of 1989 (see page 166). He was replaced as first secretary of the Czechoslovakian Communist Party by Gustáv Husák. Although other Warsaw Pact troops withdrew, the Soviets maintained their grip on the country by establishing permanent garrisons throughout Czechosovakia. The Czechoslovakian population, however, passively resisted the re-imposition of party rule and reformist zeal lingered under the surface until the final collapse of communism in the late 1980s.

Reasons for the Soviet invasion

The Soviets genuinely feared attack from the West. The Vietnam War was at its height, and the Western-backed Israelis had recently won the Six-Day War against Russia's Arab allies. The Soviets thus feared that a coalition of Western states might seek to expand in Central Europe. They were also wary of the growth of West Germany, which had been rearmed by the West and had developed into a wealthy, economically powerful state. Czechoslovakia was the only Warsaw Pact country to share borders with both West Germany and the USSR; it was thus viewed as a potential invasion route of the Soviet motherland. Finally, there were real fears that Czechoslovakia's economic reforms would draw it into the Western camp. This was important because, like East Germany's, Czechoslovakia's economy was highly advanced by Eastern bloc standards, and it performed a key role in finishing industrial goods and producing high-technology items. The loss of the Czechoslovakian economy to the Eastern bloc in general and the USSR in particular might have far-reaching consequences.

Question

Why did the USSR crush the Prague Spring?

SOURCE F

How did the Soviets justify their actions in 1968? Firstly, they argued that there was an external threat to the Warsaw Pact countries; and, secondly, that internal counter-revolution with Western backing was seeking to trample the socialist achievements of the workers. Was there really an external threat? The fact that, in mid-1968, articles were appearing in the Czechoslovak press hinting at the possible withdrawal of the country from the Warsaw Pact reflected the attitudes of Czechoslovak political forces. In other words, it resulted from developments inside the country.

Extract from the memoirs of Mikhail Gorbachev, leader of the USSR 1985–91, commenting on events in Czechoslovakia in 1968.

The invasion had long-term consequences for the Eastern bloc, hindering the economic development that was the catalyst for political reform in these countries. It became clear that extensive economic reforms would result in political and social reforms at a level that the Soviet Union would not tolerate. Without being allowed to take these steps towards economic reform, the states of Eastern Europe began to fall behind their Western rivals.

Throughout the 1970s, in a process known as 'normalisation', the Czechoslovakian Communist Party was purged of reformers: 327,000 members were forcibly ousted and a further 150,000 left voluntarily. The intellectual class was also attacked, and more than 900 university lecturers were sacked. Censorship was restored, market socialism abandoned, and there was a return to centralised economic control. However, such actions gave rise to passive opposition outside the Communist Party, which was now viewed very much as a foreign entity. The new government had been imposed by the USSR, and failed to win popular acceptance.

Husák tried to rally support by establishing a 'social contract' with the people. Although money wages were lower than those in the West, the Czechoslovakian people were offered a greater 'social wage' in the form of basic economic security, full employment, free and universal health care, guaranteed pensions and even subsidised holidays. The amount of disposable income available to many people began to rise and, by the late 1980s, Czechoslovakia ranked second in the world for the number of people owning second homes (over 80% of Czech families had a country cottage in addition to their main home). Such improvements pacified the population to a certain degree, and police repression was not needed often.

However, the country's economic success did not eliminate the population's enthusiasm for political reform. Opposition continued from some quarters. For example, a group known as Charter 77 drew up a petition calling on the government to respect the 1975 Helsinki Agreement on Human Rights, which the group believed the government was in breach of (see Source G). Those who signed the petition were punished.

SOURCE G

Civic rights are seriously vitiated by interference in the private life of citizens by the Ministry of the Interior, for example by bugging telephones and houses, opening mail, following personal movements, searching homes, and setting up networks of neighbourhood informers.

Charter 77 is an association of people united by the will to strive for the respecting of human rights in our country and throughout the world – rights accorded to all by the Helsinki Charter.

Prague, 1 January 1977.

Extract from Charter 77's Declaration. Quoted in Cannon, M. et al. 2009. 20th Century World History. Oxford, UK. Oxford University Press. p. 427.

The events of 1968 became deeply rooted within Czechoslovakia's social consciousness. The Communist Party was by this time alienated from the masses, so when the political system in Eastern Europe began to change again in the late 1980s, the party in Czechoslovakia was viewed by the people as an obstacle that had to be removed.

What brought about the end of Soviet control after 1968?

Fact
Economic decline led to problems for the workers, and the 'social contract', established after 1968, began to be eroded. This removed a major bank of support for the Husák regime. As social mobility slowed, party membership also began to decline.

Between 1968 and the late 1980s, the situation in Czechoslovakia stagnated. The police state remained as strong as ever and the political system was highly regulated. The Czechoslovakian leader Gustáv Husák hinted at economic reform and the decentralisation of planning, but the experiences of 1968 made the communists wary of taking real steps that might weaken their grip on power. Even by December 1987, when Milouš Jakeš became general secretary of the Communist Party in Czechoslovakia, there were few hopes for change. It seemed the country would continue under conservative communist rule.

The impact of Mikhail Gorbachev

By the mid 1980s, a crisis had emerged within the Eastern bloc. In 1979, the Soviet Union invaded Afghanistan, prompting the USA to increase the financial and military support it was already giving to fundamentalist Islamist terrorist groups within the country, who now became anti-Soviet insurgents. The West decided to interpret the USSR's invasion as a change in general Soviet policy, despite the fact that the West had for a long time accepted Afghanistan as part of the Soviet sphere of influence. Thus began a second Cold War, and under US president Ronald Reagan, the USA and NATO greatly extended their military capacity. The Soviets soon realised that they could not match Western military spending, and began to seek diplomatic solutions.

Mikhail Gorbachev (b. 1931)
Gorbachev was general secretary of the Communist Party of the Soviet Union from 1985 to 1991, and the last head of state of the USSR from 1990 to 1991. He linked political and social reform with economic development, initiating policies of *glasnost* (openness), *demokratizatsiya* (democracy) and *perestroika* (economic reform and restructuring). However, he feared that swift change would create political unrest within the USSR, and attempted to develop market principles within a Soviet framework. He was unable to control the pace of reform, and this led to the collapse of communism in the USSR and Soviet withdrawal from Eastern Europe.

In order not to fall too far behind the West's military lead, the Warsaw Pact countries spent more money than their relatively weaker economies could afford. The case for market socialism – abandoned after the Prague Spring in 1968 – was once more raised, but the Soviets realised that, as in the 1960s, it would be difficult to introduce such economic reforms without prompting political change. The situation was worsened by the rapidly widening technological gap between the West and the East. It was clear that, without reform, the West would soon outstrip the Eastern bloc both technologically and economically, and that the internal problems of product shortages and lack of economic infrastructure might even cause the socialist societies of the Warsaw Pact to fail.

Into this situation stepped **Mikhail Gorbachev**, who became leader of the Soviet Union in 1985. Gorbachev's policy of *perestroika* meant the relaxation of central planning and the introduction of market economic forces. Overall, his calls were similar to those made during the Prague Spring of 1968, and this made life difficult for Husák's supporters, who had rejected the idea of 'socialism with a human face'. Gorbachev also explicitly rejected the Brezhnev Doctrine, which had justified Soviet intervention in Warsaw Pact countries. Instead, Gennadi Gerasimov, the new Soviet foreign ministry spokesperson, spoke of the 'Sinatra Doctrine'. This policy effectively stated that, when it came to reform, Warsaw Pact countries were free to 'do it their way'. These developments in the Soviet Union removed an important external support for Husák's government.

Encouraged by Gorbachev's statements, many Czechs and Slovaks began to voice their opposition to various policies, and single-issue protest groups began to emerge. For example, the Bratislava Aloud group published a report in 1987, criticising the government's lack of an environmental policy. Non-communist student groups also formed. Some churches became centres of opposition, calling for religious freedom. Václav Havel was imprisoned for his involvement in anti-government demonstrations. This led to further protests, which eventually resulted in Havel's release.

The fall of communism, 1989–91

SOURCE H

Socialism With a Human Face Again

The face was familiar, although it showed the passage of years spent in hiding. Dubček, the tragic hero of the 1968 Prague Spring, returned triumphantly to join the huge protests. A week earlier, riot police had attacked student demonstrations, but now playwright Václav Havel could speak of 'the power of the powerless.' Soon the Communists yielded power to a non Communist majority.

Václav Havel writes about developments in Czechoslovakia, 24 November 1989.

Discussion points

How do Sources H and I support each other? Source H is a primary source and source I is a secondary source – what are the advantages and disadvantages of using each kind of source? How does the attitude of the crowd described in Source I reflect the information in this unit about the outlook and traditions of the Czech people?

SOURCE I

Students and dissidents led the revolution, but it was made on the streets, and above all in Wenceslas Square in central Prague. Here, from Saturday 18 November, Czechs gathered every day to hear veteran dissidents, students, actors, priests and workers demand change. The demonstrations were peaceful, cheerful and determined. Every day they got larger: and not just in Prague, but throughout the country. … As the days went by, it was clear that the future of the Communist regime was at stake.

The demonstrations reached a climax on Friday 24 November when Alexander Dubček, the Communist leader during the 'Prague Spring' of 1968, came to Prague. For over twenty years he had been silenced by the regime. Now as he stepped out onto a balcony to speak, a great roar met him. Dubček! Dubček! Echoed off the tall houses up and down the narrow square. … As the demonstration ended, the people in the square, in a spontaneous gesture, took keys out of their pockets and shook them, 300 000 key-rings producing a sound like massed Chinese bells.

Burke, Patrick. 1995. Revolution in Europe, 1989. *London, UK. Wayland. pp. 31–33.*

SOURCE J

In recent days the so-called protest marches, organized by the so-called Independent Peace Association, have continued in Prague. Approximately 100 individuals attended these activities. Saturday's marches were recorded by British and Austrian television companies. Charter-77 has been divided over policy and tactics in preparation for a confrontational rally. The older members are determined to stop any activities on 21 August while the more radical youth groups want an open clash with state authority. They have declared they are even willing to allow themselves to be shot for their cause.

Extract from Czechoslovak Secret Police (StB) memorandum, 20 August 1989. Adapted from http://www.cwihp.org.

A mass rally in Wenceslas Square, 21 November 1989

The effect of Gorbachev's rise to power was to cut Soviet support for the communist leaders of Eastern Europe. With the threat of invasion by the Red Army removed, these regimes found it impossible to control the frustrations and tensions that had been building for years within their societies. In Czechoslovakia, the final stage of events in the success of the nationalist movement began with demonstrations in January 1989 to commemorate the death of Jan Palach (see page 161). Initially the police attempted to suppress the demonstrations, but as the year went on attitudes softened, and they were noticeably absent from the demonstrations marking the anniversary of the Soviet invasion. In November 1989, the government announced that exit visas would no longer be required for those wishing to travel to the West.

On 17 November 1989, an officially approved rally to commemorate the death of Jan Opletal and the execution of nine students at the hands of the Nazis in 1939 turned into an anti-government protest. Riot police reacted violently, sparking off even more protests. This marked the start of what became known as the 'Velvet Revolution' – the non-violent overthrow of the existing government.

Václav Havel used this unrest as an excuse to form the Civic Forum, which put forward the demands of the people. The Communist Party, purged of reformers, had nothing to offer except a continuation of 'normalisation'. However, Husák also felt unable to order outright suppression of the protests. In fact, even the loyalty of sections of the police and the military was being eroded in the face of mass opposition. In Slovakia, People Against Violence was formed (the equivalent of the Civic Forum in the Czech regions). These two bodies began demanding concessions from the government.

On 24 November 1989, Milouš Jakeš resigned as first secretary of the Communist Party. Three days later, a general strike showed that the Velvet Revolution had spread from intellectuals and students to the ordinary people and organised workers. Over the next few days, the Communist Party renounced its leadership role and made plans for free elections. On 28 December, Dubček was elected speaker of the new parliament and, the following day, Václav Havel was elected president of Czechoslovakia. By early 1990 the communist system in Czechoslovakia had been completely dismantled.

Activity

The collapse of communism in Czechoslovakia in December 1989 is sometimes called the 'Velvet Revolution'. What does this term imply? Research this topic further, and explain how and why the events of 1989 differ from those that occurred in 1968.

The speed of change

The change of regime in Czechoslovakia occurred much more swiftly than it did in several other Eastern European states. In many ways, Czechoslovakia was more prepared for the events of 1989–90 than the rest of the Eastern bloc. It was one of the most industrially developed states in the region, with a history (though limited) of democracy. The German occupation during the Second World War had halted the development of Czechoslovakia's economy and culture, a situation that was not rectified by the liberation of the country by the Red Army in 1945. The imposition of communist rule in 1948 was initially tolerated because of the perceived security of having strong links with the USSR. However, after the rebuilding of the country and the economic stagnation of the early 1960s, the need for economic reform was recognised. The events of 1968 proved that economic reform would not work without associated political and social reform.

Question

Why did Czechoslovakia make the transition to post-communism so easily?

Without the military intervention of the Warsaw Pact in 1968, Czechoslovakia may have moved to a more democratic social system, albeit more slowly than it did in 1989. The re-imposition of Communist Party dominance in the 1970s did not crush the reformist tendencies of the Czechoslovakian population; rather it drove them underground and formed, effectively, a government in waiting. Furthermore, these socio-economic pressures for change could not be offset by the rise in living standards experienced in the 1970s and 1980s. Once Gorbachev had made it clear that he would not repeat the repression of 1968, it was only a matter of time before civic unrest toppled the communist government. Without the support of a state apparatus of social control, the party could not survive, and reformists such as Havel moved to fill the political vacuum.

Discussion point

Establish why Gorbachev felt that the USSR and Eastern bloc needed reform, and assess the impact of these reforms.

Why did Eastern European states last so long?

The main reasons for the longevity of Soviet control of Eastern Europe are related to factors common to *all* states: coercion, persuasion and consensus. Coercion – whether internal or external – was important, but the states could not have survived for nearly 50 years without some consent, based on both propaganda and persuasion, and on the impact of policies. One important factor was the 'nomenklatura' – the party appointments that were filled by workers and peasants, and which were an important source of social mobility. Also, the Soviet-style socialist economic model had proved successful in modernising what were largely backward agricultural economies. It had also provided unprecedented levels of social welfare. The period 1945–73 saw real improvements in standards of living, education and health care, accompanied by full and secure employment and pensions.

For most Eastern European economies, the real problems began in 1973, with the worldwide oil crisis. Although this affected economies in both the West and the East, the more flexible nature of the capitalist system allowed Western countries to shift their economic emphasis away from industry and towards the service sector. Countries in the Eastern bloc, structured for years around a highly industrialised communist economic system, were unable to adapt so easily.

The affluent populations in Eastern Europe, who had become used to economic growth, health and welfare provision, became increasingly discontented when the economy began to slow down. This led to growing numbers of protestors who, ironically, were assisted in articulating their concerns and demands by the high-quality, universal and free state education these regimes had provided.

End of unit activities

1. Design a spider diagram to illustrate some of the problems created by the five-year plans in Czechoslovakia.
2. Find out about the role played by youth groups in the Prague Spring. To what extent were they influenced by youth-organised revolutions in other parts of the world in 1968?
3. In the margin is a street cartoon that appeared during the Soviet-led invasion of 1968. Who do the figures in the cartoon represent? How does it reflect the changing nature of the relationship between Czechoslovakia and the Soviet Union? What sort of reaction is it designed to evoke?
4. 'The Soviet treatment of its Eastern European satellites can be considered a form of colonialism.'

   Divide the class into two groups. One group should work out an argument in support of this view. The other group should work out an argument to oppose it.
5. Read the brief biography of Alexander Dubček at http://www.historylearningsite.co.uk/alexander_Dubcek.htm.

   Use the information, together with information from other websites, to draw a timeline to illustrate his role in Czech history.

3 The formation of and challenges to post-communist Czechoslovakia

Timeline

1989	**Nov:** parliament abolishes the Communist Party as the central feature of Czechoslovakian civic life
	Dec: Dubček elected speaker of the Czechoslovakian parliament; Havel elected president
1991	rapid rise in inflation; Czechoslovakia leaves the Warsaw Pact
1993	Slovakia breaks away from the Czech Republic
2004	Czech Republic and Slovakia join the European Union

Key questions

- What problems faced Eastern Europe after 1989?
- What challenges faced post-communist Czechoslovakia?
- What part has Václav Havel played in the formation of post-communist Czechoslovakia?

Overview

- A series of challenges faced post-communist Czechoslovakia after 1990.
- The political reforms after the collapse of communism caused serious problems. Havel failed to mediate between the various competing groups within the new, post-communist states.
- Another pressing problem was reform of the economy along more Western lines, so that the country could begin to trade and function effectively. Here, the major issue was not the nature of the reforms but the speed at which they should be implemented.
- Czechoslovakia was particularly affected by national tensions, the most serious of which was the division between the Czechs in the west and the Slovaks in the east. There was considerable historical antipathy between these two groups, which had been made worse by the early history of communist Czechoslovakia.
- In 1993, Czechoslovakia was divided along national lines into the Czech Republic and Slovakia.
- By the end of the 20th century, both new states had entered the European Union and once more taken their historical place at the heart of European economic and cultural development.

Czechs collect information about the country's accession to the European Union in 2004

What problems faced Eastern Europe after 1989?

There were four main problems facing the countries of Eastern Europe in the transition from a command economy to a capitalist market economy, and from a one-party state to a multi-party democracy.

1 Lack of democratic traditions

Only Czechoslovakia had had any experience of democracy – and that had been very short. Also, the groups that had led opposition to the communist governments were not democratic political parties, but rather disparate groups united mainly by their opposition to one-party rule.

2 Limited nature of the revolutions

Because the revolutions in Eastern Europe in 1989 were peaceful (with the exception of those in Romania), they only swept away the top party leaderships. The state structures, and those party appointees running them, largely remained in place. The new regimes were thus reliant on communist-appointed administrators to carry out the transition to a capitalist economy and a liberal democracy.

3 Economic problems

Some historians have argued that, had the economic growth of the 1950s been maintained, the 1989 revolutions might not have taken place. The post-communist rulers, largely in power because of an economic crisis, now had to solve it. In general, they decided to abolish the command economy that the communist states had set up and which, to a large extent, had protected the people's welfare.

4 Socio-cultural issues

The transition to a capitalist economy was accompanied by poverty and hardship, and the loss of traditional support structures, which resulted in uncertainty. Some people turned to religion, others to nationalism and even racism – the very irrational elements that 'scientific socialism' (another name for communism or Marxism) had tried to eradicate or at least control. The new political leaders exploited these sentiments, sometimes resulting in racist attacks particularly against Jewish and Roma minorities. In fact, such developments had been predicted by the Marxist historian Eric Hobsbawm, who pointed out that as a condition for receiving loans from the West the new governments would be applying neo-capitalist policies in relatively backward economies. This would cause great hardship for the majority of the population, as both jobs and social services would be cut, although the changes would provide opportunities for a small minority to become very wealthy.

Theory of knowledge

Historical interpretation

Eric Hobsbawm was one of very few historians who, though welcoming the moves to democracy, warned that the collapse of one-party regimes in Eastern Europe would not necessarily result in tolerant and popular successors. In particular, he pointed out that before 1945 the governments in that region – with the exception of Czechoslovakia – had been authoritarian and often racist, especially towards the Jewish, Roma and Sinti minorities. He also questioned the likelihood of genuine democracy being established. How far have his concerns been borne out by events since 1989?

What challenges faced post-communist Czechoslovakia?

The new government of Czechoslovakia faced a number of social, political and economic challenges.

National tensions

Before the Second World War there had been considerable national, ethnic and racial tensions, including anti-semitism, in Central and Eastern Europe as a whole. The communist regimes had managed to keep these tensions in check. This was partly due to ideology – communism is hostile to such prejudices and equates them with bourgeois capitalist society. The communist states

Fact

The Jewish population of Czechoslovakia suffered badly under the Nazis. Before the Second World War, there were 281,000 Jews living there. An estimated 277,000 of them died in the Holocaust. It is estimated that in 2006 the Jewish population of the Czech Republic was only 6000.

believed that such attitudes were undesirable, even impossible, in a workers' state, and usually stepped in to prevent any potential social disorder such hatreds might cause before it could get out of hand.

Czechoslovakia was more susceptible to certain national tensions than, for example, Poland. Czechoslovakia emerged from the wreckage of the Austro-Hungarian Empire in 1919 as a mix of competing nationalities. The most extreme manifestation of this was the lack of harmony between the Czechs and the Slovaks. There had been tensions between the Czech and Slovakian halves of the country from the creation of Czechoslovakia after the 1919 Treaty of Versailles. Slovakia briefly became a nominally independent – and pro-Axis – state during the Second World War. In the wake of the communist takeover, purges in the later 1940s had been directed disproportionately at the Slovakian population. Antonín Novotný had played a major role in these purges and it was not until 1962 that the sufferings of the Slovaks were recognised. Some executions, such as that of Rudolf Slánský (see page 146), were deemed to have been in contravention of party rules, but few were punished. The communist government's reaction to the issue seemed to Slovaks to be grudging and half-hearted. In 1960, a new constitution divided the Slovakian region into three, diluting Slovakian influence in the state. To the Slovakian population there appeared to be disproportionate Czech influence at the heart of government. This was held in check by Novotný by the use of the apparatus of state control, but was broken by the elevation of a Russian-educated Slovak, Alexander Dubček, to the position of first secretary in May 1963.

Fact
Rudolf Slánský became general secretary of the Czechoslovakian Communist Party in 1946. He was one of 14 people arrested in 1951 during Stalin's anti-Titoist purges. Following a show trial in November 1952, he was executed with ten others later that month.

The division of Czechoslovakia

Following the end of communist rule in 1989, problems between Czechs and Slovaks quickly re-emerged. In the communist era the parliament had been subservient to the party, but in the new democratic era each side blocked legislation until it gained concessions from the other.

In addition, the Czechs and Slovaks had different ideas about how the post-1989 state should be structured. On 1 January 1993, Czechoslovakia ceased to exist. It disintegrated peacefully – in what was called the 'Velvet Divorce' – into two independent states: the Czech Republic and Slovakia. There are different historical explanations of this split. One view sees 1989 as a 'return to history': the Cold War and Marxist–Leninist ideology had held nationalism in check, but once the Cold War was over, these nationalist tensions resurfaced.

The Czechs were the larger and more powerful nation and were thus less likely to question the existence of 'Czechoslovakia'. In 1990, the 'hyphen war' occurred, when the Slovaks wanted the newly independent state to be called 'Czecho-Slovakia'. Before 1989, Czech representatives wielded the real power in decision-making and the Slovaks largely deferred to them. After 1989, there had to be consensus before changes to the constitution could be made or new laws introduced, but a minority could block them. Decisions about how best to introduce change were increasingly split along nationalist lines. Václav Klaus (right-wing) in the Czech area – which had a more industrialised economy than Slovakia – advocated the rapid transition to a capitalist economy. However, Vladimír Mečiar in Slovakia wanted a more gradual approach. Havel tried to effect a compromise, but a split between the two halves seemed to offer a solution. Although this division occurred without violence, the decision was made by a political élite without much in the way of popular support. There was no referendum, and opinion polls showed that the majority of people were against the split.

Question
What have been the main national tensions in the Czech Republic and Slovakia since 1990?

Economic problems

The Czechs faced the same basic question as other post-communist states in Eastern Europe – at what pace should reform be made? In Czechoslovakia, however, the national tensions made the decision more difficult. The sharp **economic shock therapy** of the Czech government resulted in the Czech Republic having, by the mid 1990s, one of the most rapidly expanding economies of all the post-communist Eastern European states. However, while a small minority became extremely wealthy as a result of these developments, the social costs were high, and many people suffered unemployment and a drop in living standards. While the majority had wanted political freedoms and wider consumer choices, they did not bargain for the unemployment, poverty and loss of social services that hit them after 1989. In the former USSR, where several billionaire oligarchs (the 'Chicago Boys') emerged alongside 140 million Russians falling below the poverty line, it was described as 'all shock, no therapy'.

SOURCE A

Our country is not flourishing. Entire branches of industry are producing goods that are of no interest to anyone, while we are lacking the things we need. A state which calls itself a workers' state humiliates and exploits workers. Our obsolete economy is wasting the little energy we have available. The country spends so little on education that it ranks today as seventy-second in the world. We have polluted the soil, rivers and forests that we have today the most contaminated environment in Europe. Adults in our country die earlier than in most other European countries.

Václav Havel's New Year's Address to the Nation, 1 January 1990.

SOURCE B

In Czechoslovakia the economic transformation was started in early 1991 when prices were freed, the currency could be traded, tax was lowered, retail trade was privatised and property restored to its former owners. In 1992 mass privatisation was started. The social costs of these reforms have also proved higher than expected which, along with the awakening of nationalist feelings, led to the split of the country into the Czech Republic and Slovakia in January 1993.

Extract from a lecture given by W. Roszkowski and J. Kofman in 1997. Adapted from http://www.cerc.unimelb.edu.au/bulletin/bulmay97.htm.

As the former Czechoslovakia entered the market economy, problems became evident. Inflation had rocketed by 25% in 1991, with wages rapidly following. However, as consumers were only able to purchase essential items, by 1992 inflation had dropped to 3%. Heavy industry felt the greatest impact. These industries had been the backbone of Czechoslovakia's communist economy; without the support of the central government and the command economy the inefficiencies of these industries, largely caused by obsolete equipment, rapidly put them out of business, causing widespread unemployment. These problems created increasing racial tensions as workers reacted adversely to the impact of the rapid introduction of a capitalist market economy – there was even some anti-semitism, despite the fact that Jews were only a small minority. By the mid 1990s, however, the situation had stabilised, and both the Czech Republic and Slovakia had made the transition to a Western-style economy. However, large numbers had paid a high social price for its introduction.

The present situation

At the time of writing, both states of the former Czechoslovakia are members of the EU and part of mainstream European culture and politics. Both have made the transition from communism, and have developed – or begun to develop – capitalist economies. The overarching institutions of the EU and NATO have allowed the two states to divide and prosper, and some sections of the Czech and the Slovak populations have been positively affected by these developments.

economic shock therapy
The policies behind economic shock therapy were based on the ideas of Friedrich Hayek and Milton Friedman who, from the 1960s, advocated policies (such as monetarism and 'rolling back' the welfare state) for 'free-market' or unrestrained capitalism. The ideas of this 'Chicago School' were first applied in the military dictatorships of Chile and Argentina in the 1970s, and were later adopted by the Reagan and Thatcher governments in the US and UK.

What part has Václav Havel played in the formation of post-communist Czechoslovakia?

Václav Havel is a playwright, dissident and politician. He emerged from the final phase of communism as president of Czechoslovakia, and held the post until the division of the country into the Czech Republic and Slovakia in 1993. Thereupon he became president of the new Czech Republic, a post which he held until 2003. He is a noted intellectual and has published many plays and numerous works of literature. He is interesting for our study because he is very different from the other leaders of independence movements under discussion. As we have noted, intellectuals played an important role in opposition to the Communist Party's centralising role in Czechoslovakian politics and society. Havel first emerged as part of this general movement in 1960, when he began to publish overtly political works. The Prague Spring and the subsequent government backlash prompted him to become the leader of the opposition group Charter 77 (see page 163), which led to his imprisonment.

SOURCE C

Extract from an article written by Václav Havel in 1984.

I am convinced that what is called 'dissent' in the Soviet bloc is a specific modern experience, the experience of life at the very ramparts of dehumanized power. As such, that 'dissent' has the opportunity and even the duty to reflect on this experience, to testify to it and to pass it on to those fortunate enough not to have to undergo it. Thus we too have a certain opportunity to help in some ways those who help us, to help them in our deeply shared interest, in the interest of mankind.

Quoted in Havel, V. 1990. Living in Truth, Essays on Politics and Conscience. *London, UK. Faber and Faber.*

Question

Why was the change to a free market economy not an easy process?

Havel was born in 1936 into a middle-class family that had been closely involved in the politics and cultural developments of post-1919 Czechoslovakia. He was forced to study economics at university, but the course did not suit him and he dropped out after two years. In 1957, he worked as a stage hand in the theatre and studied drama by distance learning. In 1963, his first play, *The Garden Party*, was performed. This was followed by numerous other works, and in 1968 his play *The Memorandum* brought him international acclaim after performances in New York.

Like many others, Havel was caught up in the events of 1968. He broadcast for Radio Free Czechoslovakia, an activity which drew the attention of the authorities in the wake of the Soviet invasion. Havel was banned from the theatre and not allowed to leave the country. His international standing remained, however, and to an extent this protected him from the more extreme measures of state repression. His literary activity simply went underground and a series of autobiographical plays, in which Havel appears as the character 'Vaněk', propelled him to the forefront of the dissident movement. This development illustrates well the difficulty the Czechoslovakian communist regime had in suppressing free expression within the state.

In 1977, Havel became a leading figure in the Charter 77 movement and co-founded the Committee for the Defence of the Unjustly Persecuted in 1979. This drew the attention of the authorities once more, and between this time and the fall of communism, Havel spent much time in confinement, most notably between 1979 and 1984. During this period he wrote the famous essay 'Power of the Powerless'. This articulated the nature of totalitarianism in the communist bloc and presented a blueprint for resistance. It is noteworthy that Havel, like Gandhi, believed that Czechoslovakian society – and indeed all the societies of the Eastern bloc – contained so many contradictions that it was inherently unstable. He argued that passive, non-violent opposition to such a regime would, in the long run, bring about reform.

Havel was a leading figure in the Velvet Revolution of 1989 as a key member of the opposition group Civic Forum. On 22 December 1989, he was elected president. His time as president was controversial and he was unable to hold together the two halves of the country. He did, however, negotiate Czechoslovakia's exit from the Warsaw Pact, and by 1991 Soviet forces had withdrawn from the country. He also facilitated his country's entry into NATO, a remarkable development given the history of Eastern Europe since the Second World War. Havel also pushed for the extension of the NATO alliance to all the former Soviet satellite states of Eastern Europe.

Havel left office in 2003 and became a full-time human rights activist. He has hosted an international forum that lobbies for human rights and related issues, Forum 200, since 1997. Since the end of his political life he has also pursued an academic and literary career in the USA.

Activity

Compare and contrast Havel's and Gandhi's approaches to resistance to oppression.

Fact

Havel can be used in an IB History assessment to illustrate the force of the intellectual in creating historical change. Further, his pacifism and non-violent agitation can be compared with that of Gandhi. However, it is important to recognise that Havel is very much a product of Czechoslovakia's intellectual, artistic and political tradition. It is difficult to see a similar figure being effective in the other case studies in this book.

Theory of knowledge

History and the arts

How does Havel's career illustrate the link between history and the arts? Would he have been such a leading figure in the Velvet Revolution if he had not also been an acclaimed playwright?

End of unit activities

1 Alexander Dubček died in 1992. Write a newspaper obituary for him, outlining and evaluating his role in Czechoslovakia's history.

2 Draw up a table listing the problems facing Czechoslovakia in 1990, adding information about the causes of each and suggesting possible solutions.

3 Who deserves the title of the greatest hero in modern Czech history – Václav Havel or Alexander Dubček? Divide the class into two groups. Each group should prepare an argument to support one of these candidates.

4 Read the country profiles on these two websites:

   https://www.cia.gov/library/publications/the-world-factbook/geos/ez.html (for the Czech Republic)

   https://www.cia.gov/library/publications/the-world-factbook/geos/lo.html (for Slovakia).

   In each case, click on the icon labelled 'People'. Look at factors such as population size, average life expectancy, literacy levels, unemployment, health care, religion, language, etc. Explain the differences between the two countries. Which of these can you attribute to their history? Which country seems to be in a more favourable position?

5 'To what extent was the collapse of Czechoslovakia as a state the logical outcome of the collapse of communism?'

   Write an essay to answer this question. Start by producing a single index card for each factor involved in the collapse of communism. The cards should have both the evaluative point that will drive the essay and evidence to support it.

   The final essay should point to two broad themes. Firstly, that the history of Czechoslovakia since 1919 was in many ways artificial, with the state lacking the qualities of a coherent nation state. Secondly, that communism suppressed the forces that were pressing for the collapse of a united Czechoslovakia. When the latter were removed, two states swiftly replaced one in this key region of Central Europe.

End of chapter activities

Paper 1 exam practice

SOURCE A

In connection with the events in Czechoslovakia the question of the correlation and interdependence of the national interests of the socialist countries and their international duties acquires particular topical and acute importance. The measures taken by the Soviet Union, jointly with other socialist countries, in defending the socialist gains of the Czechoslovakian people are of great significance for strengthening the socialist community, which is the main achievement of the international working class. ... The peoples of the socialist countries and Communist parties certainly do have and should have freedom for determining the ways of advance of their respective countries. However, none of their decisions should damage either socialism in their country or the fundamental interests of other socialist countries, and the whole working class movement, which is working for socialism. This means that each Communist party is responsible not only to its own people, but also to all the socialist countries, to the entire Communist movement.

Extract from the Brezhnev Doctrine, 25 September 1968. Quoted on http://www.fordham.edu/halsall/mod/1968brezhnev.html.

Question

According to Source A (left), why were Soviet and Warsaw Pact forces sent into Czechoslovakia in 1968?
[2 marks]

Skill

Comprehension of a source

Examiner's tips

Comprehension questions are the most straightforward questions you will face in Paper 1. They simply require you to understand a source **and** extract two or three relevant points that relate to the particular question. As only 2 marks are available for this question, make sure you don't waste valuable time that should be spent on the higher-scoring questions by writing a long answer here. All that's needed are a couple of short sentences giving the necessary information to show that you have understood the source. Basically, try to give one piece of information for each of the marks available for the question.

Fact
Events in Czechoslovakia in 1968 resulted in the 'Brezhnev Doctrine', which defined a communist state as a one-party state belonging to the Warsaw Pact. It also justified the right of the Warsaw Pact to intervene in any member country where communism was under threat.

Common mistakes

When asked to show your comprehension/understanding of a particular source, make sure you don't comment on the **wrong** source! Mistakes like this are made every year – remember, every mark is important for your final grade.

Simplified markscheme

For **each item of relevant/correct information** identified, award **1 mark**, up to a **maximum of 2 marks**.

Student answer

Source A claims that the invasion was justified because the fundamental national interests of all socialist countries were interdependent.

Examiner's comments

The candidate has selected **one** relevant and explicit piece of information from the source – this is enough to gain 1 mark. However, as no other reason/information has been identified, this candidate fails to gain the other mark available for the question.

Activity

Look again at the source and the student answer above. Now try to identify **one** other piece of information from the source, and so obtain the other mark available for this question.

Summary activity

Copy the spider diagram opposite and, using the information in this chapter, make notes in point form under each heading.

Turning points in Czechoslovakia's history

1948

- Key event
- Leaders involved
- Political situation
- Linked economic, religious, cultural issues
- Changes that occurred
- Challenges to Soviet or centralised control

1968

- Key event
- Leaders involved
- Political situation
- Linked economic, religious, cultural issues
- Changes that occurred
- Challenges to Soviet or centralised control

1989

- Key event
- Leaders involved
- Political situation
- Linked economic, religious, cultural issues
- Changes that occurred
- Challenges to Soviet or centralised control

Paper 2 exam practice

1 To what extent did social and economic issues play an important role in one independence movement in one Soviet satellite state?

2 How, and for what reasons, did Czechoslovakia achieve independence from centralised communist control and Soviet domination?

3 To what extent can the Prague Spring and the Velvet Revolution be attributed to the part played by individuals?

Further reading

Try reading the relevant chapters/sections of the following books:

Calvocoressi, Peter. 1987. *World Politics Since 1945 (5th Edn)*. London, UK and New York, USA. Longman.
Crampton, Richard J. 1994. *Eastern Europe in the Twentieth Century – And After*. London, UK and New York, USA. Routledge.
Dubček, Alexander. 1993. *Hope Dies Last*. New York, USA. Kodansha America.
Kenny, Padraic. 2006. *The Burdens of Freedom: Eastern Europe since 1989*. London, UK. Zed Books.
Longworth, Philip. 1994. *The Making of Eastern Europe*. Basingstoke and London, UK. St Martin's Press.
Pittaway, Mark. 2004. *Brief Histories: Eastern Europe 1939–2000*, London, UK. Hodder Education.
Stokes, Gale. 1993. *The Walls came Tumbling Down: The Collapse of Communism in Eastern Europe*. Oxford, UK. Oxford University Press.
Vadney, Thomas. E. 1998. *The World Since 1945*. London, UK. Penguin Books.
Webb, Adrian. 2002. *Central & Eastern Europe Since 1919*. London, UK. Routledge.

6 Poland

Tsarist Russia A term applied to the highly autocratic pre-revolutionary Russian state, ruled by the tsar (from the Latin *Caesar*, meaning emperor). Tsarist Russia was a dictatorship that ruled a huge empire stretching from Poland in the west to the Pacific Ocean in the east.

Catholic and Orthodox Christianity During the medieval period, the Christian Church split into two distinct forms – Catholic in the West and Orthodox in the East. Under Byzantine influence, Russia became Orthodox whilst most of Europe, including Poland, became Catholic. Thus, the Russian domination of Poland was seen by the Poles as a religious struggle between these two branches of Christianity.

Introduction

Until the 18th century, Poland had enjoyed a long history as an independent state. However, during the later part of the 1700s it was partitioned by and absorbed into its neighbouring states of Prussia, Russia and Austria. The largest portion was allocated to the Russian Empire. Nationalism remained strong, despite attempts by **Tsarist Russia** to extinguish Polish national consciousness in the 20th century, including an attempt to impose **Orthodox Christianity** on a **Catholic** nation. These events left a legacy of bitterness between Poland and Russia.

Polish independence was at last achieved by the defeat of Germany, Austria-Hungary and Tsarist Russia in the First World War and the events of the Russian Revolution in 1917. Taking advantage of the chaos that followed these events, the Poles declared an independent state on 9 November 1918. On 28 June 1919, the new state of Poland was recognised by the victorious powers as part of the Paris peace settlements of 1919–20, and was re-created from German, Austrian and Russian territory. In 1920, Poland's army, led by Marshal Piłsudski and encouraged by Britain and France, invaded the Russian territories of Belorussia and the Ukraine. An attempt by the Red Army to invade Poland was beaten back, and in the 1921 Treaty of Riga, Poland took these western territories from the new Bolshevik state.

Events in Poland in the 19th and early 20th centuries created a strong feeling of nationalism based on the Catholic Church and a deeply rooted sense of traditional Polish culture. In 1939, at the start of the Second World War, the West effectively abandoned Poland to its fate after it was invaded by Nazi Germany on 1 September. Sixteen days later, the USSR invaded eastern Poland to take the lands assigned to it in the Nazi–Soviet Non-Aggression Pact. Events such as the Katyn Massacre in 1940 (see page 178), and the Warsaw Uprising of 1944 (see page 179), only increased Polish bitterness towards the Soviet Union. This bitterness was worsened by the fact that, as the Red Army pushed back the Germans and advanced into Poland, Polish industrial equipment was dismantled and sent to the USSR as reparations. For many Poles, 'liberation' by the Red Army soon began to feel like 'occupation'. Thus, in the period after the Second World War, many Poles saw the imposition of Soviet-style communism and the reduction of their country to a satellite of the USSR as part of a repeating historical pattern.

Map of Poland, showing territory gained from other countries by 1921

1 The origins and growth of movements challenging Soviet and centralised control of Poland

Key questions

- How did a communist-dominated, pro-Soviet state emerge in Poland after the Second World War?
- How did de-Stalinisation affect Soviet control in Poland?

Timeline

1919 establishment of independent Poland after Versailles

1919–21 Russo–Polish War

1939 Second World War begins; Poland is conquered after German and Soviet invasions

1940 Katyn Massacre

1944 Warsaw Rising begins

1945 Lublin Committee convenes

1947 communists win Polish elections

1947–53 purges in Poland

1953 death of Stalin

Overview

- A pro-Soviet communist Poland was established after the Second World War, which created a historical problem that influenced events up to 1990.
- The Poles were promised independence after the Second World War by the Allies, but were 'short-changed' by the West.
- As a result of this, the USSR acquired Poland as a satellite state. Poland had a long-standing historical antipathy to Russia, yet some of its population were prepared to accept Soviet domination as a guarantee against future German aggression.
- Poland lost much of the eastern part of its pre-war territory to the USSR. In return, its borders were shifted westwards at Germany's expense.
- Initial resistance to the domination of the USSR was crushed by 1953.
- A situation developed that accommodated both sides and established a workable communist state in Poland. However, it left an undercurrent of anti-communist feeling that re-emerged a few years later, as a series of economic crises hit the country in the 1960s and 1970s.

How did a communist-dominated, pro-Soviet state emerge in Poland after the Second World War?

Poland in the Second World War

On 1 September 1939, Germany attacked Poland. Two days later, Britain and France declared war on Germany. On 17 September, the USSR attacked eastern Poland. Pressed from two sides, the Polish armed forces rapidly collapsed.

Armoured vehicles of the Soviet Red Army drive alongside German troops, as the two forces meet up inside Poland

Historical debate

The issue of territorial changes along the border between Poland and the Soviet Union continues to be hotly debated. Much of this land had been old Poland before the partitions of the 18th century, but had belonged to Russia from 1772. In 1921, in the Treaty of Riga, Poland took land that is now in Lithuania, Ukraine and Belarus – about 200 km (125 miles) east of the Curzon Line recommended by the British in 1920, and in areas where the Poles were an ethnic minority. In fact, Poland had seized much of this land from Lithuania in the 16th century.

The declarations of war from the West did not come quickly enough for the Poles, and they viewed the events of 1939 as a betrayal by both the West and the USSR. This sense of betrayal was reinforced by decisions made by the Western Allies at the end of the war (see page 180), which left Poland firmly in the Soviet sphere of influence. The role of the USSR in the events of 1939 was even more significant, as the Red Army's attack appeared to be an attempt to reverse Poland's takeover of Russian land following the Russo–Polish war of 1919–21, and to re-establish traditional Russian control of the country.

The Germans treated the Polish population badly, committing atrocities on a grand scale. Poland also suffered during the brief period of Soviet rule, from 1939 to 1941. Stalin was determined to put in place a programme of Sovietisation. The purpose of this policy was to establish communist rule and suppress all members of Polish society who might potentially engage in anti-communist activities after the expected German invasion – which came less than two years later. The opening up of Soviet archives after 1990 revealed that the number of Poles who died during the Soviet occupation of their country may have been as many as 40,000.

Bodies are retrieved from the mass grave in which Polish officers were found after the Katyn Massacre in 1940

Fact

The most infamous of the atrocities in Poland at this time was the massacre of Polish officers at Katyn on 5 March 1940, during which 5000 men died. The officers were drawn from the Polish upper and middle classes and had military training. Thus, they posed a clear threat to the new communist order. The massacre was made public by the Germans in 1943, placing considerable strain on Polish–Soviet relations.

The suffering of the Polish people in the Second World War was extreme. It has been calculated that about 22% of the original 1939 population died during German occupation. The Germans systematically exploited Poland's people and resources to sustain their war effort. Estimates suggest that the country lost a third of its housing stock, most of its schools, and almost all of its railways and port facilities. More than any other Eastern European country, Poland had to be totally rebuilt at the end of hostilities. This placed serious socio-economic stress on the country and provided the post-war communist government with an ongoing problem.

Polish resistance to the invasion continued even after the collapse of its armed forces. This resistance came from three main groups: Polish troops serving in both the Allied and the Soviet armies; two governments in exile (in Britain and the USSR); and a domestic resistance force, the Polish Home Army. As the war went on, the existence of these resistance movements created considerable political tension, as both Britain and the USSR tried to promote the interests of the Poles based in their respective countries to be the next rulers of Poland.

Governments in exile

There were two governments in exile – one in Britain, known as the London Poles, and one in the USSR, which was known as the Lublin Poles. In addition to opposing each other, both governments were used to give legitimacy to either Western or Soviet plans for post-war Poland, as well as to defeat the German invaders. Relations between the two governments improved slightly after the USSR's entry into the war in 1941, but in the long run they were never able to establish an amicable relationship.

From 1943 onwards, with the tide of battle turning in favour of the Allies on the Eastern Front, it became increasingly clear that Nazi Germany was going to be defeated. The Red Army – in the process of liberating Eastern Europe from Nazi occupation – would therefore end the war in Central and Eastern Europe. To meet the USSR's security needs, Stalin wanted to redraw Poland's eastern frontier, determined to recover land taken by Poland in 1921 as well as to retain land seized in 1939. The London Poles could not accept this, and in July 1943 the USSR broke off relations with them. It was clear that, while the West was preparing the way for a pro-Western Polish government after the war, Stalin was working for a pro-Soviet Polish communist takeover. Furthermore, the Soviet leader was in a strong position to do so, given that the Red Army would be physically present in Poland when hostilities ceased. The reality of this situation was recognised by the Allied leaders at the Tehran Conference in 1943 and was reinforced at Yalta in 1945.

The Warsaw Rising

In mid 1944, the Red Army crossed the pre-1939 Polish–Soviet border. In August, as the Soviets approached the Polish capital of Warsaw, the Polish Home Army rose up against the Nazi occupiers. The Polish government in exile in London had ordered the rising so that a pro-Western independent Poland might be established before the capital was liberated. This would give the London Poles a chance of setting themselves up as the legitimate leaders of Poland. The Warsaw Rising was also an effort to divert German military resources away from the battle against the Red Army. Stalin could have ordered his troops to press forward to support the rising – but he did not. His plans for post-war Poland did not include the London Poles; he intended to establish a pro-Soviet communist satellite state in this most important part of Eastern Europe.

Question

Who were the London Poles and the Lublin Poles?

Fact

The Tehran Conference was held in 1943 and began the process by which the Allied powers established the form of post-war Europe. The Yalta Conference was held in February 1945. By this point it was obvious that Nazi Germany would be defeated and the Allied powers – Britain, the USA and the USSR – sought to define the post-war map of Europe. This process not only established national boundaries, but also set the spheres of influence of the main contenders.

Question

Why have the events surrounding the Warsaw Rising been the subject of historical debate?

The Red Army halted its advance, and by October 1944 the Warsaw Rising had been ruthlessly crushed by the German army. When the Red Army liberated the city it did so without the aid of domestic resistance fighters. In fact, the Germans had eliminated a potential post-war anti-communist force. Stalin's failure to support the Home Army in 1944 reinforced anti-Russian feeling amongst the population. However, many also bitterly resented the fact that, as in 1939, the Western Allies had provided no practical help.

SOURCE A

In the event of the fall of Warsaw you are not to surrender but to withdraw from the city and attempt to link up with Soviet forces to the east of Zoliborz. Should it be impossible to cross the river Vistula retreat along the river to the south, where Soviet forces will do the utmost to help you cross in boats.

Instructions issued to the commander of the Polish Home Army, General Skokowski, from General Berling, a Polish general in the Red Army, regarding possible outcomes of the Warsaw Rising in 1944.

Discussion point

In groups of two, examine the reasons why there was considerable historical antagonism between the Poles and the Russians.

The post-war reorganisation of Poland along communist lines

At Yalta (see page 179), the Allies agreed that the Soviet Union could move its border with Poland westwards, thereby regaining territory it had lost to Poland in the 1921 Treaty of Riga. Although Poland lost a great deal of land to the USSR, it was allocated a large – though not equivalent – block of land in the east of Germany. Despite this, many Poles looked on Yalta as a 'betrayal' by the West, in much the same way that many Czechoslovakians viewed the decisions at Munich as a betrayal by the same powers (see page 142).

The Polish communists – the Polish Workers' Party, or PWP – faced serious problems in establishing power. Firstly, they were opposed by traditional power groups that had historically opposed communism. Secondly, the communists had been prime targets for the Nazis, and the only activists left were the few who had survived by going underground or those who had fled to the Soviet Union. Finally, association with the USSR was a drawback because of the deep-rooted Polish distrust of all things Russian.

Fact

The Polish Communist Party had also been purged in 1938 on Stalin's orders – several Polish communists had continued to support Trotsky after his expulsion from the USSR in 1929.

However, the communists did have an advantage in that they faced no domestic political opposition. Unlike Czechoslovakia, Poland did not have a strong democratic tradition in the period 1918–39. It was briefly a democracy from 1918, but Marshal Piłsudski (who had been chief of state from 1918 to 1922) led a military coup in 1926, and remained effective dictator until his death in 1935. There were thus no strong popular political organisations. Many leaders of Poland's public opposition to the communists had been eliminated in the Warsaw Rising. The communists were also supported by the Red Army, which had significant numbers of troops in Poland at the end of the Second World War.

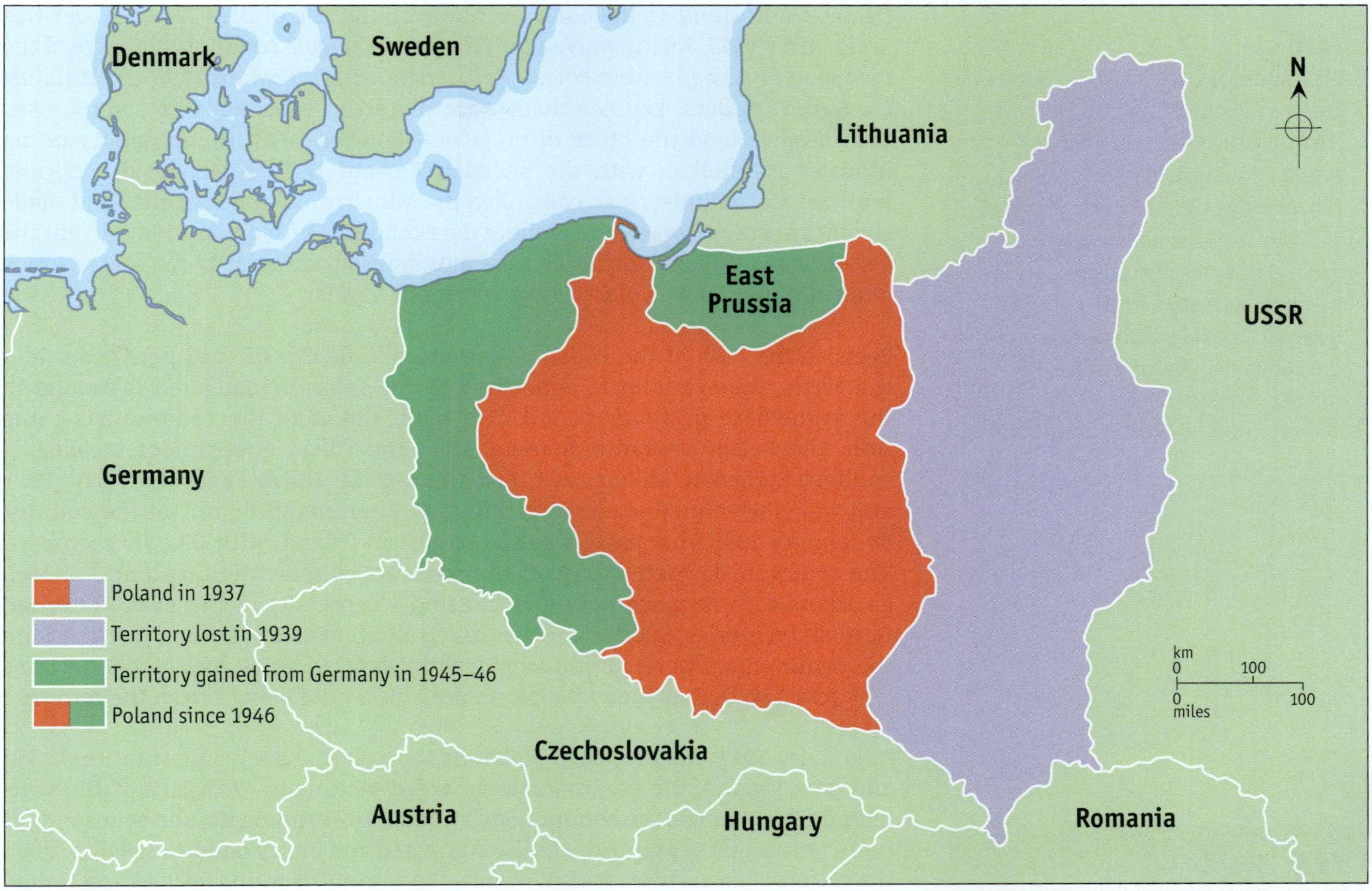

Map showing territories lost and acquired by Poland as a result of the end of the Second World War

Establishing Soviet/communist control

Upon liberation, the Soviets established the Lublin Committee to oversee the administration of Poland during the transition to the post-war period. In July 1944, this Polish Committee of National Liberation at Lublin was recognised by the other Allies as Poland's provisional government, rather than the London-based group. On 19 January 1945, the Soviets transformed this body into a provisional government. In March, leading members of the London government in exile and key members of the Home Army – especially its commander general, Leopold Okulicki – were invited to discuss the country's future. Despite guarantees to the contrary, the Soviets arrested the delegation.

The provisional government contained some PWP members, but initially the party was very much in the minority. From 1943, the PWP was led by **Władisław Gomułka**; it had hardly any members and was forced to ally itself with the Polish Socialist Party (PSP). Ranged against it was the powerful Peasant Party under Stanisław Mikołajczyk, who had been a leading member of the Polish government in exile in London, and the relatively weak Labour Party and Democratic Party. At the Yalta Conference, Stalin had promised free elections in Poland, and in early 1945 it was difficult to see how the PWP would survive these, let alone emerge as the ruling party.

Władisław Gomułka (1905–82) Gomułka had been part of the communist government in exile in the USSR. He emerged as leader of communist Poland in 1947, but fell from power in 1954 as a result of infighting within the party. He was later rehabilitated and served as party leader in 1970.

Fact
With Soviet aid, the PWP also set up a secret police, the Urząd Bezpieczństwa (UB), and the Volunteers' Citizens Militia Reserve, numbering 100,000. The militia was established initially to crush an anti-communist guerrilla war conducted by members of the pre-war Polish Home Army from 1945 to 1947. However, both the secret police and the militia soon became arms of a totalitarian state.

Despite indications to the contrary, however, the rise of the PWP to power was rapid. After 1945, Poland moved quickly from a 'bogus' coalition – in spite of the inclusion of some London Poles – to an increasingly obvious PWP dictatorship. On Stalin's orders, key positions were placed in the hands of communists. Communists held the office of president (Bolesław Bierut) and deputy prime minister (Gomułka), with the socialist Edward Osóbka-Morawski as prime minister. Communists also controlled the Ministry of Public Security and made significant steps towards controlling the economy. On 3 January 1946, all but the very smallest Polish companies were nationalised, and in 1947 the massive task of reconstruction was placed in government hands.

Because the bulk of the Polish upper and middle classes had perished under the Nazis, there was little opposition to the reforms instigated in Poland in the immediate post-war period. The main threat to the communists came from the Polish peasants. A member of the Polish government in exile in London, Stanisław Mikołajczyk, had formed the Polish Peasants' Party (PPP), and was determined to derail communist attempts to dominate the country. By January 1946, this party was the largest in Poland, with 600,000 members. The communists tried to buy off the peasants by redistributing land – as well as animals, farm machinery and housing – especially in the newly acquired German territories. Such action was taken all over Eastern Europe, but in Poland the communists were careful to parcel out land in small lots of 2–3 hectares (5–7 acres) so that as many people as possible would benefit from the reform.

Fact
Nationalisation took place quite gradually in Poland, compared to other East European countries, and there were no mass purges or show trials in the years that followed.

In January 1947, the promised elections took place. As a result of intimidation and vote rigging, the communists emerged victorious, with 80% of the vote. Before the elections, the communists arrested 142 candidates, and thousands of non-communist supporters were also arrested and imprisoned. Mikołajczyk fled the country; his party was taken over by the communists and became the United Peasants Party. The communists swiftly created a constitution based on that of the USSR, and the socialist Józef Cyrankiewicz was installed as prime minister. On 1 May 1947, Gomułka merged all leftist parties into a single, Marxist-dominated Polish United Workers' Party (PUWP). Industries were nationalised and peasant lands became part of collectives known as the Polish Agricultural Enterprises.

The presence of the Red Army on Polish soil and Stalin's actions at the end of the Second World War meant that the pro-Western Poles in London simply did not have the political leverage to put up a credible fight. However, the Sovietisation of Poland was not as extreme as it was in other parts of the Eastern bloc. The Catholic Church, with its deep roots in the country, was actually treated well by the communists. It retained its property until 1950, and religion remained on the school curriculum. As a result, the church continued to be one of the main focuses of Polish life, both spiritual and social.

The Soviet grip tightens

The motive behind the Soviet domination of Eastern Europe was primarily defensive. Poland was the largest country in the region and it had been one of the main routes taken by invaders of Russia in the past. Stalin simply could not tolerate policies that might create an independent Poland. The event that triggered a Soviet clampdown on Poland was Stalin's confrontation with Tito's Yugoslavia and that country's subsequent expulsion from **Cominform** in 1948. Thus, the imposition of a more orthodox Soviet-style communist system in Poland was a reaction to the potential collapse of the USSR's dominance in Eastern Europe.

Cominform An international organisation of communist parties dominated by the USSR. Cominform was established in 1947 and dissolved in 1956.

The backlash began with attacks on Gomułka by pro-Soviet members of the PUWP, in which Gomułka was accused of having right-wing nationalist tendencies. This soon developed into a full-scale purge of the PUWP, and by 1952, 25% of its membership had been ejected from the party. The Soviets ordered the arrest of potential dissidents. Many were executed, but it is probably the case that the country suffered less than its Eastern European neighbours due to Gomułka's unwillingness to apply the purges with full force.

Gomułka's wartime career had marked him out as a loyal ally of the USSR. He was, however, a strong Polish patriot and believed that his country could follow a separate communist path to that of the USSR. Although they had a good relationship to begin with, it is clear that Stalin became increasingly suspicious of many of Gomułka's policies. Gomułka had opposed the collectivisation of Poland's farms on the grounds that it would give rise to peasant resistance. Gomułka had also failed to crack down on the Catholic Church, and had opposed the formation of Comintern. In addition, his open support for Tito in Yugoslavia was considered totally unacceptable by Stalin.

However, the Soviets feared that military intervention to bring Gomułka into line might not have the desired effect. Furthermore, at this time the first steps were being taken in Europe towards the formation of **NATO** in 1949. This meant that the Soviets faced the added danger of a potential war with the West should they decide to exert their dominance in Poland by force of arms. To add to these fears, ongoing anti-communist resistance in Poland could destabilise the country so much that the communist regime would collapse completely, perhaps pushing Poland into the Western camp.

NATO The North Atlantic Treaty Organisation, a Western European and North American military alliance dominated by the USA.

It can be argued, therefore, that the USSR was unable to impose purges in Poland on a scale experienced in other parts of Eastern Europe simply because it did not feel confident enough to back up its threats with force. Gomułka, a communist with strong Polish nationalist leanings, managed to survive the crisis and remained as leader of his country until 1951. He was then removed from power, but re-emerged to play a part in the nationalist movement nine years later.

Soviet leader Nikita Khrushchev (left) meets secretary of the Polish Communist Workers Party Władisław Gomułka in 1960

How did de-Stalinisation affect Soviet control in Poland?

Stalin's death in 1953 brought a new reformist faction to power in the USSR, which was eventually led by Nikita Khrushchev. The impact of the Second World War and the effect of the purges had a devastating effect on economies across the communist bloc, and it was agreed that changes were essential if the Soviet Union and its allies were to keep up with developments in the West and create an economy strong enough to deter a Western military attack.

Unrest in 1956

Fact

In his secret speech, Khrushchev attacked Stalin's policies and accepted that there could be 'national roads to socialism' that did not necessarily have to follow the Soviet model. Although intended to have only a domestic impact – to achieve de-Stalinisation or liberalisation – it rapidly caused serious problems in Eastern Europe.

The change of leadership in Moscow triggered internal unrest in Poland. In fact, it was Polish communists who leaked Khrushchev's 'secret' speech of February 1956, in which he attacked Stalin. By then, Poland had already begun its own process of de-Stalinisation. However, in June 1956, there were strikes and riots in the city of Poznán after wage cuts and changes to working conditions were announced. Two days of fighting between workers and the police left 53 dead and over 300 injured. The PUWP was divided on how to respond – a pro-Soviet faction was against change, while a reformist communist wing wanted liberalisation and economic reform.

There were three main reasons for the public unrest.

1. The Poles still harboured resentment towards the Russians based on their historical relationship.
2. Since 1948, the USSR had taken a notoriously heavy-handed approach to certain aspects of Polish civic life (for example, the USSR had imposed a Russian officer, Konstantin Rokossovsky, on Poland as its minister of war).
3. Poles faced continuing economic austerity as the country struggled to recover from the devastating effects of the war. In 1951, rationing was introduced, followed by large price increases in 1953 and a drop in real earnings by 1955.

The reforms pioneered by the USSR after 1953 also had a serious effect on the Polish population. Intellectuals began to discuss the future form of socialism – one with a distinctly Polish flavour. Many clubs sprang up in this period, including the Crooked Circle, which encouraged open discussion of issues affecting Polish citizens. Young people were exposed to an influx of Western popular culture in the form of jeans and jazz. Student groups began to produce satirical theatre. All these developments inevitably led to increasing criticism of the PUWP.

Tensions in the upper echelons of the party began to weaken the apparatus of state control. In 1954, the party leader, Bolesław Bierut, died and was replaced by Edward Ochab, who advocated the return of Gomułka. The party also embraced the reformist message coming from the USSR and allowed the formation of a Catholic youth organisation and the release of former members of the Home Army then being held in detention camps.

In summary, the initial trigger to the unrest that surged through Poland in 1956 was economic, with Poznán's railway workers striking and demonstrating for better living conditions. The strikers were shot at – an action that released the underlying tension in Polish society. This was no longer a campaign for better living conditions. It became a much wider issue that questioned Poland's role in the post-war order. The public perception of events in Poznán was that the USSR was acting behind the scenes. Furthermore, the PUWP was not isolated from these developments. Members of the party, including its leadership, were genuinely distressed by the events in Poznán and sought to distance themselves from the shootings by promising further reform. Collectivisation was slowed, former members of the Home Army were fully readmitted to civic society and workers' councils were formed. Gomułka, who had suffered in the purges of 1949, became a pro-reform symbol in the party. In August 1956, he was readmitted to party membership and appointed to the Politburo (see page 147) – without this action being approved by the USSR. From the outside, this seemed like the start of a process that could easily lead to the collapse of socialism in Poland.

Question

How did events following the death of Stalin affect Poland?

SOURCE B

On 25 October this year in Warsaw an enormous rally was held, where Gomułka said that Khrushchev had agreed that Soviet troops would withdraw to their former positions in Poland. However, they would still remain in Poland because of the West German militarists' threat. This is accepted by the greater part of the Polish people. There were some isolated anti-Soviet demonstrations under the slogans: 'For a free Poland', for the return of Rokossowski to Moscow and support for the Hungarians and demands for the release of leading Polish churchmen.

Extract from a Bulgarian military intelligence report on the situation in Hungary and Poland, 1 November 1956. Adapted from http://www.cwihp.org.

The restoration of stability

The Soviets now had to consider the best way of bringing the Poles back into line without using force. More serious anti-Soviet activity was taking place in Hungary, and military intervention in two Warsaw Pact countries would have stretched the USSR's resources to the limit. In addition, it was clear from the outset that the leadership of the PUWP would not tolerate the reinstatement of the pro-Stalinist faction that had been agitating for a return to more extreme measures of social control.

On 19 October 1956, Khrushchev visited Warsaw, and Soviet troops in Poland were told to prepare to move on the capital. However, the Politburo then elected Gomułka as secretary general. After Soviet fears about a possible 'sell-out' to the US had been addressed – and in return for Poland's promise to remain loyal to the Warsaw Pact – the USSR had no option but to allow the PUWP leadership to follow a reformist Polish 'road to socialism'. Gomułka was confirmed as first secretary of the PUWP, and a series of concessions were offered to the Poles, including promises not to interfere in Poland's internal affairs. In practice, this meant Poland had moved from the position of **puppet state** to that of a **client state**. The workers' councils were retained and collectivisation was abandoned. The land was returned

puppet state A state which has a nominal leader but which in reality is controlled by a foreign power.

client state A state which, usually in return for economic or political support, gives uncritical allegiance to another state.

to peasants and land ownership on a relatively large scale was permitted. Greater freedom of speech and of expression in the arts, along with greater personal freedom, was also allowed. The church was given guarantees of limited freedom, making it the only fully independent church in the Eastern bloc.

SOURCE C

The Polish leaders, especially Gomułka, sought to defend everything that was happening in their country. They assured the Soviet delegation that the measures being taken would not have an adverse effect on Poland's relations with the USSR. On the question of why so many changes had occurred in the Polish Communist leadership Gomułka said that the comrades who had not been re-elected to the Politburo had lost the confidence of the party masses. We are very worried because the comrades who were replaced were known to the USSR as trustworthy revolutionaries who were faithful to the cause of socialism.

Extract from the minutes of a meeting of the Politburo of the USSR, 24 October 1956, detailing the report of a Soviet commission sent to Poland. Adapted from http://www.cwihp.org.

Fact

The Polish border was a key point of contention between Poland and Germany in the west and Poland and the USSR in the east (see page 176). In 1939, the Soviets had occupied (or reoccupied) land taken from Russia by Poland in 1921, and in 1945 they refused to return it. To compensate the Poles, the Allies shifted Poland's western border further west at Germany's expense. This realignment of Poland's frontiers involved mass resettlement of Germans.

These measures brought the situation in Poland back under control, and stability returned. In effect, a small revolution took place in 1956, but it was channelled through, and resolved by, the communists, whose leading role was not seriously challenged. Gomułka realised that some reform was necessary if the PUWP was to survive. In fact, in the long term, he managed to restore party dominance. For example, by the 1960s the workers' councils were effectively functioning as extensions of the party. It was difficult to resist this development because there was no real organised political movement outside the PUWP. Gomułka also believed that the USSR was Poland's only protection against a resurgent Germany. In 1955, West Germany became a member of NATO and started rearming. The West Germans pointedly refused to recognise the new western border of Poland as it had been established along the Oder–Neisse line, and fear of a future attempt by the Germans to recover this territory influenced Gomułka's decisions in 1956.

The main trend evident from the events of 1956 is the effect of reform within an authoritarian political structure – that is, reform tended to spark off radicalism. The events also show that the use of force, a common reaction by Eastern bloc regimes to popular unrest, was not always appropriate or effective. Gomułka restored order and stability through a degree of compromise. In some ways his policy worked because he knew he could eventually restore communist dominance. In other ways, however, his policy made problems worse because it did not address fundamental issues such as social organisation and freedom, and it allowed the survival of elements of Polish society that later became a focus for resistance. In particular, an independent Catholic Church that was diametrically opposed to many of the basic principles of Marxism developed into a powerful political force in Poland. The failure to carry through collectivisation also allowed for the survival of a bourgeois class that agitated for further reform as time went on.

Question

How and to what extent did religion play a role in undermining communist control in Poland?

Gomułka's solution to the events of 1956 began to fall apart in the mid 1960s. The compromises to which he had agreed did not address the underlying tensions within Polish society. In particular, Gomułka was at heart an authoritarian. As he slowly reinstated communist dominance in Polish society, rifts began to appear once more. As social tension rose in Poland, communist chiefs within the country, and outside observers like the Soviets, perceived events as part of a wider pattern and thus interpreted them as a greater threat to the PUWP and communism than they perhaps were.

End of unit activities

1 Using the information in this chapter, draw up a table to clarify the role played by each of the organisations listed below in the history of Poland after 1939. For each, include information (if available) on leaders, who the organisation represented, what it wanted for Poland, and what actions it took.

- Polish Home Army
- London Poles
- Polish Workers' Party
- Peasant Party
- Lublin Committee
- Polish United Workers' Party

2 Choose one of the following topics and carry out some research on it. Then prepare an oral presentation to explain clearly how the incident contributed to anti-Soviet feelings in Poland. You may start by consulting one of the websites below, but look for other information as well.

The Katyn Massacre (1940)
http://news.bbc.co.uk/2/hi/europe/8606126.stm
https://www.cia.gov/library/center-for-the-study-of-intelligence/csi-publications/csi-studies/studies/winter99-00/art6.html

The Warsaw Rising (1944)
http://www.warsawuprising.com/
http://www.warsaw-life.com/poland/warsaw-1944-uprising

3 'The communists used a combination of persuasion and intimidation to consolidate their hold on power in post-war Poland.'

Carry out some research into this statement. Then divide the class into two groups. One group should prepare an argument to support the statement and the other an argument to oppose it.

4 Draw a spider diagram to illustrate the factors contributing to unrest in Poland in 1956. Include information on political, economic and cultural factors, as well as external influences.

5 Select evidence from the text in this unit to prepare an argument to support (or oppose) the view that Gomułka was a Polish nationalist as well as a communist. Write up your findings in the form of a newspaper article, with a suitable headline.

2 Methods of achieving independence from Soviet and centralised control

Timeline

1956 USSR agrees not to interfere in the internal affairs of Yugoslavia; severe civil disturbances in Poznán and other parts of Poland

1968 disturbances in Poland

1973 oil crisis plunges the world economy into crisis

1976 Committee for the Defence of the Workers (KOR) founded

1978 Karol Wojtyła elected first Polish pope, John Paul II

1979 papal visit to Poland

1980 more unrest leads to formation of Solidarity (Solidarność)

1981 military coup by General Jaruzelski

1985 Mikhail Gorbachev becomes leader of the USSR

1989 fall of communism in Poland; Wałęsa, becomes president

Mieczysław Moczar (1913–86)
Moczar was a high-ranking member of the Polish Workers' Party and an army general. Famous for his virulent anti-semitism and his extreme nationalism, he headed a faction of party hardliners in 1968.

Key questions

- What role did Mieczysław Moczar play in challenging Soviet and centralised control?
- What was the contribution of Edward Gierek?
- What organisations challenged Soviet/centralised control?
- What brought about the end of communism and Soviet control?
- What part did Lech Wałęsa play?

Overview

- During the 1960s, opposition to the communist regime in Poland increased.
- Like other Eastern bloc states, Poland was affected by the events of 1968.
- Increasing economic problems in Poland from the late 1960s onwards created a workers' movement, Solidarność (Solidarity), which initially agitated for better wages and working conditions.
- Solidarity soon became an influential political movement, challenging many of the basic precepts upon which the communist state was based.
- Initially, Solidarity was very effective, but in the medium term it failed in the face of state repression.
- By the mid 1980s, the state had restored order and pushed Solidarity underground.
- By the late 1980s, a situation was evolving that provided the context for the fall of communism in Poland.
- Solidarity played an important role in these events, but there were other key factors too, including continuing economic problems and changes in the USSR.

What role did Mieczysław Moczar play in challenging Soviet and centralised control?

Initially, pressure for change came from an unexpected quarter. A Polish general, **Mieczysław Moczar**, formed a veterans' association to bring together members of the communist resistance and the Home Army. He also began to severely criticise the USSR for its actions during the Second World War, especially the Katyn Massacre (see page 178). Moczar did not call for reform – despite being a leading communist, he was also a strong nationalist and even resorted to stirring up anti-semitism in order to gain support for his ideas. In fact, in 1952, he was dismissed from office because of these views, and spent a brief time in prison. The thrust of his campaign was the establishment of a more nationalist approach to communism in Poland. The effect of his actions, however, was to bring Poland's relationship with the USSR into sharp focus once more. In 1966, there was a direct clash between the communists and the church. On the 1000th anniversary of the foundation of the Polish church, bishops wrote to their German counterparts seeking reconciliation for the events of the Second World War. The PUWP immediately accused the church of undermining Poland's national interests. Thus, as the important year of 1968 and the Prague Spring (see page 155) approached, Poland's internal political and social stability was beginning to show signs of weakness.

The events of 1968

The events in Poland in 1968 were not as dramatic as those that occurred at the same time in Czechoslovakia, but they cast doubt on Gomułka's ability to maintain communist dominance in Poland. There was also a danger that events in Czechoslovakia would incite similar actions in Poland – one of the most important members of the Warsaw Pact. In January 1968, a production of the strongly anti-Russian 19th-century play *The Forefathers* encouraged student protest againsts the centralised regime, which led to calls for a general strike. These popular acts of passive opposition to Soviet control turned into direct action in March, as events in Czechoslovakia unfolded. In Warsaw, violent clashes took place between students and the police, and it seemed that military intervention might be necessary to restore order. Gomułka's position as PUWP leader was also directly threatened by Moczar. Order was restored by force and by targeting Jews as the alleged instigators of anti-socialist activity. This anti-semitism played to a deep-rooted prejudice in Polish society. Gomułka was lucky to survive the crisis, and the USSR played a key role in ensuring he retained his position. Given the events in Czechoslovakia, which had diverted the Warsaw Pact's military resources, Moscow could not allow another socialist state to stray from the communist mainstream.

Thus, by 1968, political agitation within Poland had twice been prevented by the party. The underlying economic and social forces that had caused the unrest in the first place had not been addressed, however.

What was the contribution of Edward Gierek?

Economic and political developments in the 1970s

The events of 1968 had shaken the USSR, and it decided that a new form of socialism would have to be imposed to maintain the stability of the communist bloc. Since Khrushchev's time, the concept of market socialism (see page 149) had driven reform, and the Soviets decided to place greater emphasis on changes in the economic structure of Eastern Europe – in particular the production of consumer goods – to prevent a repeat of the events of 1968. There were problems with implementing this policy, however. To begin with, workers were not used to manufacturing high-quality goods. Furthermore, technological development had tended to be confined to the military sector of the economy and it was difficult to expand this to cover consumer items. Finally, capital was needed to finance these changes, and the only real source of such funding was the West. In part, it was this need for financial aid to implement economic changes in the Eastern bloc that encouraged the interval of détente which characterised this period of the Cold War, and which led to the **Helsinki Agreements** of 1975.

Theory of knowledge

History and ethics

The tactic of using anti-semitism to win popular support raised issues of deep concern, as well as questions about the attitude of many Poles towards Nazi actions during the German occupation. About 3 million Jews died – 90% of the Jewish population of Poland – and many of the most notorious Nazi death camps, including Auschwitz and Treblinka, were in Poland. Read this review of a study of post-war anti-semitism in Poland, and comment on the attitude of the Catholic Church towards it. http://www.nytimes.com/2006/07/23/books/review/23margolick.html?_r=1

Helsinki Agreements A series of documents signed by all European states and the USA, amongst others, in which they undertook to improve East–West relations.

Edward Gierek and events in the 1970s

Even before 1975, Poland and other Eastern bloc states began to seek loans from the West. At first Western banks were eager to lend money, but in 1973 the October War in the Middle East and the ensuing oil crisis transformed the situation. Poland's plans to change the direction of its economic development were stopped in their tracks.

The first major signs that the settlements of 1956 and 1968 were about to break down emerged in December 1970. The economic problems that had plagued the country since 1948 resurfaced, and strikes and riots broke out in reaction to the government's announcement of a 36% increase in food prices just before Christmas. Workers at the Gdańsk and Gdynia shipyards led these demonstrations, and their protest movement this time was largely outside any communist-controlled bodies and structures. Instead, workers wanted their independent trade union to be legitimised. The Lenin shipyard in Gdańsk later became the birthplace of the Solidarity trade union, and one of the leading members of the strike committee in 1970 was Lech Wałęsa, who later played a key role in developments in Poland.

Edward Gierek (1913–2001)
The leader of the PUWP from 1970 to 1980, Gierek was a reformer who oversaw a period of expansion and prosperity in Poland in the 1970s. He was also an advocate of better relations with the West. He was ousted in 1980, after the Polish economy went into rapid decline and unrest grew.

Initially, Gomułka's reaction was characteristically repressive, and police were ordered to crush the 'counter-revolutionaries'. Order was restored, but in the process 75 people were killed and 2000 injured. Public outrage at these events placed so much pressure on the government that Gomułka – who had already lost much credibility in the 1968 crisis – was forced to resign as first secretary of the PUWP. He was replaced by **Edward Gierek**. The fall of the party's leader showed the extreme pressure it was under, and demonstrated the power of popular opposition to the government. The events of 1970 provided a model for later political action.

Gierek rushed to make concessions to restore order. Price increases were cancelled, and wages and social security benefits were increased. In January 1971, he successfully appealed to strikers to return to work. He also launched an ambitious plan for 'consumer socialist' economic regeneration, based on Western loans and imported technology. Attempts were also made to increase the import of luxury goods from the West, at considerable cost to the government. Over half of the personnel in the middle and upper ranks of the PUWP were changed. For a short period of time, between 1972 and 1974, the press was given extensive freedoms. These radical steps had the desired effect, and not only did the disturbances of 1970 abate but the living standards of average Poles

SOURCE A

Eastern European GNP as a percentage of the European average.

Country	1910	1938	1973
Europe	100	100	100
Czechoslovakia	98	82	117
Hungary	75	67	89
Poland	70	55	89
Romania	61	51	66

From Berend, I. T. 1996. Central and Eastern Europe, 1944–1993. Cambridge, UK. Cambridge University Press. p. 188.

genuinely improved by up to 40%. Gierek also negotiated personally with the strikers and promised them greater inclusion in government decisions.

In 1972, wages were again increased to encourage harder work and thus greater productivity. By the following year, agricultural and industrial production, investment and wages were all up. In addition, prices had stabilised and the prospect of a genuine economic boom within a structure of market socialism seemed to be within Poland's grasp. Political change, however, had not kept up with economic reform. Much more seriously, Poland had dangerously exposed itself in order to finance the consumer demand and industrial development that lay behind this progress. When the world economy went into rapid decline, new loans from the West dwindled and existing ones were subject to far higher interest rates. All these developments created a massive national debt, just as the world was hit by the 1973 oil crisis. Furthermore, by 1974 half of Poland's trade was with the West rather than with its Comecon (see page 147) partners, so when Western demand for Polish goods evaporated, an economic crisis ensued in Poland.

Workers' expectations had been raised by the reforms of the early 1970s. Now, however, the government could no longer meet these expectations. In 1976, attempts to increase food prices by 60% resulted in a renewed wave of strikes, protests, civil unrest and riots. These were met with a heavy-handed police reaction. Gierek managed to stave off a major crisis by withdrawing the food-price increase and instead begged the West successfully for food and economic support. However, this could not halt Poland's ongoing economic problems.

Gierek had reorganised some parts of Polish industry into what were called Large Industrial Concerns. Wages in these organisations were allowed to rise steeply. Poland faced a housing crisis, with chronic shortages in the cities and low standards of amenities in rural dwellings. Public services such as health care collapsed under the pressure. Four million Poles left the country to settle in the West, and these were mainly highly skilled workers. These problems were exacerbated by social inequalities – the privileges enjoyed by party members caused resentment in others. Such discontents were heightened by the fact that 30% of the industrial working class was under 25. Though these young people were often better educated than older workers, most of them had ended up in the factories, as the nomenklatura system (see page 167) meant there were limited opportunities for significant social mobility.

There was also discontent within the PUWP. Polish communism had always had nationalist leanings and, as we have seen, this created friction between elements of the party and the USSR. By 1979, the large debt owed to the West had created a new insult to Polish national pride. The PUWP was, however, unable to control the situation. Managing wages and prices was difficult due to the potential for civic unrest. The country's debts could only be serviced by more borrowing – so much so that, by 1979, 92% of Poland's export earnings were being used to pay off its international debt.

Gierek's attempts to find a political solution to these economic problems had little effect. In 1977, an amnesty was granted to all those involved in the disturbances of 1976. In the same year, Gierek met Cardinal Wyszyński (a leading figure in the reform movement) and Pope Paul VI in the hope of enlisting the support of the Catholic Church. This was simply interpreted as a sign of weakness. Gierek even appealed to the country's deep-rooted sense of nationalism by allowing a statue of Marshal Piłsudski, the right-wing nationalist dictator of Poland from 1926 to 1935, to be erected. But nothing could quell the rising unrest in the country.

What organisations challenged Soviet/ centralised control?

The problems of the late 1970s created a new feature of opposition in Poland – organised groups that could articulate the demands of civil society in a more coherent and effective manner than striking and rioting. In particular, the teachings of Karl Marx on issues such as egalitarianism led many well-educated young workers to criticise the privileges of the communist élites. The first of these groups to emerge was the Committee for the Defence of the Workers (KOR), in reaction to the events of 1976. Initially this body – led by Jacek Kuroń and Karol Modzelewski – was a welfare organisation established to provide support for those in prison and the families of those who had died in the labour strikes. Within a year, however, KOR had become politicised and renamed itself the Committee for Social Self Defence, or KSS/KOR. It began to criticise the inability of the PUWP to protect the rights and interests of workers.

Finlandisation A term derived from the political situation in Finland after the Second World War. Although a free, liberal democratic state with a capitalist economic system, Finland lived in the shadow of its former wartime enemy the USSR. It was therefore very careful to accommodate Soviet wishes. The term Finlandisation therefore refers to a Western-style state under heavy Soviet influence.

One of the most significant aspects of KSS/KOR was that it drew support from Warsaw intellectuals from outside the communist structure, teaming up intellectuals who had protested in 1968 with workers who had protested in 1970. This was an entirely new and very dangerous development, because until this time the PUWP had been able to control dissident elements within society by offering concessions and then absorbing them into party structures. KSS/KOR began to argue for the **Finlandisation** of Poland, to create a truly independent Polish form of socialism. The group created an underground press and produced newspapers such as *Robotnik* ('The Worker'). By September 1976, the Ministry of the Interior had identified 26 anti-socialist groups in the country, including the right-wing Confederation for an Independent Poland. It was KOR, however, that began the movement which led to the launch of the first of the independent trade unions on 1 May 1978 in Gdańsk. This was the Free Trade Unions of the Coast, and one of its leaders was Lech Wałęsa.

On 16 October 1978, Karol Wojtyła was elected Pope John Paul II. Wojtyła had been a professor at the Catholic University of Lublin and Archbishop of Krakow. His election as the first Polish pope provided an immediate focus for Polish national aspirations. Although he never openly criticised the communist regime, he had spoken out about the dignity of humankind and the right for personal freedom. In June 1979, he visited his native country, where his meetings attracted huge crowds. While in Poland, he highlighted human-rights issues. Wojtyła's popularity with the Polish masses only emphasised how unpopular the PUWP had become. By 1979, the party had developed into an organisation of élite workers. By the end of the 1970s, the Polish opposition – KOR, workers' unions and the church – was thus more united than it had ever been.

In the later part of the 1970s, the Polish authorities experienced a period of crisis. Throughout the 1950s and 1960s, a pattern of civil unrest in the form of strikes and riots was repeated again and again. This unrest was normally prompted by economic problems often brought into focus by price rises. In each case, the situation was brought under control by a mixture of force and concessions. With regard to the latter, the party had often been able to reinstate political reforms and always managed to infiltrate any new bodies that threatened democratic reform. As a result, communist rule retained its central position in

Pope John Paul II visits Poland in June 1979

Polish society. Economic reforms, however, were almost impossible to stop once set in motion. This would not have been a problem if Poland had not embarked on an ambitious programme of reform at the same time that the West entered a period of prolonged economic crisis. By 1979, rapid economic decline in Poland led to the emergence of a genuine alternative to the PUWP, a development that had been accelerated by Wojtyła's election as pope.

The crisis of 1980 and the rise of Solidarity

The trigger for the crisis of 1980 was, as always, economic. Poland's international debt had led Western creditors to call on the Polish government to apply price increases. On 1 July 1980, Gierek agreed to increase the price of meat, prompting some small protests as well as strikes at the Ursus tractor factory in Warsaw. However, in August, the sacking of a popular female union activist led to demands for her reinstatement. By 18 August, over 200 factories in the Gdańsk region had joined a strike committee established by Lech Wałęsa. It was from these crises that the unofficial trade union Solidarność (Solidarity) emerged. Solidarity produced its *21 Demands*, which included calls for improved pay and conditions, and for the right to form independent trade unions. Solidarity's demands were supported by both KOR and the Catholic Church.

Theory of knowledge

History and religion

Poland is an example of a situation where nationalism and religion overlapped to become a powerful political and historical force. Can you think of an example in the world today where this overlap exists, or where it is used by politicians to incite support?

Questions

What were the long-term economic problems faced by the communist regime in Poland? Why did they lead to political agitation?

This was the first major challenge to communist control in Eastern Europe since the Prague Spring of 1968. The Politburo decided to negotiate, and on 31 August 1980 the Gdańsk Agreement was reached. In exchange for acknowledgement of the PUWP's leading role in society, Solidarity secured for itself and for all Polish workers a series of remarkable concessions, including the right to establish independent trade unions and the right to strike.

Lech Wałęsa (b. 1943) Wałęsa was a political and union activist, and the leader of the trade union Solidarity from 1980. He later became a key player in the collapse of communism in Poland. He was the first post-communist president of his country in 1990, a position he held until 1995.

The success of Solidarity and its leader **Lech Wałęsa** would be challenged by the authorities in 1981, and in the short term the movement was countered by the imposition of martial law and the use of the apparatus of state control. However, Solidarity was a unique development in the communist bloc, and eventually played a significant role in the collapse of communism.

Workers outside the Lenin shipyard in Gdańsk in July 1980, catching leaflets being distributed by strikers

Historian Jacques Rupnik described the rise of Solidarity as Europe's 'first genuine workers' revolution since the Paris Commune of 1871'. The significance of Solidarity was the source of its power – the industrial working class. In other communist countries, protest had always come from intellectual sources. This is not to say that there were no intellectual influences on Solidarity, but rather that the core of its support was rooted in the mass of the working-class population. No other communist regime had to accommodate such a movement.

There are several reasons why Solidarity was so important to the independence movement in Poland. Firstly, the emergence of this organisation fundamentally undermined the ideology of Eastern European and Soviet-dominated socialism, in which workers and their practices were controlled by the state. Secondly, Solidarity soon evolved into a political organisation, campaigning for more than just changes in workers' pay and conditions, making demands for greater freedom of expression and religion, and for the release of political prisoners. Furthermore, the politicisation of Solidarity led to it being supported by both Polish intellectuals and, critically, the Catholic Church in Poland. Finally, the organisation provided a channel through which Polish national consciousness could find expression. This created a momentum that was difficult for the PUWP to counteract and was the reason why, despite its immediate authoritarian reaction, the party was eventually forced to negotiate with the movement.

What brought about the end of communism and Soviet control?

Impact of the Solidarity strikes

In February 1981, the moderate general **Wojciech Jaruzelski** became prime minister. He faced the first crisis of his administration just one month later, when a demonstration in Bydgoszcz in favour of the farmers' trade union Rural Solidarity was dealt with harshly by the security forces. On 27 March, Solidarity called a four-hour general strike in protest. The strikes were causing significant damage to Poland's fragile economy, and the constant pressure of servicing the country's debts forced the government to negotiate and concede some rights. Successes such as this gained Solidarity further recognition, and by mid 1981 the organisation had 10 million members. This was not just an important development in Poland – it also provided an inspiring example for other Eastern European states.

Solidarity supporters take part in a May Day march in 1985

Wojciech Jaruzelski (b. 1923)
Jaruzelski was the last commander in chief of the Polish People's Army (LWP), and the chair of the PUWP from 1981 to 1989. He was prime minister from 1981 to 1985, and then president 1985–89. He resigned as head of state after the Polish Round Table Agreement in 1989 was followed by democratic elections. Previously, as minister of defence in 1968, he had ordered the Polish 2nd Army to join in the Warsaw Pact invasion of Czechoslovakia. In 1970, he had helped Gierek oust Gomułka.

On 10 February 1981, a court decided that Rural Solidarity could register as an association but not as a union. This group represented Poland's 3.2 million smallholders, and they demanded the right to engage in collective bargaining. When the state reacted by arresting and beating up Rural Solidarity's leader, Jan Rulewski, calls went out for a general strike. Although this did not challenge the state directly, the government once again compromised, formally recognising Rural Solidarity in May 1981. However, many of the rank-and-file members began to champion more extreme action than Lech Wałęsa and other members of Solidarity's leadership were happy with.

By this time Gierek was coming under increasing political pressure from within the PUWP. His political base lay in the coalfields of his home province of Silesia, and the workers there had engaged in widespread industrial action, destroying his credibility.

Furthermore, Gierek was not certain that elements of the armed forces and police would co-operate in crushing the strikers by force. In fact, Gierek stuck to the same strategy that had worked in the past – offer concessions then regain control by making any independent organisation subservient to the party. Now, though, this strategy failed to work, and as a result, Gierek was replaced as first secretary by Stanisław Kania. However, Kania had no new solutions, resorting instead to simply sacking discredited officials and engaging in rhetoric.

The October Programme

In October 1981, Solidarity's October Programme directly challenged the party's leading role for the first time. The programme came at a time when the economic crisis meant rationing was widespread and the government was consistently unable to meet its debt payments. On 3 October Solidarity moved to force the government's hand, staging a one-hour national strike. Kania tried to buy off the workers with a 12% pay rise, but this simply worsened Poland's economic woes and was not enough to appease Solidarity.

Kania flew to Moscow to reassure the Soviets that the situation was under control, whilst East Germany and Czechoslovakia closed their borders with Poland. Tensions grew with the first arrest of a Solidarity member, Jan Narozniak, and when a leading member of the Warsaw branch of the movement, Zbigniew Bujak, demanded an investigation into the secret police and the circumstances surrounding the deaths of protesters in 1970 and 1976. As far as the PUWP was concerned, Solidarity had now become an open political threat.

Despite this, there was no direct confrontation between Solidarity and the party. This was partly due to the personalities of the key players in the leadership – both Wałęsa and Kania were instinctively more inclined to compromise than fight. The church also began to call for restraint. All sides were also afraid of a Soviet invasion and, indeed, troops were massing on the Polish frontier in the Baltic States and the Ukraine.

Solidarity demanded legal recognition, and this was formally granted in a Warsaw court on 24 October. The court, however, inserted a series of caveats into the legal document of recognition, including agreements that the union would not become a political party or undermine Poland's alliances. Many Solidarity members believed that the court had acted beyond its jurisdiction, and at an open-air mass on All Saints Day, Solidarity leaders both commemorated the Katyn Massacre and called for a general strike.

Question

Why were the communist authorities forced to officially recognise Solidarity in 1981?

The Communist Party regains control

At this point, the PUWP began an attempt to regain control of the situation, after considerable pressure was placed on the party by the USSR. In July 1981, the party held its ninth congress, in the course of which it voted a number of members who also belonged to Solidarity on to its central committee. Secret voting in party elections was also introduced. Although radical, these acts did little to change the basic outlook of PUWP members, which was conservative in the extreme and sought to protect the privileges of its members. Furthermore, the congress was overshadowed by Solidarity's first national congress in September. This meeting demanded that a referendum should be held on party reform. Solidarity also decided to publish books on Polish history, and even publicly declared it would support the peoples of other Eastern bloc states in setting up similar unions. In November 1981, Solidarity members went further still, openly attacking the Soviet leadership in Moscow and demanding full-scale reform in Poland. The government then began talks with Solidarity on the formation of a 'Front of National Unity'. These developments were a direct threat to Soviet **hegemony** in Eastern Europe, and prompted action by the new first secretary, ex-minister of war Wojciech Jaruzelski, who had replaced Kania in October.

hegemony The dominant influence of one region or country over others in political affairs. It can also refer to the power and influenceof some social classes or groups over others.

SOURCE B

In regard to the situation in the Polish People's Republic the Politburo of the USSR recommends:

1. The endorsement of Comrade Brezhnev's information about the situation unfolding in the Polish People's Republic.
2. The establishment of a Commission to deal with this matter.
3. To instruct the Commission to pay close attention to the situation unfolding in Poland and to keep the Politburo regularly informed about the state of affairs in Poland and about possible measures on our part.
4. In the event of dangerous development the Commission is to bring suggestions about necessary courses of action before the Politburo.

Extract from Top Secret Politburo instructions about how to deal with the Polish crisis, 25 August 1980. Adapted from http://www.cwihp.org.

Imposition of martial law

Despite reformers in the Communist Party having gained greater internal democracy, hardliners now began to call for strong action to deal with both the economic and the political crisis. The government struck first at Solidarity's most radical centres, in Wrocław and Katowice. On 2 December 1981, riot police landed by helicopter on the roof of a fire officers' training school to break up a strike there. This act shook the union's leadership and they met in secret in Radom to plan their response. The meeting was radical, and some argued for a full-scale revolt. Unfortunately, the meeting had been bugged by the secret police. The tapes were doctored to make the Solidarity leadership seem a threat to public order, and then published. This prompted a full-scale government crackdown.

Historical debate

There is some historical debate over the extent to which the concerns of the Soviet and Polish governments about the intentions of Solidarity leaders were justified. Robert Gates, for instance (in *From the Shadows*), has commented on how the CIA actively engaged in covert action against Soviet influence in Eastern Europe by providing Solidarity with 'printing materials, communications equipment and other supplies for waging underground political warfare ...'.

On the night of 13–14 December 1981, Jaruzelski imposed martial law, and Poland's borders and cities were sealed off. The authorities rounded up and imprisoned most of Solidarity's leadership, including Wałęsa, along with thousands of activists and strikers. Political authority was placed in the hands of a military council, all civil rights were suspended and public services were placed under military control. Although some workers fought back, especially in the Silesian coalfields, the state had overwhelming force at its disposal and any attempts at protest were quickly suppressed. By Christmas 1981, Solidarity seemed finished, and the government was in total control of the country. The reason that the Polish army co-operated with Jaruzelski's action was simple – fear of Soviet invasion.

However, Jaruzelski did not attempt to use the 'normalisation' approach followed by Gustáv Husák in the wake of the Prague Spring (see page 155). Instead, he announced that the measures he had taken were temporary and would be rescinded once order was restored. He realised that Solidarity had changed Polish politics, creating an alternative to the PUWP, which had now lost all credibility in the eyes of the Polish people. So, although the media and artists were once again placed under government control, they were left alone as long as they avoided involvement with the banned Solidarity. Similarly, the Catholic Church, under Archbishop Glemp, reached agreement with Jaruzelski's government. However, in the long term it would become impossible to relax the grip that the military had on the state without the political situation once again spiralling out of control.

A few activists escaped arrest and continued their opposition underground. KOR pursued a form of 'anti-politics' protest, by creating an underground alternative society which spread rapidly in different localities. However, this made it difficult to conduct any national resistance or co-ordinated protest, and a generational divide began to emerge within the opposition movements.

Fact
The events of 1981 have parallels with the Prague Spring in Czechoslovakia in 1968. When faced with economic stagnation and collapse, the ruling parties in both states had to resort to the use of armed force.

In addition, Jaruzelski's actions did nothing to solve the economic problems that were at the root of the crisis. Indeed, the military coup of 1981 prompted economic sanctions by the West – one of Poland's major trading partners. Economically, the situation in the country worsened. The role of the Soviet Union in these events is also significant: behind every action that occurred throughout 1981 lay the threat of the Red Army. However, the USSR was facing problems of its own and, as the 1980s wore on, the fear of Soviet military action against anti-communist forces and in support of the oppressive regime in Poland and the other states in the Eastern bloc began to wane.

The fall of communism in Poland

Between 1981 and 1984, Jaruzelski slowly relaxed his hold on the country. Lech Wałęsa was released from detention in December 1982 and martial law was suspended. During 1983 and 1984, other Solidarity leaders were also released. In 1984, an amnesty was declared for all those who had been caught up in the events of 1981. However, there was no doubt that Solidarity had suffered a major setback, which became clear during the 1984 local elections. Although Solidarity had called for a boycott, the turnout was over 60%.

Jaruzelski also carried out reforms and changed the party's approach to dealing with crises. When the pro-Solidarity priest Jerzy Poiełuszko was kidnapped and murdered for his anti-communist preaching, the security police responsible were put on public trial.

Solidarity members celebrate the first anniversary of the recognition of Rural Solidarity, outside Warsaw Cathedral, May 1982

Question

Why do you think Solidarity members chose to commemorate their victory at Warsaw Cathedral?

In 1985, prices were increased in an attempt to bring the economy under control. This resulted in a predictable repeat of the events of previous years and Solidarity once more became active, demanding a boycott of that year's elections. Once again, this was only partially successful, and caused Wałęsa to be imprisoned for a second time, in February 1986. Later that year, Jaruzelski granted an amnesty to all those who had been arrested under martial law.

In 1985, Mikhail Gorbachev became leader of the Soviet Union, and his reforms in the USSR began to have an impact in Poland. In particular, it was becoming obvious that, far from threatening to invade to restore communism, Gorbachev would no longer back Jaruzelski's regime with armed force. Jaruzelski moved quickly to support Gorbachev's policy of *glasnost* (freedom), and Poland soon became the most liberal state in the Eastern bloc. This led to the lifting of international economic sanctions. In September 1987, the US vice-president George Bush made an official state visit, during which he met both Jaruzelski and Wałęsa.

SOURCE C

Acting on the basis of a mandate given to me in democratic elections at the First Congress of Solidarity in 1981 as chairman of that Union, led by an opinion expressed by the leaders of national and regional authorities, I am calling on the government to take measures, which would enable the realization of the principle of union rights and put an end to the martial law which constrains the development of trade unionism.

I am also concerned about progress towards further economic development, particularly in relation to the West.

Extract from a letter from Lech Wałęsa to the Polish communist government, 2 October 1986. Adapted from http://www.cwihp.org.

The main problem the regime now faced was that Solidarity's leadership and example had created a deep-rooted opposition to the PUWP in Polish society. By 1986, there were six underground newspapers and even an anti-government radio station, Radio Solidarity. Thus, when the government attempted radical economic reforms in October 1986, the population was able to co-ordinate resistance. However, the economy was once again on the point of collapse, and this led to a new political crisis. Jaruzelski agreed to the formation of private firms, but the austerity measures imposed resulted in major price rises. So, in November 1987, the government held a national referendum to seek approval for the changes. Significantly, Solidarity called for boycotts and the government lost the vote.

More radically, in January 1988, a co-ordinated wave of strikes brought the Polish economy to a standstill. These strikes were led by younger Solidarity – as well as non-Solidarity – workers, and were beyond the control of Solidarity's leadership.

SOURCE D

Generally, anxiety is rising due to the prolonged economic crisis. The opinion is spreading that the economy instead of improving is getting worse. As a result, an ever greater difference is developing between the optimism of the authorities and the feeling of the mass of society. Criticism directed at the authorities is rising because of the 'slow, inept and inconsistent' introduction of economic reform. Dissatisfaction is growing because of the rising costs of living. The opinion is spreading that the government has only one answer, price increases. Against this background the mood of dissatisfaction is strongest among the workers.

Extract from a Polish government report, 28 August 1987. Adapted from http://www.cwihp.org.

In August 1988, the coal industry went on strike, forcing the government to negotiate. At this point Jaruzelski made Wałęsa an offer – if Solidarity's leadership could persuade the militants to call off the strikes, the government would legalise Solidarity. Wałęsa convinced the union to accept, and after three days the strikes were called off.

SOURCE E

Right now we can begin to discuss the topics for negotiations. I think we should be concerned with two questions:

1) implementation of the promise made by the authorities that there would be no repression toward striking workers.
2) the legalization of Solidarity, consistent with the wishes of the striking workers.

A positive consideration of the above-mentioned questions will allow for a broader debate on economic and political reforms in our country.

Extract from a memorandum from Lech Wałęsa to the Polish communist government, 4 September 1988. Adapted from http://www.cwihp.org.

There were widespread changes in the upper echelons of the government and a new reformist, Mieczysław Rakowski, came to power as prime minister, alongside Jaruzelski. These changes in the Polish leadership – and the crippling nature of the industrial action – made it easier for Jaruzelski to overcome the divisions in the party and convince the Central Committee to agree to talks, which began on 18 January 1989.

Initially, these negotiations were simply to discuss legalising the union, but they soon took on a political tone. On 6 February, they became round-table talks, involving not just the government and Solidarity, but also other trade unions, opposition parties, intellectuals and the church. These were the first steps in the dismantling of communist rule in Poland.

The discussions came to an end on 5 March. Solidarity was to be given legal recognition by the state, as well as minority representation in a new parliament, while wide-ranging economic changes were to be put in place. The Catholic Church was to be given full legal status. Most radically, the political system was to be completely overhauled. A new parliament with two houses, an upper house called the senate and a lower house, the *sejm*, was to be set up and truly free elections would follow. The senate could veto decisions unless they were backed by a 65% majority in the *sejm*.

On the surface it might seem that Wałęsa was foolish to have accepted the conditions laid down by the government. Firstly, he agreed to an election within only two months of making the accord with the government. Solidarity had no experience of administering a nationwide election and had none of the infrastructure needed to guarantee success. Even Wałęsa despaired at having to agree to such a swift election in return for the recognition of the union for the second time. Secondly, not all of the seats in the parliament were contested. Voting for the senate was to be completely open but the phrase 'non-confrontational election' was used to describe the voting arrangements for the *sejm*. These arrangements meant that 65% of the seats in the *sejm* were contested unopposed by the PUWP and its allies. Solidarity and all the other opposition parties would contest only 35% of the available seats.

SOURCE F

Outlawed for seven years, Solidarity became the government's negotiating partner in February and a full-blown opposition party in the summer's parliamentary elections. Running largely on their identification with Lech Wałęsa, the Solidarity candidates so completely defeated the communists that the regime felt it had no choice but to form a coalition. President Jaruzelski settled on Walesa's handpicked choice for the premiership, the lawyer Tadeusz Mazowiecki. Now the once jailed and their former jailers share a common enemy: a bankrupt economy.

Extract from an article by Adrzej Wojda, a senator in the sejm, *August 1989. Quoted on http://web.archive.org/.*

Free elections

The Polish elections in June coincided with the first free elections in the USSR. Solidarity was elected with a staggering 99% of the openly contested seats, and some voters simply crossed off those they did not want elected from the ballot papers. In all, Solidarity candidates won all 161 seats in the *sejm*, and 99 out of the 100 seats in the senate; 33 of the 35 main communist leaders – including the prime minister, Rakowski – failed to secure seats in the *sejm*. Most significantly, the PUWP was prepared to accept this outcome. The only concession to the past was that Jaruzelski kept his position as head of state, and Solidarity even contrived to keep enough of its members absent from parliament to ensure his position could be secured by vote. Jaruzelski diplomatically resigned all his posts in the PUWP, but remained head of the army. This concession to the old regime was designed to allay Soviet fears and prevent a possible invasion by the USSR. It is clear from subsequent events, however, that such an invasion was never likely to happen.

Jaruzelski proposed that Solidarity enter into a coalition government, but Wałęsa insisted that their candidate, Tadeusz Mazowiecki, a Catholic intellectual and long-standing political advisor to Solidarity, should be prime minister. The communists attempted to secure Soviet support, but when Rakowski spoke to Gorbachev in late August, the Soviet leader stated that he was not concerned about the internal politics of Poland, although he would give Jaruzelski his nominal support. Only if the situation in Poland seemed to be a direct threat to the security of the USSR would he act. Once Gorbachev had been given assurances by Solidarity leaders that Poland would not leave the Warsaw Pact, Jaruzelski accepted Wałęsa's proposal and on 18 August, an interim administration was set up. On 21 August, on the 21st anniversary of the Warsaw Pact invasion of Czechoslovakia, 10,000 demonstrators took to the streets, chanting: 'Long live Dubček' and 'Long live Poland'. Poland thus led the way in 1989, holding the first free elections, with Mazowiecki becoming the first non-communist leader in the Eastern bloc. These events in Poland were followed by upheavals right across Eastern Europe.

Fact
Gorbachev had abandoned the defence policy established by Stalin in the immediate post-war period, and had come to the conclusion that the USSR could not afford to garrison Eastern Europe and pay for military interventions to support the region's communist leadership.

On 29 December 1989, the Republic of Poland was declared and the deputy prime minister, Leszek Balcerowicz, implemented his 'big bang' economic reforms (see page 208). Overnight, communism had ceased to exist in Poland.

Reasons for the communist collapse in Poland

The reasons for the collapse of communist power in Poland are twofold. Firstly, the country, like many of its neighbours, was at least partly reliant on the threat of Soviet intervention for the maintenance of its communist political system. Although the Soviets had not actually applied military power to the Polish situation – as they had in Czechoslovakia – the threat was always there. Indeed, fear of Soviet military intervention was a factor in maintaining relatively cordial relations between the government and the opposition. Furthermore, in the events that unfolded after 1980, the party had made concessions to Solidarity simply because it did not want the Red Army restoring order in its country.

The second factor, however, was almost uniquely Polish. The course taken by opposition in the country had been dictated by Poland's history. The strength of the Catholic Church in the country had protected it from direct attack by the party, and as the church became more politicised it had created a lasting and well-organised opposition. The Soviets represented more than a new order in the country after 1945; they were seen as a foreign invader who had stabbed Poland in the back in 1939 and 1945, and seemed to be attempting to reverse the events of the Russian Revolution, which had seen Poland regain its independence from the Russian Empire. This meant that, when opposition appeared, it was sustained over a period of time and grew into the KSS/KOR and, eventually, into Solidarity. Solidarity was a unique development because it directly challenged the idea that workers were the social élite in Poland – a belief that lay at the heart of communist ideology – and slowly eroded the legitimacy of the PUWP. Thus, as economic crisis followed economic crisis, the government lost the support of all but a few members of Polish society. This, combined with developments in the Soviet Union following the rise of Gorbachev in 1985, meant it could not retain its hold on power.

SOURCE G

In 1980–1981, the Solidarity movement drew the support of ten million Poles (that is, almost all the adult Poles of working age). A deep dent was made in the monolith of the Soviet bloc, whose fate would be soon sealed by its defeat in the Soviet–US economic struggle played out as the 'star wars' armament race. The national minorities, so invisible to the average Pole, considered Solidarity a 'Polish affair', into which they would not meddle. This was also due to the fact that most Solidarity members chose to express their anti-communist yearning for Poland's independence through Polish nationalism centered on the Roman Catholic Church. Prior to the imposition of martial law (1981–1983), however, Solidarity issued a statement, in which it obliged itself to guarantee 'full civil rights for all Poles in spite of their national origin'.

Kamusella, T. 'Poland's Minorities in the Transition from Soviet-Dominated Ethnic Nation-State to Democratic Civic Nation-State'. Quoted on http://www.yorku.ca/soi/_Vol_3_4/_HTML/kamusella.html

Questions

What does this academic think caused the success of Solidarity? Are there any flaws in his argument?

What part did Lech Wałęsa play?

Lech Wałęsa was born in 1943 to a working-class family. He entered the Lenin Shipyard in Gdańsk as an electrician in 1966. In 1980, he became the leader of the Solidarity trade union and after a period as a political prisoner he became a major figure in the final days of communist rule in Poland. In 1983, he was awarded the Nobel Peace prize. He was president of his country between 1990 and 1995. A charismatic leader with no higher education, he was propelled to the forefront of world politics by the events of the 1980s.

Lech Wałęsa addressing a Solidarity demonstration

Wałęsa was active as a trade unionist before the formation of Solidarity. Initially, he was interested in mainstream trade union issues: pay and conditions of service. The events of 1980, however, pushed Wałęsa over the line into politics. The reason for this was the nature of the communist state in Poland. At the heart of the state's ethos was the concept of 'workerism' – the idea that the workers of Poland were the élite of society. The problem was that the economic issues faced by the country in the later part of the 1970s put great stress on the relationship between the working classes and the Communist Party. Thus, when the demonstrations of 1980 began they were initially over pay, conditions and food.

Once it became obvious that the state could not easily fulfil the workers' needs, full-scale political activity became the next obvious step. Wałęsa recognised that the needs of the workers could only be met by internal reform of Poland's political system.

Solidarity leader

Wałęsa's career as a trade unionist began in 1968, when he encouraged his co-workers in the Gdańsk shipyards to boycott government-organised rallies that condemned recent student strikes. In 1970, he organised strikes in the shipyards against government plans to raise food prices. The heavy-handed reaction of the government to this industrial action, which resulted in the deaths of 30 workers, started Wałęsa on the road to full-scale political activity. In 1976, he was sacked from his job for his trade-union affiliations. As a result he suffered from long periods of unemployment.

In the later part of the 1970s, Wałęsa and his family were placed under surveillance by the secret police, and Wałęsa was arrested several times during this period. In 1976, he worked closely with KOR. By this point it is possible to argue that Wałęsa had become a full-scale political dissident.

The Gdańsk strike

Wałęsa was not actually a shipyard employee when he became the leader of the Gdańsk strikers in 1980. He soon rose to become leader of the Inter-Enterprise Strike Committee that turned what was a limited dispute into a genuine threat to the government. As a result, he became both a key player in the subsequent Solidarity movement and a figure of international renown. He was eventually arrested and imprisoned between 1981 and 1982, after which he attempted to return to the shipyards as an ordinary electrician. It was at this point that he was awarded the Nobel Peace prize.

Throughout the 1980s he continued his underground pro-Solidarity activities, until 1988, when he helped organise more strikes in Gdańsk. In December of that year he co-founded the Solidarity Citizens' Committee, effectively a political party, which emerged as the most powerful bloc in the *sejm* after the events of 1989. As leader of this bloc he backed Mazowiecki as Poland's first non-communist prime minister since 1939. In 1990, Wałęsa was elected president, a post he held until 1995.

Fact

The Inter-Enterprise Strike Committee was formed by Wałęsa and others in August 1980. It was best known for the issuing of its *21 Demands*, which led to the Gdańsk Agreement. The demands included the right to form free and independent trade unions, pay increases, and compensation for workers participating in the strikes.

Presidency

During his presidency Wałęsa oversaw the difficult transition to a market economy, although he actually left most of the decisions regarding this development to his prime minister, Hanna Suchocka. He was criticised for being over-authoritarian, especially within Solidarity, and proved ill-equipped either to lead the state or to handle the media. He was defeated in the presidential election of 1995 by Aleksander Kwasniewski.

Wałęsa was not a typical worker. He was essentially a political activist from 1970 onwards. Where he differed from other key players, such as Václav Havel in Czechoslovakia, was his background. He was not highly educated and saw the way to political reform through the organisation of workers and the use of industrial muscle in the form of strikes. During the period of opposition to the government he was a highly effective leader. In the more open and sophisticated political environment of a fully democratic state, however, he was found wanting and was soon marginalised.

End of unit activities

Activity

Historians discuss the role of individuals in the historical process. Consider Wałęsa as an individual who may have changed the course of history. Use him as a case study in a general essay based on the question below.

'To what extent is the historical process driven by the influence of individual human beings?'

Discuss your answer. Try to compare Wałęsa to other similar figures who might have changed the course of history.

1 Identify each of the following leaders and briefly explain the political role he played:
   - Moczar
   - Gierek
   - Kania
   - Jaruzelski
   - Mazowiecki.
2 Write an argument to support or oppose the view that economic issues were the basis of the dissatisfaction with communist rule in Poland.
3 Draw a spider diagram to illustrate the significance of the emergence of Solidarity as a political force in the early 1980s.
4 Draw up a table to summarise the reasons for the collapse of communism in Poland in 1989. Include issues such as economic problems, the political situation, the role of the church, external factors and the rise of Solidarity.
5 Write a critical biography of Lech Wałęsa in the form of a newspaper article. In it, examine how he emerged as a political activist, whether he deserved to win the Nobel Peace prize in 1983, and explain how someone who was so admired as a national hero could be voted out of office within five years.
6 'Lech Wałęsa's leadership was the critical factor in the collapse of communist control in Poland.' Discuss.

   In pairs, produce a profit/loss account for Wałęsa on a single piece of paper. On one side list positive factors which support the statement, on the other negative factors which challenge it. Then rate the factors from 1 (least convincing) to 5 (most convincing). Use the results as the basis for an essay plan.

3 The formation of and challenges to post-communist Poland

Key question

- What problems faced post-communist Poland?

Overview

- The biggest problem Poland faced after 1990 was the creation of a market economy. The leaders of the new Poland had to decide how this was to be achieved without inflicting unacceptable damage on the social fabric of the country. As in Czechoslovakia, some argued for a short, sharp shock, others for a slower conversion.
- The second issue was the creation of a democratic constitution along Western lines; this was achieved relatively easily and with great success.
- A rapid privatisation of the economy – the 'big bang' – was initiated, intended to launch Poland in the global capitalist market. One result of this was that, by 1990, Poland enjoyed the lowest rates of unemployment in Europe.
- The largest political problem lay with the new president, Lech Wałęsa. He had been an excellent campaigner for reform but he proved to be a poor leader of state. He soon fell from power.
- Solidarity, the movement that had so influenced the collapse of communism in Poland, was unable to adapt to the needs of the new state and rapidly declined. It eventually reverted to its former status as one of several national trade unions.
- Hanna Suchocka became prime minister in 1991 and managed to pilot the state through the complexities of the early 1990s.
- Since Poland made the transition from communism, it has become a mainstream European state.

Historical debate

Historian Francis Fukuyama's view that the 1989 events in Poland – and in the rest of Eastern Europe – marked the 'end of history' has been criticised by several historians as being an example of 'retrospective determinism'. Timothy Garton Ash, for example, questions whether the 'triumph' of free-market capitalism and the collapse of communism were 'inevitable'.

Timeline

1990	Solidarity wins the first free local elections in Poland; Wałęsa becomes first president of the country
1991	Hanna Suchocka made prime minister and effects successful economic reforms
1993	Solidarity's influence declines in the elections
1999	Poland becomes a member of NATO
2004	Poland becomes a member of the European Union

Fact

When, on 12 September, the *sejm* voted to accept Mazowiecki and his government, it meant that – for the first time in over 40 years – Poland had a government led by non-communists. In July 1990, the coalition cabinet was re-shuffled to remove the last remaining communists; and in October, the constitution was amended so that Jaruzelski could be replaced by a new president. This happened in December 1990, when Wałęsa became the first Polish president elected on a popular vote.

What problems faced post-communist Poland?

Economic problems

The new Polish government's first priority was economic reform. The country's economic weakness had always been at the root of the political problems faced by the former communist regime. Under the PUWP, the economy was over-centralised and dependent on heavy industry. This made it inflexible in the global capitalist marketplace, which increasingly dominated the late 20th century. Furthermore, the construction of a more consumer-oriented economy had only been achieved by borrowing heavily from the West. This created a serious debt crisis that Poland had been unable to control. These factors had conspired to set in train the events that had led to the collapse of communism in 1989. It was important that they were put right if the planned new liberal capitalist democracy was not to face the same fate.

SOURCE A

The first country to institute a 'shock therapy' was Poland, in 1989. Under the pressure of a clear economic disaster, its initial objective was basically to overcome hyperinflation and then introduce a market economy. Initial hyperinflation made the social costs very high. High unemployment and the economic ruin of individual farmers created widespread discontent. These social costs resulted in the defeat of the Solidarity reformers in the election of September 1993. The new government generally continued earlier policies but slowed down privatisation. Nevertheless, the overall growth rate of the Polish economy remains one of the highest in Europe.

Extract from a lecture delivered in 1997 by W. Roszkowski, the director of the Institute of Political Studies at the Polish Academy of Sciences. Quoted on http://www.cerc.unimelb.edu.au.

The new finance minister was American-educated Leszek Balcerowicz, supported by the Harvard economist Jeffrey Sachs. They proposed a rapid privatisation of the economy along Western lines, which they called the 'big bang'. A two-phase approach was put into action. Firstly, the currency was to be stabilised and inflation brought under control. This would allow Poland to enter the global capitalist market. Then the plan would enter phase two, in which mass privatisation would take place. A reluctant *sejm* passed the reform act in December. The reaction of the West – and Western firms – was predictably positive, and new loans were offered to help cushion Poland during the period of transition. The reforms had an instant effect, as small businesses began to flourish. However, this success was also due in part to the existence of a bourgeois farming class that had always indulged in small-scale free market trade, but that was now released from the constraints of the planned economy with the 'big bang'. The reforms also allowed what had been a black market to come out into the open. What is more, with the establishment of a stable currency with a favourable exchange rate with Western currencies, exports expanded considerably.

Fact

The reforms were not without problems. The transition created fluctuation in prices – an effect that Poles were not used to in the communist era. In addition, the move to free-market capitalism initially pushed down wages by almost 30%.

Solidarity, a workers' movement, had swept aside a state which had in many ways been a workers' state, in that for almost 50 years it had provided significant social and welfare benefits for the majority of the population. In its place, along with the political freedoms and democracy that the workers desired, came the economic liberalism of free-market capitalism. The effects of this economic system in Poland soon disillusioned the workers who had brought Solidarity to power, as they quickly found themselves suffering from the effects of global capitalism. The early imposition of Western-style 'economic shock therapy' to post-communist Poland caused similar social suffering and deprivation to that which occurred later in Czechoslovakia and the other Eastern bloc countries after the fall of communism.

SOURCE B

Key economic indicators in the Soviet Union and Eastern Europe, 1988–90

Country	Economic growth (%)			Inflation (%)		
	1988	1989	1990	1988	1989	1990
USSR	6	3	–4	7	9	10
Poland	5	0	–12	60	241	800
Czechoslovakia	2	1	–3	0	1	14
Hungary	2	1	–5	16	17	29
Romania	0	-11	–12	1	2	20

Cannon, M. et al. 2009. 20th Century World History. *Oxford, UK. Oxford University Press. p. 440.*

SOURCE C

When Solidarity won, Polish workers lost. ... with the one group that could control them [the workers], Solidarity, chiefly interested in promoting the marketization causing the emotional distress, a political crisis was inevitable.

Ost, D. 2005. The Defeat of Solidarity: Anger and Politics in Postcommunist Europe. *New York, USA and London, UK. Cornell University Press.*

Question

What were the initial effects of Western-style capitalist economic policies and privatisations on the Polish economy?

From January 1990, the Polish economy – and the Polish people – were subjected to the demands of a capitalist market economy. Price controls and trade barriers were removed, as were many state subsidies. The Polish złoty was made convertible with foreign currencies. Inflation was brought under control – but at a massive social cost. Industrial output fell by 30%, wages by 40% and unemployment rose from almost nil (under the communists) to over 1 million by the end of 1990. Poland soon had the highest unemployment rate in the whole of Europe.

Fact

It must be remembered that at the root of the events of 1991 was Solidarity, which was a union whose prime reason for existence was the protection of workers' rights. As a result, it was difficult or impossible for the government to push ahead with reform if it would create undue suffering to workers.

Privatisation soon followed, and by the end of 1991 almost half of all small firms were in private hands. Balcerowicz was more reluctant to privatise large-scale economic concerns, though. These remnants of the communist era were highly inefficient, and if they were reorganised along Western lines many of them may have gone bust and all would have had to shed labour. The new government feared that this would create mass unemployment and create further political instability.

In 1991, when five of the largest concerns in Poland were offered for sale, the response of potential owners was lukewarm at best. An attempt to broaden the privatisation plan by offering vouchers to all Polish citizens (which were in effect shares) floundered in 1990, as a new political crisis developed.

Political problems

In May 1990, the first free local elections confirmed Solidarity's domination. In July 1990, the coalition cabinet was reshuffled to remove the last remaining communists. On 12 September, the *sejm* voted to accept Mazowiecki and his government – for the first time in over 40 years, Poland had a government led by non-communists.

However, during September 1990, political pressure caused by the rapid 'Westernisation' of the country's economy came to the surface when the United Peasants' Party withdrew its support for the government coalition because of the end of state farming subsidies. Wałęsa followed suit when he began to politicise Solidarity due to frustration at the pace of reform. Wałęsa sacked the head of the Citizens' Committee, Wujec, prompting a political crisis. The *sejm* soon called for new elections and, in October, the constitution was amended so that Jaruzelski could be replaced by a new president. This happened in December 1990, when Wałęsa became the first Polish president, elected with 40% of the popular vote. However, the outcome of the election was not decisive enough to prevent Wałęsa being overruled on reforms to the electoral system, and, at the behest of the *sejm*, a new system of **proportional representation** was introduced.

proportional representation
A method of voting whereby each party gains representation in parliament more closely related to the proportion of the total votes it receives in an election.

The following year saw another election, with a large number of parties competing for seats. A coalition of six parties emerged. Significantly this election eliminated the last of the communists and the nationalist Confederation for an Independent Poland, which had come into being as an underground opposition movement in 1982. Solidarity was slowly collapsing in this new political environment. It had held together prior to the fall of communism as the primary opposition group, but once it had to compete in a proper political battle, cracks started to appear in its ranks and the interests of different members of the organisation began to create friction.

Solidarity supporters increasingly began to oppose the government, and this led to divisions and the creation of new political parties. Although Wałęsa defeated Mazowiecki in the presidential elections, the election contest had been bitter, and Solidarity became even more divided. The much-delayed parliamentary elections finally took place in October 1991 and gave further evidence of the political divisions in Poland. There followed a series of weak and short-lived coalition governments.

At the time of writing, Solidarity has returned to its roots and now serves Polish workers in the same capacity as a Western trade union – the only difference is its vast size and its legitimacy as the force that brought down the PUWP. Eventually, Eastern Europe's first female prime minister, **Hanna Suchocka**, emerged as leader of a disorganised *sejm* under a hostile president, Lech Wałęsa.

Hanna Suchocka (b. 1946)
Suchocka had a legal background and emerged as Poland's prime minister in 1992, a position she held for a year. Her mix of leftist economic politics and right-leaning social politics made her a compromise candidate who appealed to all wings of the *sejm* and allowed her to successfully pilot economic reform in Poland in the immediate post-communist years.

Suchocka created a programme for full-scale privatisation. She made a deal with organised labour called the Pact on Enterprises – a transfer of the remaining large-scale sectors of the Polish economy to private ownership. This would be phased to allow the economy as a whole time to adjust to the changes in the labour market. By 1993, Suchocka had managed to halt the decline of Polish production and create economic growth without simultaneously creating mass unemployment.

However, the September 1993 elections showed the continuing disintegration of Solidarity and the political impact of the introduction of capitalist free-market economic policies. Solidarity received less than the 5% necessary to obtain representation in the new parliament, while the 'former' communists gained a clear majority.

In the presidential elections of 1995, ex-communist Aleksander Kwasniewski defeated Wałęsa by a narrow margin. Capitalist economic shock therapy (see page 171), and Wałęsa, had done what Jaruzelski and martial law had failed to do – destroy Solidarity. As one Gdańsk worker commented in 1999: 'Yes, we have freedom: but what good is that if you have no money to buy the shiny goods in the shops?' Solidarity continued, but as only one of several national unions, and with a membership of only a few hundred thousand, compared to its 10 million members during the mid 1980s.

SOURCE D

The irony is painful. Workers started the great changes, yet have paid the highest price. Solidarity was originally a trade union, yet the result of its triumph is that Gdańsk workers are employed by their former workmates, now turned capitalist, in private firms with no trade unions at all.

Garton Ash, T. 2002. The Polish Revolution: Solidarity. *New Haven, USA. Yale University Press. p.* 380.

Poland and the wider world

Despite the political changes of 1993–95, the free-market policies of privatisation and de-regulation continued. As the millennium approached, Poland began to enter the European mainstream, not just politically and economically, but also culturally. By 2000, Poland was fully integrated with the capitalist nations in the West, and the most extreme expressions of the development of the country were its entry into NATO in 1999 and the European Union in 2004.

In some ways this is a return to Poland's historical position – later medieval and early modern Poland was one of the most powerful of European states. In others it marks real change: post-communist Poland is, like many other states, not a fully independent country. It is part of larger trans-national organisations like the European Union and is heavily under the influence of capitalist globalisation. The main difference experienced by Poland since 1989, however, is self-determination. Prior to that date the country had not been independent since the 18th century, apart from a short period in the inter-war years. It had been an outpost of the Tsarist Russian Empire, then it had fallen under Nazi tyranny and finally it operated as a satellite of the USSR. In none of these periods could Poland act independently. So too today, but the difference now is that it is a fully integrated part of Western European liberal democracy and Poles can influence their fellow Europeans via democracy, diplomacy and negotiation. Poland's economy is more efficient, and a stable and forward-looking country has been created. Whether this will last is, obviously, open to debate. The recent economic crisis has placed a burden on all developed states that has not yet been resolved.

Since 1990, Poland has enjoyed the relative weaknesses – political, economical and military – of the Soviet Union and then its successor Russian state. With a resurgent Russia, can Poland maintain its Western orientation without some kind of accommodation with its powerful Eastern neighbour?

Theory of knowledge

History and reason

On 10 April 2010, the Polish president, Lech Kaczynski, together with 89 other high-ranking Polish officials, including the head of the army and the head of the central bank, died in a plane crash in Smolensk, Russia, on their way to a ceremony to mark the 70th anniversary of the Katyn Massacre. Some people immediately assumed that the Russians were responsible. Explain why this is an example of bad reasoning. Find out what you can about relations between the two countries since the collapse of communism, and whether this accident revived old tensions.

End of unit activities

1. Draw a spider diagram to illustrate the impact of the 'big bang' reforms on the Polish economy in the early 1990s.
2. Poland joined the European Union in 2004. Find out how EU membership has affected the Polish economy, as well as the impact it has had on other aspects of economic life, such as migration to other EU member states.
3. Design a flow chart to illustrate the transformation of Solidarity from its establishment as an unofficial trade union in 1980, to its dominant role as an opposition political movement by 1989, and then its position in post-communist Poland.
4. Use the information in this unit, together with more from books and websites, to find out how successfully democracy has worked in Poland since 1990.
5. Hot-seating exercise:

   The character in the hot seat is Lech Wałęsa, and he will be interrogated in two sittings. Allow the individual who volunteers for the hot seat time to prepare a case, perhaps with the support of a team. The two sittings address the two phases of his political life, as a trade union and political activist and as president of Poland. The thrust of the questioning will demand explanations for success in the former, failure in the latter.

End of chapter activities

Activity

'What we may be witnessing is not just the end of the Cold War, or the passing of a particular period of post-war history, but the end of history as such. ... That is, the end point of mankind's ideological evolution and the universalization of Western liberal democracy as the final form of human government.'
Fukuyama, F. 1989. 'The End of History'

To what extent is this perspective a valid one when applied to the situation in post-communist Poland?

Summary activity

Copy the diagram below and, using the information in this chapter, make point form notes under each heading.

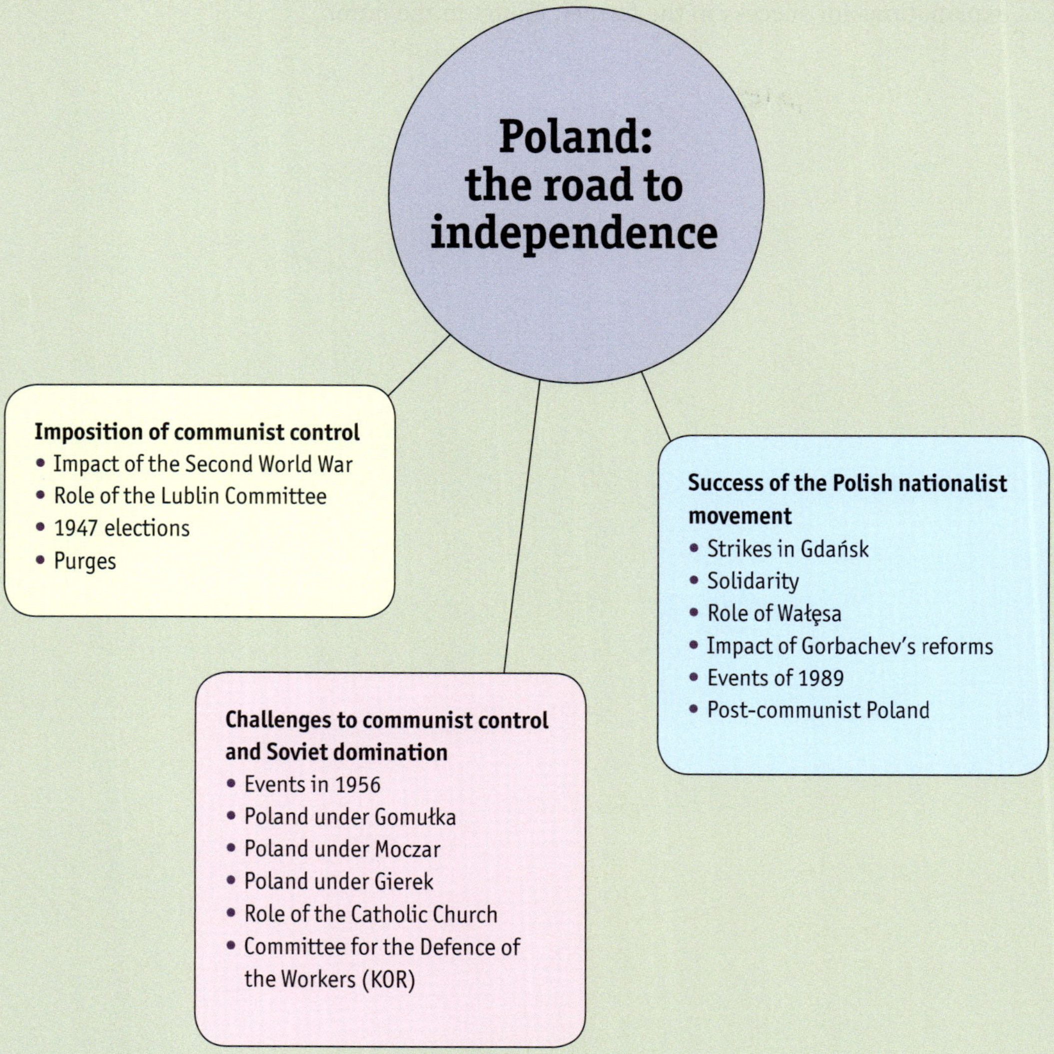

Paper 2 exam practice

1 'Non-violent movements rarely achieve political and social change.' How far do you agree with this assertion?

2 Why did Poland achieve independence from centralised Communist control and Soviet domination?

3 Analyse the role of religion and nationalism in Poland's quest for independence from communist control and Soviet domination.

Further reading

Try reading the relevant chapters/sections of the following books:

Calvocoressi, Peter. 1987. *World Politics Since 1945 (5th Edn)*. London, UK and New York, USA. Longman.

Crampton, Richard J. 1994. *Eastern Europe in the Twentieth Century – And After*. London, UK and New York, USA. Routledge.

Dubček, Alexander. 1993. *Hope Dies Last*. New York, USA. Kodansha America.

Kenny, Padraic. 2006. *The Burdens of Freedom: Eastern Europe since 1989*. London, UK. Zed Books.

Longworth, Philip. 1994. *The Making of Eastern Europe*. Basingstoke and London, UK. St Martin's Press.

Pittaway, Mark. 2004. *Brief Histories: Eastern Europe 1939–2000*, London, UK. Hodder Education.

Stokes, Gale. 1993. *The Walls came Tumbling Down: The Collapse of Communism in Eastern Europe*. Oxford, UK. Oxford University Press.

Vadney, Thomas E. 1998. *The World Since 1945*. London, UK. Penguin Books.

Webb, Adrian. 2002. *Central & Eastern Europe Since 1919*. London, UK. Routledge.

7 Exam practice

Introduction

You have now completed your study of the main aspects and events of nationalist and independence movements in Africa and Asia and post-1945 Central and Eastern Europe. In the previous chapters, you have practised answering some of the types of source-based question you will have to deal with in Paper 1. In this chapter, you will gain experience of dealing with:

- the longer Paper 1 question, which requires you to use both sources and your own knowledge to write a mini-essay
- the essay questions you will meet in Paper 2.

Exam skills needed for IB History

This book is designed primarily to prepare both Standard and Higher Level students for the Paper 2 Nationalist and Independence Movements in Africa and Asia and post-1945 Central and Eastern Europe topic (Topic 4). However, by providing the necessary historical knowledge and understanding, as well as an awareness of the relevant key historical debates, it will also help you prepare for Paper 1. The skills you need for answering both Paper 1 and Paper 2 exam questions are explained in the following pages.

The example below shows you how to find the information related to the 'W' questions that you will need to evaluate sources for their value and limitations.

SOURCE X

The situation in Indochina is not that of open military aggression by the Chinese Communist regime. Thus, in Indochina, the problem is one of restoring tranquillity in an area where disturbances are fomented from Communist China, but where there is no open invasion by Communist China. This task of pacification, in our opinion, cannot be successfully met merely by unilateral armed intervention. Some other conditions need to be established. Throughout these Indochina developments, the United States has held to a stable and consistent course and has made clear the conditions which, in its opinion, might justify intervention.

Extract from an address by US secretary of state John Foster Dulles, 11 June 1954 on the situation in Indochina, delivered to the World Affairs Council.

address WHAT? (type of source)
John Foster Dulles WHO? (produced it)
11 June 1954 WHEN? (date/time of production)
situation in Indochina WHY? (possible purpose)
World Affairs Council WHO? (intended audience)

Paper 1 exam practice

Paper 1 skills and questions

This section of the book is designed to give you the skills and understanding to tackle Paper 1 questions. These are based on the comprehension, critical analysis and evaluation of different types of historical sources as evidence, along with the use of appropriate historical contextual knowledge. For example, you will need to test sources for reliability and utility – a skill essential for historians. A range of sources has been provided, including extracts from official documents, personal diaries, memoirs and speeches, as well as visual sources such as photographs, cartoons and paintings.

In order to analyse and evaluate sources as historical evidence, you will need to ask the following **'W' questions** of historical sources:

- **Who** produced it? Were they in a position to know?
- **What** type of source is it? What is its nature – is it a primary or secondary source?
- **Where** and **when** was it produced? What was happening at the time?
- **Why** was it produced? Was its purpose to inform or to persuade? Is it an accurate attempt to record facts, or is it an example of propaganda?
- **Who** was the intended audience – decision-makers or the general public?

This will help you to become familiar with interpreting, understanding, analysing and evaluating different types of historical sources. It will also aid you in synthesising critical analysis of sources with historical knowledge when constructing an explanation or analysis of some aspect or development of the past. Remember, for Paper 1, as for Paper 2, you need to acquire, select and deploy relevant historical knowledge to explain causes and consequences, continuity and change. You also need to develop and show an awareness of historical debates and different interpretations.

Paper 1 questions will thus involve examining sources in the light of:

- their **origins** and **purpose**
- their value and limitations.

origins The 'who, what, when and where' questions.

purpose This means 'reasons, what the writer/creator was trying to achieve, who the intended audience was'.

The **value and limitations** of sources to historians will be based on the **origins and purpose** aspects. For example, a source might be useful because it is primary – the event depicted was witnessed by the person producing it. But was the person in a position to know? Is the view an untypical view of the event? What is its nature? Is it a private diary entry (therefore possibly more likely to be true), or is it a speech or piece of propaganda intended to persuade? The value of a source may be limited by some aspects, but that doesn't mean it has no value at all. For example, it may be valuable as evidence of the types of propaganda put out at the time. Similarly, a secondary – or even a tertiary – source can have more value than some primary sources, for instance, because the author might be writing at a time when new evidence has become available.

Remember – a source doesn't have to be primary to be useful. Remember, too, that content isn't the only aspect to have possible value. The context, the person who produced it, and so on, can also be important in offering an insight.

Finally, when in the exam room, use the information provided by the Chief Examiner about the five sources, as it can give some useful information and clues to help you construct a good answer.

Paper 1 contains four types of question. The first three of these are:

1 **Comprehension/understanding of a source** – some will have 2 marks, others 3 marks. For such questions, write only a short answer (scoring 2 or 3 points); save your longer answers for the questions carrying the higher marks.

2 **Cross-referencing/comparing or contrasting two sources** – try to write an integrated comparison, e.g. comment on how the two sources deal with one aspect, then compare/contrast the sources on another aspect. This will usually score more highly than answers that deal with the sources separately. Try to avoid simply describing each source in turn – there needs to be explicit comparison/contrast.

3 **Assessing the value and limitations of two sources** – here it is best to deal with each source separately, as you are not being asked to decide which source is more important/useful. But remember to deal with **all** the aspects required: **origins**, **purpose**, **value and limitations**.

These three types of questions are covered in the chapters above. The other, longer, type of Paper 1 question will be dealt with in this section.

Paper 1 – judgement questions

The fourth type of Paper 1 question is a judgement question. Judgement questions require a *synthesis of source evaluation and own knowledge.*

Examiner's tips

- This fourth type of Paper 1 question requires you to produce a mini-essay to address the question/statement given in the question. You should try to develop and present an argument and/or come to a balanced judgement by analysing and using these **five** sources **and** your own knowledge.
- Before you write your answer to this kind of question, you may find it useful to draw a rough chart to note what the sources show in relation to the question. This will also make sure you refer to all or at least most of the sources. Note, however, that some sources may hint at more than one factor/result. When using your own knowledge, make sure it is relevant to the question.
- Look carefully at the simplified markscheme below. This will help you focus on what you need to do to reach the top bands and so score the higher marks.

Simplified markscheme

Band		Marks
1	**Developed and balanced** analysis and comments using **BOTH** sources **AND** own knowledge. References to sources are precise, and sources and detailed own knowledge are used together; where relevant, a judgement is made.	8
2	**Developed** analysis/comments using **BOTH** sources **AND** some detailed own knowledge; some clear references to sources. But sources and own knowledge not always **combined together**.	6–7
3	**Some developed** analysis/comments, using the sources **OR** some relevant own knowledge.	4–5
4	**Limited/general** comments using sources **OR** own knowledge.	0–3

Common mistakes

When answering Paper 1 argument/judgement questions, make sure you don't just deal with sources **or** own knowledge! Every year, some candidates (even good ones) do this, and so limit themselves to – at best – only 5 out of the 8 marks available.

Student answers

The student answers that follow have brief examiner's comments in the margins, as well as a longer overall comment at the end. Those parts of the answers that make use of the sources will be highlighted in green. Those parts that deploy relevant own knowledge will be highlighted in red. In this way, you should find it easier to follow why particular bands and marks were – or were not – awarded.

Question 1

Using Sources A, B, C, D and E on pages 219–20, **and** your own knowledge, explain why the NVA/VC won the Vietnam War by 1975.
[8 marks]

SOURCE A

Viet Cong guerrillas.

SOURCE B

The Pentagon was recommending that the US mobilize for virtually total war and this in an election year. The war had already exacerbated the rate of inflation, and taxes would have to be increased. It was a fact that opinion polls during the Tet crisis indicated that the American public favoured a stronger military response, but it was also the case that Johnson's standing with the people was plummeting. Americans wanted to win, but the president seemed incapable of delivering. The scene was set for the most dramatic turnabout in the war.

Vadney, T. E. 1987. The World Since 1945. London, UK. Penguin. pp. 327–28.

SOURCE C

The US military never successfully resolved the tension between 'clearing and holding' and 'searching and destroying'. The effort against the VC was largely successful, however, and pacification programmes did show some effectiveness over the medium term. Operational errors on the part of the VC (most notably, the Tet Offensive) also contributed vitally to erosion of the internal rebellion; over time, the NLF became an enormously less important part of the military equation in South Vietnam. These successes were, however, undermined by US willingness to undertake a serious effort to control infiltration into South Vietnam: as the VC withered, the NVA took responsibility for fighting the communist ground war in South Vietnam.

Walton, C. Dale. 2005. The Myth of Inevitable US Defeat in Vietnam. London, UK. Frank Cass. p. 56.

SOURCE D

The situation in Indochina is not that of open military aggression by the Chinese Communist regime. Thus, in Indochina, the problem is one of restoring tranquillity in an area where disturbances are fomented from Communist China, but where there is no open invasion by Communist China. This task of pacification, in our opinion, cannot be successfully met merely by unilateral armed intervention. Some other conditions need to be established. Throughout these Indochina developments, the United States has held to a stable and consistent course and has made clear the conditions which, in its opinion, might justify intervention. These conditions were and are (1) an invitation from the present lawful authorities; (2) clear assurance of complete independence to Laos, Cambodia, and Viet-Nam; (3) evidence of concern by the United Nations; (4) a joining in the collective effort of some of the other nations of the area; and (5) assurance that France will not itself withdraw from the battle until it is won.

Extract from an address by US secretary of state John Foster Dulles, 11 June 1954, on the situation in Indochina, delivered to the World Affairs Council.

SOURCE E

Comments made by North Vietnamese politician Pham Van Dong in 1964.

The US can go on increasing aid to South Vietnam. It can increase its own army. But it will do no good. I hate to see the war go on and intensify. Yet our people are determined to struggle. It is impossible for westerners to understand the force of the people's will to resist and to continue.

Quoted in Chandler, M. and Wright, J. 1999. Modern World History. *Oxford, UK. Heinemann. p. 110.*

Student answer

There are a number of reasons why the North had won the Vietnam War by 1975, and these five sources offer a range of examples. Firstly, Source A shows that the NVA/VC fought a guerrilla rather than a conventional war. The US found this very difficult to counter. However, some historians believe that the US had found an effective military answer to the nationalist guerrillas, as Source C demonstrates. It was not purely military factors that led to communist victory, however. The events on the ground had a seriously negative effect on US domestic opinion, as Source B shows. This finally forced the US to withdraw from Vietnam, allowing a victory for the North.

Examiner's comment

This is a good, well-focused, start. Sources A, B and C are referred to, interwoven and used, along with a little own knowledge, to set up a sustainable line of debate.

Sources A, B and C all relate to each other. Sources A and D show that the guerrilla offensive in the South was effective because of the support of Communist China, which supplied military materiel. Source D comes from a US government source and overstates the Chinese threat. Source E, however, shows the determination of the Vietnamese people to resist whatever actions the US took. So, Sources D and E are also linked, because the US feared that the Vietnam War was part of a larger communist plot to dominate the whole of Southeast Asia. This was one of the reasons that the US resorted to a full-scale military reaction to the guerrilla threat in the South, rather than seeking a diplomatic solution to the Vietnamese problem. In the long term, this tied the USA's hands and created the domestic pressures to withdraw as laid out in Source B.

Examiner's comment

All five sources are clearly referred to and used, showing a good understanding of their content, as well as a little own knowledge. There is also a comment at the end that hints at a wider understanding of the developments in Vietnam and develops the initial line of debate.

Finally, Source C is a revisionist theory which challenges the impact of the guerrilla strategy on the outcome of the war. Because of the nature of the war and its high media profile, the US was often depicted in sources and, hence, modern histories of the conflict, as incapable of checking the guerrillas. Source C challenges this, arguing that actually the US military reaction was both well thought out and effective. It argues that, militarily, the Tet Offensive of 1968 was a massive military setback for Hanoi. This 'truth', however, was not reflected in the media coverage of the war in America, and led the US public to come to the wrong conclusions, prompting the political opposition to the war outlined in Source B. This both lends weight to the original line of debate and shows how perspectives can be affected by depictions of events on television.

Examiner's comment

As before, sources (C and B) are clearly used and, in this case, linked. There is also relevant own knowledge and evidence of a high-level response pointing to the way in which historians revise their views of the past, and how the same events can be interpreted in radically different ways.

In conclusion, these five sources touch on all the main reasons why the NVA/VC won the Vietnam War by 1975. Overall, the main reason was probably the one shown in Source B – the impact of events in Vietnam on US domestic opinion. The other sources, however, all interlink to set up the outcome described in Source D, thus showing that, although reasons for historical change can be laid out in an order of hierarchy, in reality factors are linked to each other to produce historical change.

Examiner's comment

The conclusion shows that the student has kept the question in mind and has attempted to make a judgement.

Overall examiner's comments

There is good use of most of the sources, with clear references to them. However, Source E is not used extensively. The response displays a good grasp of the historical process. There is some use of own knowledge, mainly integrated with comments on the sources. There are, however, some omissions. For example, the strong willingness to resist – and the methods used – by the Viet Cong and the North Vietnamese are not dealt with. Also, the unstable political situation in South Vietnam is not mentioned by the sources nor brought in by the candidate. Hence, this is a good Band 2 answer, but it fails to get into Band 1.

Activity

Look again at all the sources, the simplified markscheme on page 218 and the student answer on pages 220–21. Now try to write a few paragraphs to push the answer up into Band 1, and so obtain the full 8 marks.

Question 2

Using Sources A, B, C, D and E below, **and** your own knowledge, analyse reasons for the Soviet intervention in Czechoslovakia in 1968.
[8 marks]

SOURCE A

Ulbricht, who was already concerned with Czech co-operation with West Germany, became alarmed. Moscow, though still generally supportive of Dubček, felt uncomfortable. For his part, Dubček welcomed the Warsaw Pact manoeuvres on Czech soil as a means of demonstrating loyalty to the alliance. But when Pact forces withdrew, Dubček's meetings with the Soviet Politburo showed how seriously his allies regarded Czech developments. They were afraid that he would not be able to contain the situation; and that he had already opened Pandora's box.

Adapted from Longworth, P. 1992. The Making of Eastern Europe. *London, UK. Macmillan. p. 25.*

SOURCE B

US troop build-up in Vietnam in the years running up to 1968.

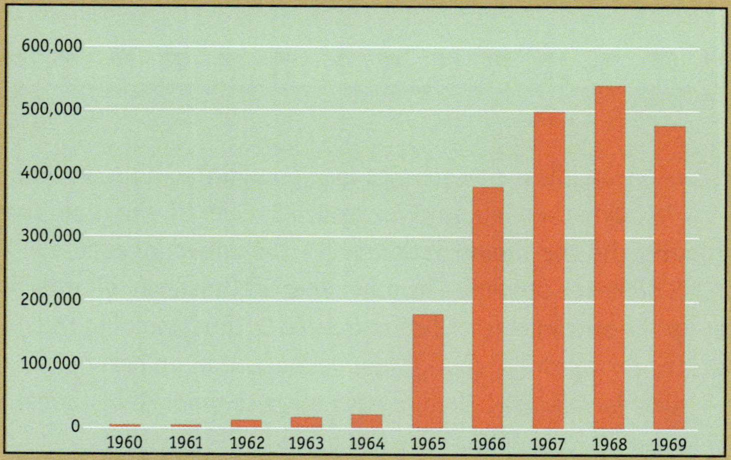

SOURCE C

The principles of peaceful coexistence, friendship, and cooperation among all states have always been and still form the unshakable foundation of the foreign relations of the U.S.S.R. This policy finds its most profound and consistent expression in the relationship with socialist countries. Socialist nations can build their relations only on the principle of full equality, respect of territorial integrity, state independence and sovereignty, and non interference in one another's domestic affairs.

This does not exclude, but on the contrary presupposes, close fraternal cooperation and mutual aid between the countries of the socialist commonwealth in the economic, political, and cultural spheres. It is on this basis that after World War II and after the rout of fascism the regimes of the people's democracies came into being in a number of countries of Europe and Asia.

Extract from an official Soviet Statement titled 'Friendship and Co-operation Between the Soviet Union and Other Socialist States'. 30 October 1956. The Department of State Bulletin XXXV, No. 907. pp. 745–47.

SOURCE D

A map showing Czechoslovakia as a potential invasion route into the USSR.

SOURCE E

It's no secret that the KGB played an important role in many decisions concerning foreign policy matters. This applies to the events of 1968 in Czechoslovakia. The KGB stirred up fears among the country's leadership that Czechoslovakia could fall victim to NATO aggression or a coup unless certain actions were undertaken promptly. At about the same time, I reported from Washington that the CIA was not involved in the developments of the Prague Spring. But my attempt at an even-handed report simply did not fit in with the KGB's concept of the way events were shaping up in Czechoslovakia, and therefore never got beyond the KGB. My information was wasted.

A Russian spy working in America during the Prague Spring, commenting on events in 1990. Cold War International History Project Bulletin no. 3. p. 6. http://www.cwihp.org.

Student answer

There were several main factors behind the Soviet intervention in Czechoslovakia in 1968. Most of these are mentioned by the five sources. The main ones are Soviet fear of internal changes in socialist societies and fear of the West. The Soviet-style economies established in Eastern Europe after the Second World War were not efficient and needed reform. The Prague Spring was part of a general reform of these economies that was sweeping across Eastern Europe. Czechoslovakia was at the forefront of this development. The Soviet Union feared that economic reform would be followed by pressure to change the societies of the Eastern bloc, perhaps putting communism in jeopardy.

Examiner's comment

This is a good introduction, showing a clear understanding of the topic and the question.

Source A shows the fears of communist leaders, especially the East German leader Ulbricht. They were afraid that the situation within Czechoslovakia would spiral out of control. Socialism would be threatened not only there, but also in neighbouring countries. One of the reasons that this fear might have been understandable was Czechoslovakia's recent history – before the Second World War, Czechoslovakia had been a vibrant democracy within the Western European mainstream. Ulbricht's views would have been influenced by this and popular pressure within the country to move to a more Western-style society. It is interesting, however, that Source A also shows that the Czech leader did not want to break away from the socialist bloc, and went to extreme lengths to convince the other communists of this.

Examiner's comment

There is good use of Source A, and the use of some precise own knowledge integrated in the answer.

Sources C and D touch on another important reason – the growing fear of the extension of Western influence into a socialist country. Source C makes two statements. Firstly, it notes a Soviet promise to protect and maintain alliances with other socialist states. It promises that the USSR will respect the sovereignty of fellow socialist states. At first sight this seems to contradict Soviet actions in 1968. However, in the second part of Source C there is a clear statement of Soviet intentions to maintain 'close fraternal co-operation and mutual aid' between socialist countries. It also refers to the defeat of Nazi Germany 'after the rout of fascism'. To an extent, Source A echoes this with its references to 'Czech co-operation with West Germany'. Thus, the Soviets intervened in Czechoslovakia because of wider fears of threats to their security. Source D shows clearly that there is a direct route from the West and the NATO alliance through Czechoslovakia to the frontier of the USSR.

Examiner's comment

There is good understanding and clear use of two, or even three, more sources. There is also integration of some sound and relevant own knowledge. However, an opportunity has been missed to integrate the response further by commenting on Source B. This source is by far the most difficult of the three to use, and you will note it gets hardly any attention from the candidate. The response could have argued that Source B reinforced Soviet paranoia by showing a build-up of anti-communist forces in a region of the world where the two ideologies were in open conflict.

The final reason for the Soviet intervention is suggested by Source E. This source is important firstly because it was written in 1990, after the opening of the Soviet archives, and secondly because it shows the views of a Soviet agent. He states that the KGB deliberately manipulated intelligence to paint a picture of US and NATO threats to the Eastern bloc. This reinforces the arguments given in Sources C and D.

Examiner's comment

This is a good analysis because it focuses on the provenance of Source E to reach a judgement. However, a criticism of this evaluation is that the candidate takes what is written at face value.

Source B shows American troop build-ups in Vietnam in 1968. This is proof that the USA was becoming more involved in the Vietnam War.

Examiner's comment

This is little more than a fragment. It is a simple description and makes only a limited evaluative point. The candidate cannot link this source to the question set and has simply inserted this section because they realise they must address all the sources. This is an example of a weak response to a source.

Consequently, the most important reasons for the Soviet intervention in Czechoslovakia in 1968 were fear of attack from the outside and internal threats to communism. The Soviets had expanded into Eastern Europe after the Second World War to create a buffer zone to stop an attack like the one launched by the Nazis in 1941. The second factor was due to the failings of the communist economies of the Eastern bloc and the need for reform, which might encourage social upheaval.

Overall examiner's comments

There is good and clear use of most sources throughout, and constant integration of precise own knowledge to both explain and add to the sources. There are weaknesses, however. Source B is used poorly. Source E could have been subject to further scrutiny about its reliability. Finally, the candidate mentions two reasons for Soviet intervention – fear of invasion and a collapse of socialist society. The former reason is dealt with very well, with sound integration of sources. The latter is almost an aside. The candidate is using own knowledge to reach these two conclusions, but the sources do not easily allow access to the second. A better tactic would have been to state openly that the sources are weak on the second half of the line of debate. This would have allowed this part of the argument to be used in the essay under the question prompt '**and** your own knowledge', and it would have allowed for a further layer of analysis of the limitations of the sources as a set. Overall, however, this is a strong response and would have been marked into Band 2, scoring 6 marks out of the 8 available.

Activity

Look again at all the sources, the simplified markscheme on page 218, and the student answer above. Now try to write your own answer to this question and see if you can remedy the weaknesses noted in the overall examiner's comments to score maximum marks.

Paper 2 exam practice

Paper 2 skills and questions

For Paper 2, you have to answer two essay questions from two of the five different topics offered. Very often, you will be asked to comment on two states from two different IB regions of the world. Although each question has a specific markscheme, you can get a good general idea of what examiners are looking for in order to be able to put answers into the higher bands from the 'generic' markscheme. In particular, you will need to acquire reasonably precise historical knowledge in order to address issues such as cause and effect, or change and continuity, and to learn how to explain historical developments in a clear, coherent, well-supported and relevant way. You will also need to understand and be able to refer to aspects relating to historical debates and interpretations.

Make sure you read the questions carefully, and select your questions wisely. It is a good idea to produce a rough plan of **each** of the essays you intend to attempt, **before** you start to write your answers. That way, you will soon know whether you have enough own knowledge to answer them adequately.

Simplified markscheme

Band		Marks
1	Clear analysis/argument, with very specific and relevant own knowledge, consistently and explicitly linked to the question. A balanced answer, with references to historical debate/historians, where appropriate.	17–20
2	Relevant analysis/argument, mainly clearly focused on the question, and with relevant supporting own knowledge. Factors identified and explained, but not all aspects of the question fully developed or addressed.	11–16
3	**EITHER** shows reasonable relevant own knowledge, identifying some factors, with limited focus/explanation – but **mainly narrative** in approach, with question only implicitly addressed **OR** coherent analysis/argument, but limited.	8–10
4	**Some limited/relevant** own knowledge, but **not linked effectively** to the question.	6–7
5	**Short/general** answer, but with very **little accurate/relevant knowledge and limited understanding** of the question.	0–5

Remember, too, to keep your answers relevant and focused on the question. For example, don't go outside the dates mentioned in the question, or answer on individuals/states different from the ones identified in the question. Don't just describe events or developments – sometimes, students just focus on one key word or individual, and then write down all they know about it. Instead, select your own knowledge carefully, and pin the relevant information to the key features raised by the question. Also, if the question asks for 'reasons' and 'results', or two different countries, make sure you deal with **all** the parts of the question. Otherwise, you will limit yourself to half marks at best.

Examiner's tips

For Paper 2 answers, examiners are looking for clear/precise analysis and a balanced argument, linked to the question, with the use of good, precise and relevant own knowledge. In order to obtain the highest marks, you should be able to refer to different historical debate/interpretations or relevant historians' knowledge, making sure it is relevant to the question.

Common mistakes

- When answering Paper 2 questions, try to avoid simply describing what happened. A detailed narrative, with no explicit attempts to link the knowledge to the question, will only get you half marks at most.
- If the question asks you to select examples from **two** different regions, make sure you don't choose two states from the same region. Every year, some candidates do this and so limit themselves to – at best – only 12 out of the 20 marks available.

Student answers

Those parts of the student answers that follow will have brief examiner's comments in the margins, as well as a longer overall comment at the end. Those parts of student's answers that are particularly strong and well-focused will be highlighted in red. Errors/confusions/loss of focus will be highlighted in blue. In this way, you should find it easier to follow why marks were – or were not – awarded.

Question 1

For what reasons were India and Pakistan granted independence in 1947? [20 marks]

Skill

Analysis/argument/assessment

Examiner's tip

At first sight this question seems straightforward, but it conceals a major potential pitfall. The combination of two states, India and Pakistan, effectively makes this a dual question.

Student answer

India and Pakistan were granted independence in 1947 essentially for two reasons. Firstly, even before the First World War, Britain had become uncomfortable with retaining its colonial possessions in India, and wished to grant independence. Colonialism did not sit well with Britain's liberal democratic political ideology. This apparent political contradiction had been exposed by the activities of Congress and Gandhi in the interwar years. The second reason was the impact of the Second World War. Prior to this, there were elements of the British establishment that could not, for ideological or economic reasons, tolerate the loss of their Indian empire. It took the Second World War to so weaken Britain as a colonial power that it had little choice but to grant independence. The fact that the British were forced to give up India as a result of the pressures of the Second World War explains why two states emerged in 1947.

Examiner's comment
This is a clear and well-focused introduction, showing a good grasp of the key requirements of the question.

It is clear from the period before the First World war that the British Empire did not want to hold on to its Indian possessions indefinitely. As early as 1909, the British minister John Morley had pushed for political concessions in the subcontinent. These came to fruition in 1910, when the first elections were held and 135 Indians took their places as legislators. But Morley was motivated by the need to maintain Britain's hold on this most important part of the empire, rather than the granting of full independence. The First World War, however, showed both Congress and the British just how dependent the colonial power was on India in terms of military power and finance. This increased the pressure on Britain to meet certain demands and grant India increasing autonomy. This can be seen in a report to the British parliament in 1917 by Edwin Montagu, the secretary of state for India. In the report, he stated the government's intention to encourage 'the gradual development of self governing institutions'. Thus, by the end of the First World War it was clear that Britain intended to modify its relationship with India. The problem, however, was that once the crisis of the First World War passed there was less incentive to actually carry out these plans.

Examiner's comment
There is a clear line of debate being developed here, with both supporting accurate own knowledge and a sense of critical judgement.

The First World War, therefore, had two effects on the process of Indian independence. Firstly, it had shown the strength of India as a potential sovereign state. Secondly, it had resulted in a grudging willingness of the colonial power to grant the subcontinent a level of autonomy. Against this, however, comes the second raft of factors, all associated with the Indian independence movement itself. At the core of the movement was Congress. This organisation had its origins in the later 19th century. Prior to the First World War, Congress had sought a negotiated solution to the question of independence. Once progress stalled after Montagu's announcements in 1917, it was clear that more militant tactics would have to be adopted to force the British out. This development was encouraged by the 1918–19 influenza epidemic, which killed over 12 million Indians, and by the bloodshed in the holy city of Amritsar in 1919.

Congress, however, was composed of an indigenous élite that had supplied the subcontinent's civil service for a century. Congress had to balance militant action against the real threat of the development of new forms of nationalist agitation so extreme that they would create a post-colonial India under the control of radicals rather than the traditional Indian élite. Proof of this was the formation of the Indian Communist Party by Manabendra Nath Roy during this period. This organisation championed armed struggle against the British – a development that would only succeed after considerable bloodshed and would probably so destabilise India as to produce chaos. Thus, Congress had to tread very carefully if it was to achieve its objectives.

Examiner's comment
There is accurate supporting own knowledge here, with explicit development of the original line of debate. Once again the answer displays both control and a sense of critical judgement.

Into this situation stepped Gandhi. He was in many ways the solution to Congress's dilemma. His political tactic of satyagraha and his public image had a devastating effect on Britain's legitimacy as a colonial power. Acts of satyagraha exposed the inherent injustice of colonial rule. A good example of this is the Salt March of 1930. Secondly, Gandhi became a world figure. His image of a quasi holy man who was resisting the might of the British Empire with reasonableness and dialogue was very appealing to both the more liberal elements of the British élite and the wider world, especially the USA. Gandhi presented the Indian nationalists with a middle way – resistance to colonial rule through non-violent action – which exposed the ridiculousness of a liberal democracy like Britain maintaining its grip on India. To some extent, this neutralised the more radical elements of both Congress, such as Subhas Chandra Bose, and the extreme left. To a great degree it also created a stable environment for political change. In this Gandhi proved to be a unique historical figure.

Examiner's comment
There is more analysis here, with supporting accurate own knowledge. The response extends the debate.

The key event was, however, the Second World War. This conflict bankrupted Britain and made maintenance of its empire impossible. Thus, in the immediate post-war period the British rushed to meet Congress's demands. By 1947, independence had been granted to the subcontinent. This period was characterised by British mismanagement, which both allowed for the emergence of two states in the region, India and Pakistan, and led to massive inter-communal violence.

The emergence of Pakistan was, in many ways, inevitable. The Muslim League had been formed before the First World War and its leader, Jinnah, had long since come to the conclusion that an independent Muslim state had to be created if Muslims were to retain political independence from the Hindu majority. The British, however, connived with the Muslim League in an attempt to control the situation and, as a result, when the two-state solution came into existence it was in an unsatisfactory form. The solution of dividing Pakistan into East and West was unworkable in the long run, and the mass movement of population resulted in killing on a huge scale.

Examiner's comment
Here the candidate extends the debate to cover the Pakistan command prompt in the question. However, the relationship between Britain and the Muslim League lacks detail, and the concluding sentence is unfocused.

Thus, Indian and Pakistani independence came about due to a combination of three factors. Firstly, the British had indicated they were willing to make serious concessions to the nationalists by the time the First World War had ended. Secondly, the Indian nationalists had set in train a very effective political campaign in the 1920s and 1930s, in which Gandhi played a key part. Thirdly, the Second World War had forced Britain to grant independence. It was the circumstances associated with this final factor that led to the specific form of independence adopted in the subcontinent, a region divided along religious grounds in the form of India and Pakistan. This unsatisfactory solution led to mass bloodshed at the time and has created instability both in Pakistan and between Pakistan and its neighbour ever since.

Examiner's comment
This is a punchy and focused conclusion that finishes with a flourish.

Overall examiner's comments

This is a good, well-focused and analytical answer, with very specific and relevant own knowledge that supports the points made without obscuring them. The answer is thus good enough to be awarded a mark in Band 1 – probably 18 marks. However, not all aspects are given equal weight. In particular, the Pakistani element of the response is unbalanced. More importantly, it would have been very useful to have some mention of **relevant specific historians/ historical interpretations**.

Activity

Look again at the simplified markscheme on page 226 and the student answer above. Now try to write a few extra paragraphs to push the answer up to the top of Band 1 and obtain the full 20 marks available.

Question 2

Analyse the successes and failures of Lech Wałęsa.
[20 marks]

Skill

Analysis/argument/assessment

Examiner's tip

This is a fairly straightforward question. It has a narrow focus on a single individual, and the response must show a balance between Wałęsa's successes and his failures. Better responses deal with this in a thematic manner. For example, you could discuss the theme of Wałęsa as president, and then in one sub-section discuss successes and failures. Weaker responses tend to deal with successes and failures as two separate parts of the essay, with paragraphs following one another, success–failure–success, and so on.

Student answer

Lech Wałęsa was born in 1943 and became an electrician in the Gdańsk shipyards in 1966. By 1980, he had become leader of the Solidarity trade union, where he became a leading agitator for workers' rights and political freedoms. He was imprisoned several times in the 1980s, but with the fall of communism in 1990 he became president of Poland, a position he retained until 1995. He is now a world figure and a Nobel Prize winner.

Examiner's comment

This is a generalised introduction that only presents background knowledge. It does not address the question.

In the later part of the 1970s, deeply rooted problems in Poland associated with economic issues came to a head when the Polish pope, John Paul II – also known as Karol Wojtyła – visited Poland in 1979. This led to a wave of civil unrest. This was most extreme in Gdańsk, where the shipyard workers went on strike. It was at this time that Wałęsa became leader of the Gdańsk strikers. He was very successful in this period and he rose to become the leader of the Inter-Enterprise Strike Committee. He was also successful because in 1980, he managed to force the government to give the strikers a series of concessions to do with their working conditions, pay and their right to free association.

Examiner's comment

The paragraph makes little attempt to engage the question. It is also mainly narrative, and therefore does not have a clear enough explanatory thrust. However, an example of his success is given at the end.

In the 1980s, Wałęsa was less successful. He was imprisoned between 1980 and 1981, and when he was released he found it difficult to find employment because the government did not trust him, and since December 1981 had been cracking down on the activities of Solidarity. Wałęsa's position in the early 1980s is proof of his failures. As the 1980s continued, however, he enjoyed a mix of success and failure. Wałęsa worked underground for Solidarity. Six underground newspapers and an underground radio station, Radio Solidarity, were set up. Wałęsa was also successful because in 1984 the government declared an amnesty for all who had been caught up in the events of 1980. But, during this period Wałesa was a failure because his efforts to advance the cause of Solidarity got nowhere. Throughout the 1980s, therefore, there was a mix of successes and failures for Wałęsa.

Examiner's comment

Again, the candidate is attempting to advance an argument. Unlike the previous paragraph, this section has more balance – there is a mix of success and failures. There is also greater balance between analytical comments and evidence. The analysis, however, is still based on assertions and the candidate is failing to develop points to give the answer a clear explanatory thrust. However, the section does have focus.

Wałęsa was successful in the events surrounding the fall of communism in Poland in 1990. He was a key player in the Solidarity agitation in the run-up to 1990 – for example, in January 1988 a wave of co-ordinated strikes were very effective. The communist leader, Wojciech Jaruzelski, also negotiated with Wałęsa when he realised the situation was getting out of hand and the USSR would not support him. These are examples of success. Wałęsa also played a key role in the elections to the sejm, where Solidarity won most of the seats. Wałęsa was also successful when he was elected president in 1990. In this period overall, he was successful.

Examiner's comment
Again, the candidate is attempting to advance an argument, but there are clear problems of development. If the examiner has to read between the lines to establish why things are happening or why they are having a particular effect then the essay will not get into the upper bands.

Wałęsa was a failure as president. He was unable to handle the move to a more Western style economy. He overreacted to pressure and sacked people such as the head of the Citizens Committee, Wujec. He clashed with his prime minister, Hanna Suchocka, who was very successful. He was a failure as president because he could not make the transition from a political agitator to a proper political leader with responsibilities. So, in this period, he was a failure.

Examiner's comment
This paragraph has shifted the other way. It has some very astute analytical observations that are focused, if underdeveloped. Here, the weakness is a failure to support points with evidence.

On balance, Wałęsa was a success. On reviewing the evidence we see that he was very successful in the early period, a limited failure in the 1980s and a failure as president. Wałęsa was most successful in 1980 and 1990, when he played a key role in Solidarity.

Examiner's comment
This is a very basic conclusion. It presents an argument of sorts, but is littered with assertions. On the positive side, it does make sense of the arguments that have come earlier in the essay.

Overall examiner's comments

This answer attempts to address the question explicitly, but is unable to balance the analysis with the evidence. As a result it swings from narrative, accompanied by nods at the question, to barely supported assertions. It is a real answer to the question set and it does display understanding, but it fails to develop the debate to a point where it offers the clear explanatory thrust needed to get into Bands 1 or 2. The answer is good enough to be awarded a mark at the middle part of Band 3 – probably about 9 marks. To reach the higher bands, some **specific development of the reasons for success/failure** is needed.

Activity

Look again at the simplified markscheme on page 226 and the student answer above. Now try to write a few extra paragraphs to push the answer up to the top of Band 1 to obtain the full 20 marks.

Question 3

Compare and contrast the independence movements in **two** developing states – one in Africa and the other in Asia.
[20 marks]

Skill

Analysis/argument/assessment

Examiner's tip

This question once again seems to be fairly straightforward. It allows the candidate to select the case studies to use in support of the question, and the demands of the question will be met as long as the essay discusses Asia and Africa. The potential pitfall lies in the open-ended nature of the question. What exactly is meant by 'compare and contrast'? Before embarking on the essay, therefore, you will need a clear plan, based on themes if possible. Thus, you might look at the basis of support, the historical context of each case study, the methods of achieving independence, and so on. In this way, you will be able to interweave the two case studies into the text to meet the demands of the upper bands of the markscheme.

Student answer

In Indochina, the independence movement was called the Viet Cong. They were helped by the army of North Vietnam. They were guerrillas and fought a guerrilla war against the Americans. In Rhodesia, the independence movement was ZANU and ZAPU, who were also guerrillas but who did not receive any help from outside people.

Examiner's comment
This is a very basic start, which addresses the question set only on a superficial level. There is a very limited attempt at comparison. The candidate fails to identify the outside support for the Zimbabweans.

The VC had fought the French and had been able to set up an independent North Vietnam, but when the Americans helped the South Vietnamese, the war began again. The VC fought as guerrillas and this defeated the Americans because US troops were not used to fighting in the jungle.

Examiner's comment
Some relevant knowledge is displayed, but it is not focused on the question except by inference.

In Rhodesia, the whites had total control and the black people were little more than serfs. By 1965, the whites had set up an independent Rhodesia on their own. They would not give independence to the blacks. The white leader was Ian Smith and he was an extremist. The blacks were so upset by this that they set up their own armies, called ZAPU and ZANU. Robert Mugabe led the blacks and they fought a guerrilla war against the whites. The blacks had a hard time of it because of the powerful Rhodesian army, and it was only after a long time that they were successful.

Examiner's comment

This paragraph shows some relevant knowledge, but it is even more generalised than the previous one. There are also inaccuracies – for example, ZAPU and ZANU were the organisations themselves, not the military wings.

In Vietnam there was a big battle called Tet. The VC won Tet and they captured the US embassy in the South Vietnamese capital Saigon. This was shown to the Americans on television and it so upset them that they turned against their president, Lyndon Johnson, and forced him to step down. Because of this battle the VC won. There were no battles like this in Zimbabwe.

Examiner's comment

Some relevant knowledge is displayed but it is not moulded to the question set. Some of this is on the brink of being inaccurate – Tet was in fact a big setback for the VC. Note the crude failed attempt at a comparative analysis at the end.

So, the Zimbabwean and Vietnamese independence movements were the same because they were both guerrilla wars. They also had good leaders like Mugabe and Ho Chi Minh, which allowed them to win. There were many similarities, but some factors were different. The Vietnamese had a jungle to hide in, whereas the Zimbabweans did not. So there were differences and similarities between the two movements.

Examiner's comment

This is a conclusion of sorts. The candidate realises the need for comparative analysis, but the answer fails to meet this demand of the assessment beyond assertions. This is a pity because this paragraph flags up – in red – valid points, that could have become the basis of a much better response.

Overall examiner's comments

This is weak response that barely engages the question set. It does display some valid own knowledge but has problems moulding this to the question. It flags up some interesting points but fails to develop them. It has real problems of control. It shows limited relevant own knowledge and would thus enter the markscheme in band 4. The short length of the response, however, would place it at the bottom of this band, gaining 6 marks.

Activity

Look again at the simplified markscheme on page 226 and the student answer above. Now try to write a more detailed response to push the answer up to the top of Band 1 and obtain 20 marks.

Further information

Sources and quotations in this book have been taken from the following publications.

Afigbo, A. E. et al. 1986. *The Making of Modern Africa, Volume 2: The Twentieth Century*. London, UK. Longman.
Arnold, Guy. 2006. *Africa: A Modern History*. London, UK. Atlantic Books.
Berend, I. T. 1996. *Central and Eastern Europe, 1944–93*. Cambridge, UK. Cambridge University Press.
Blake, Robert. 1977. *History of Rhodesia*. London, UK. Methuen Publishing.
Bose, Sugata and Jalal, Ayesha. 1998. *Modern South Asia*. London, UK. Routledge.
Bottaro, J. et al. 2001. *Successful Human and Social Sciences Grade 9*. Cape Town, South Africa. Oxford University Press.
Burke, Patrick. 1995. *Revolution in Europe, 1989*. London, UK. Wayland.
Buss, Claude A. 1958. *Southeast Asia and the World Today*. Princeton, USA. D. Van Nostrand.
Cannon, Martin et al. 2009. *20th Century World History*. Oxford, UK. Oxford University Press.
Chandler, Malcolm. and Wright, John. 1999. *Modern World History*. Oxford, UK. Heinemann.
Chandra, Bipan, et al. 2000. *India after Independence: 1947–2000*. London, UK. Penguin.
Cole, A. B. (ed.). 1956. *Conflict in Indo-China and International Repercussions*. New York, USA. Cornell University Press.
de Bary, William. 1958. *Sources of Indian Tradition*. New York, USA. Columbia University Press.
Demma, V. H. 1989. *American Military History*. Washington, DC, USA. US Army.
Documents from the Military Archives of Former Warsaw Pact Countries. 2000. Historical Office, Office of the Secretary of Defence and Joint History Office.
Dubček, A. 1992. *Hope Dies Last*. Tokyo, Japan. Kodansha International.
Fisher, P. 1985. *The Great Power Conflict After 1945*. London, UK. Basil Blackwell.
Galbraith, John Kenneth. 1994. *A Journey Through Economic Time: A Firsthand View*. Boston, USA. Houghton Mifflin.
Garton Ash, T. 2002. *The Polish Revolution: Solidarity*. New Haven, USA. Yale University Press.
Gates, R. 1997. *From the Shadows*. New York, USA. Simon & Schuster.
Geary, Patrick J. 2003. *The Myth of Nations*. Princeton, USA. Princeton University Press.
Guha, Ramachandra. 2007. *India after Gandhi: The History of the World's Largest Democracy*. London, UK. Macmillan.
Havel, V. 1990. *Living in Truth, Essays on Politics and Conscience*. London, UK. Faber and Faber.
Hayslip, Le Ly. 1993. *When Heaven and Earth Changed Places*. New York, USA. Plume.
James, Lawrence. 1997. *Raj: The Making and Unmaking of British India*. London, UK. Abacus.
Karnow, S. 1984. *Vietnam: A History*. Harmondsworth, UK. Penguin.
Kelly, George A. 1968. *Addresses to the German Nation*. New York, USA. Harper Torch.
Leaver, David. 2004. *Encyclopedia of African History II*. London, UK. Routledge.
Longworth, Philip. 1992. *The Making of Eastern Europe*. London, UK. Macmillan.
Meredith, Martin. 2005. *The State of Africa*. London, UK. Free Press.
Metcalf, Barbara and Metcalf, Thomas. 2006. *A Concise History of Modern India*. Cambridge, UK. Cambridge University Press.
Nehru, Jawarharlal. 1946. *The Discovery of India*. London, UK. Meridian Books.
Nkrumah, Kwame. 1965. *Neo-colonialism: the Last Stage of Imperialism*. London, UK. Thomas Nelson & Sons.
Ost, D. 2005. *The Defeat of Solidarity*. New York, USA and London, UK. Cornell University Press.
Pollock, Alan. 1995. *Vietnam: Conflict and Change in Indochina*. Melbourne, Australia. Oxford University Press.
Raftopoulos, B. and Mlambo, A. 2009. *Becoming Zimbabwe*. Harare, Zimbabwe. Weaver Press.
Santoli, Al. 1985. *To Bear Any Burden*. New York, USA. E. P. Dutton.
Talbot, Ian and Singh, Gurharpal. 2009. *The Partition of India*. Cambridge, UK. Cambridge University Press.
Vadney, T. E. 1987. *The World Since 1945*. London, UK. Penguin.
Walsh, Ben. 2001. *Modern World History*. London, UK. John Murray.
Walton, C. Dale. 2005. *The Myth of Inevitable US Defeat in Vietnam*. London, UK. Frank Cass.
Zeman, Z. A. B. 1969. *Prague Spring*. Harmondsworth, UK. Penguin.
Zhai, Q. 2000. *China and the Vietnam Wars, 1950–1975*. Chapel Hill, USA. University of North Carolina Press.

Index

Acknowledgements

The volume editor and publishers acknowledge the following sources of copyright material and are grateful for the permissions granted. While every effort has been made, it has not always been possible to identify the sources of all the material used, or to trace all copyright holders. If any omissions are brought to our notice we will be happy to include the appropriate acknowledgement on reprinting.

Cold War International History Project (CWIHP), www.cwihp.org, by permission of the Woodrow Wilson International Centre for Scholars: p. 165 (Source J) A. Lorenc et al., T8/91 vol. XIX., envelope 1, #79-84 (also vol. XXI, #2242-2247). Published in Czech in *Organizace a Rizeni, Represe v CSSR: Operaeni Staby Generala Lorence 1988–1989, Edice Dokumentu Vol. 4/II (Úrad Dokumentace a Vysetrovani Zlocinu Komunismu 1998)*, translated by Vance Whitby; p. 185 (Source B) Ministry of National Defense, Intelligence Department, Bulgaria, translated by Vanja Petkova, edited by Dr Jordan Baev, Momchil Metodiev, and Nancy L. Meyers; p. 186 (Source C) Account of a Meeting at the CPSU CC, on the Situation in Poland and Hungary; p. 197 (Source B) CPSU CC Politburo Decision Setting Up Suslov Commission, from TsKhSD, F. 89, F. 42, D. 22; p. 200 (Source C) Institute of Political Studies (Polish Academy of Sciences), Warsaw, translated by Jan Chowaniec; p. 200 (Source D) Andrzej Paczkowski Papers, translated by Jan Chowaniec; p. 201 (Source E) Andrzej Stelmachowski Papers, translated by Jan Chowaniec. p. 223 (Source E) Cold War International History Project Bulletin no. 3, p. 6.

Picture Credits

Cover Vithalbhai Jhaveri/GandhiServe; p. 16 (l) Project Gutenberg; p. 16 (r) The National Archives/HIP/Topfoto; p. 20 Time & Life Pictures/Getty Images; p. 25 AFP/Getty Images; p. 29 Getty Images; p. 30 US Department of Defense/MC2 Jesse Awalt; p. 33 Peter Jordan/Alamy; p. 37 from None but ourselves: Masses vs the Media in the Making of Zimbabwe by Julie Frederickse, Ravan Press, Johannesburg, 1982; p. 39 Gamma-Keystone via Getty Images; p. 43 Jim Barber/Shutterstock; p. 45 Brian Harris/Alamy; p. 49 AFP/Getty Images; p. 51 Philimon Bulawayo/Reuters/Corbis; p. 52 AFP/Getty Images; p. 64 Getty Images; p. 66 Mary Evans Picture Library/Alamy; p. 70 Popperfoto/Getty Images; p. 73 Time & Life Pictures/Getty Images; p. 76 Getty Images; p. 81 Dinodia Images/Alamy; p. 86 Time & Life Pictures/Getty Images; p. 88 Getty Images; p. 91 Time & Life Pictures/Getty Images; p. 104 Wikipedia; p. 106 Library of Congress; p. 111 AFP/Getty Images; p. 113 AFP/Getty Images; p. 114 NASA Headquarters/GReatest Images of NASA (NASA-HQ-GRIN); p. 115 Gamma-Keystone via Getty Images; p. 119 Tim Page/Corbis; p. 121 Getty Images; p. 122 Topham/AP; p. 125 Bettman/Corbis; p. 127 Popperfoto/Getty Images; p. 128 Time & Life Pictures/Getty Images; p. 132 AFP/Getty Images; p. 136 Popperfoto/Getty Images; p. 145 Library of Congress Prints and Photographs Division; p. 146 (t) Yugoslav People's Army; p. 146 (b) ČTK; p. 149 Getty Images; p. 157 Haak78/Shutterstock; p. 158 John Jensen/British Cartoon Archives; p. 160 Popperfoto/Getty Images; p. 161 (l) Joseph Koudelka/Magnum Photos; p. 161 (b) Bill Rowntree/Mirrorpix; p. 164 Kojoku/Shutterstock; p. 166 AFP/Getty Images; p. 167 Joseph Koudelka/Magnum Photos; p. 168 Getty Images; p. 177 Getty Images; p. 178 Gamma-Keystone via Getty Images; p. 181 Wikipedia; p. 183 AFP/Getty Images; p. 190 Wikipedia; p. 193 Getty Images; p. 194 (l) David Fowler/Shutterstock; p. 194 (r) Alain Keler/Sygma/Corbis; p. 195 Time & Life Pictures/Getty Images; p. 199 Topham/AP; p. 204 Reuters/Corbis; p. 219 Getty Images.

Produced for Cambridge University Press by

White-Thomson Publishing
+44 (0)843 208 7460
www.wtpub.co.uk

Series editor: Allan Todd
Development editor: Margaret Haynes
Reviewers: Peter Atkinson and Nigel Worden
Editor: Sonya Newland
Designer: Clare Nicholas
Picture researcher: Amy Sparks
Illustrator: Stefan Chabluk